AF522227

Sources of Research in Indian Classical Music

Sources of Research in Indian Classical Music

Dr. Ms. REENA GAUTAM (Baloria)

KANISHKA PUBLISHERS, DISTRIBUTORS

NEW DELHI - 110 002

KANISHKA PUBLISHERS, DISTRIBUTORS
4697/5-21A, Ansari Road, Daryaganj
New Delhi -110 002
Phones : 2327 0497, 2328 8285
Fax : 011-2328 8285
E-mail : kanishka_publishing@yahoo.co.in

Sources of Research in Indian Classical Music

First Published 2012
Edition-2021
ISBN: 978-81-7391-433-8

PRINTED IN INDIA

Published by Madan Sachdeva for Kanishka Publishers, Distributors, 4697/5-21A, Ansari Road, Daryaganj, New Delhi-110 002, Typeset by Sunshine Graphics, Delhi, and Printed at Rajdhani Printers, Delhi.

Acknowledgements

"God has two dwellings, one in heaven and other in meek and thankful hearts".
— Izzak Walton

Now it is time for me to thank all those that inspired guided and helped me till the very end of this book. Among them, I am grateful and sincerely express my deep sense of gratitude and indebtedness to Dr. (Mrs.) Anupam Mahajan for her valuable guidance and keen interest and her immense help in the matter of preparation of this book.

I specially thank to Sh. Mohammed Haroon (Librarian), for his constant help in providing me the relevant material of Faculty of Music and Fine Arts Delhi University.

I dedicate my book to my lovely life partner Dr. Ravinder and Baloria who not only inspired me but also encouraged me from time by time.

I cannot close without acknowledging with grateful thanks the information I derived from the various books. I thank to those scholars of India and other sectors of the world; who have written books and literature for the betterment of students in this field.

Dr. Ms. REENA GAUTAM (Baloria)

Preface

"Art is the vital force of a nation, the fountain from which the national life is inspired and sustained. In India, as no where else, her splendid art has been the essential basis of culture, the over powering tendency of her soul always illumining the mind of man, exalting his heart and enriching his life. It is doubtful, if any other country in the world can display such wealth of artistic activity, remarkable for a great depth of feeling and imaginative creativeness, or offer anything equal to the highest attainment of Indians in this sphere."

Having been a student in the Faculty of Music, Delhi University for more than a decade, I was prompted to choose this topic. The present research work is an ambitious one. Nevertheless, 1 attempted it because I am convinced that there is an urgent need for taking a fresh look at music research.

The Webster's International Dictionary proposes a very inclusive definition of research, "a careful critical inquiry or examination in seeking facts or principles, diligent investigation in order to ascertain something." This definition while helpful in indicating in a very general way what people mean when they talk about research, is not specific and precise enough to give us a complete and clear idea of what research involves. Name of research involve mainly a 're-search' i.e. activities refers to 'a critical and exhaustive investigation or experimentation having as its aim the revision of accepted conclusions in light of newly discovered facts'. The function of research is to add new knowledge to its existing store, but its power of cleansing our mind. Research is now become the prime goal all over the world. Numerous problems have been solved by it and uncountable problems are still to be solved.

Research in the humanities—literature, music and fine arts enhances the quality of life. While other disciplines deal with biological and economic realities. Although music is entertainment, classical music, specially because of its rigorous discipline and its theory bonds with the past tradition keeps us close to our cultural values e.g. A performer belonging to the modern generation during his performance wear traditional clothes, copies traditional gestures, like bowing to his elder's etc. However, a look at the history of music shows that the Natya sastra and other granthas (textbooks) follow an established pattern of inquiry. Art and Theory are both valid and complementary "Can we say that Raman's cogitation on colours are less beautiful than Nandlal Bose's painting? (Deva, S.N.A. 1970, p. 6).

The methods given in Research methodology books of other disciplines are not easily adaptable to music. Classical music is a complex art and a taste for it, is acquired over a number of years. Special techniques have to be devised to elicit responses from listeners of classical music. There is a popular fallacy that music can only be demonstrated and not written about. Music as a descriptive suffers from lack of research, so less research has been done in music than in the social sciences. Most artists feel that it is not possible to express anything their art with more words, they feel happy when they demonstrate their point by singing rather than by talking. While this is true of certain aspects like comparing two ragas, showing the shape and texture of 'gamakas' and also there are many great aspects that can be covered by language, e.g. Biographies of great musicians, study of sahitya and its decorative 'angas', sources of patronage, critical evaluation of trends and philosophical background of our Indian music.

In the present book, an attempt has been made to provide basic guidelines on research. In it, I discussed the subject matter of research. The merits, demerits, various methods like historical, case study, interviews etc. are also covered in it. Various steps mentioned in a research like selection of problem, hypothesis and sources.

The First Introductory Chapter Content

(a) What is Research: In simple word research can be defined as any scholarly investigation in search for truth. Systematized efforts to gain new knowledge are also known as research. Some of the generally accepted definitions of research by well-known scholars are quoted in this part. A research being a fact finding inquiry as certain characteristics of its own, so some of them are mentioned here.

(b) Research in Music: Research in Indian music should be under stood in the light of the uniqueness of Indian thought and values. For it, the research has been finding new facts and it is theoretical as well as practical. Indian music is very rich in traditions and has changed through a very slow process, so new in Indian classical music is not easy to locate.

The findings of research in some area of science may be truly dramatic but research in the field of performing art cannot be spectacular.

(c) Varieties of Research: Several methods or types are being used in research e.g. Pure, Action, Experimental. Any one of them can be used, but it must be carried out on a set pattern and its result should be reliable.

Second Chapter Includes

(a) Selection of Research Problem: Topic selection is an area of primary importance for the secret of success in research. The formulation of a topic with a research problem is really a first step because if the problem has been well conceived in the beginning of an inquiry, the researcher will have very few difficulties in the investigation of the problem.

(b) Formulation of Research Problem: The practical usefulness of the problem plays a significant role in guiding a research worker in selection of data. Formulation of the problems is a important step in research work. He should determine the right kind of research plan or methodology is suited for his research problem.

(c) Hypothesis: A research scholar can not go ahead in a systematic manner with his problems for investigations, without getting some kind of guidance. Such guidance is provided by a hypothesis, which prevent him from grouping in the dark. It has a very important place in research work because without it, research worker cannot proceed in his work. Hypothesis may be developed from a variety of sources e.g. theory, personal experience etc. By discussing the characteristic of good hypothesis, it comes to know that hypothesizes performs their designated functions *vis-a-vis* research and the growth of knowledge generally.

(d) Collection of Data (Primary and Secondary): After formulating a problem, hypothesis, the next step is of assembling the data, standardized research tools may be used for data collection and it begins when most of the things pertaining to the nature and mode of enquiry. Data can be interpreted easily and objectively. They are directly linked with conclusions and are always collected with a sense of purpose. Data are may be either Primary and Secondary. Primary sources are the first appear and the secondary came next. The distinction between these two is very subtle.

Third Chapter only Deals with Primary Sources: In this we discuss various types of methods the interview, questionnaires, historical, case study etc. their advantages and disadvantages, merits, demerits, their types with examples.

Fourth and Final Chapter Contents only secondary sources with their varieties like sculpture, paintings, manuscripts, text books, oral traditions, by them, we not only come to know our great glorious past of our classical music but also its changes from past to present, its various instruments, their changed structure from present, valuable old textbooks, musical gharanas, new discoveries of science used in music e.g. C.D., tapes, A.I.R.'s contribution in expanding our soothing lyrics etc.

I do not claim that the matter contained in this book is original, as the ideas of several learned researches scholars have been gathered and quoted in this work. A list of these standard books is given in the bibliography. I have mainly employed sources from books, periodicals, references in the literature, printed materials, sculptures, paintings, interviews, radios and live concerts. It provides factual knowledge, which encourages independent thinking a growing under-standing and increased appreciation of fundamental principals and values in music.

Dr. Ms. Reena Gautam (Baloria)

List of Illustrations

Contents

1
Sources of Research in Indian Classical Music

INTRODUCTION

Why a research on music? Music is meant to be listened to and enjoyed, not to be read and thought about, as some of our music lovers say that 'music is an art, the fantastic, sophisticated pleasing art of sound. It is a performing art, to be learnt practically from a guru through oral tradition method'. But there is another aspect of this art, made up of its history, its norms, and its forms and formal rules, its style and, together with these, its ethnic and social implications. The study of the inter-relationship and development of all these would certainly improve one's understanding of this beautiful art. "If the art of music be so natural to man that vocal melody is practiced wherever articulate sounds are used, there can be little reason for deducing the idea of music from the whistling of winds through the reeds that grew on the river Nile. And indeed, when we reflect with how easy a transition, we may pass from the accents of speaking to diatonic sounds, when we observe how early children adopt the language of their amusements to measure and melody, however rude, when we consider how early and universally these practices take place there is no avoiding the conclusion, that the idea of music is conatural to man and implied in the original principles of his constitution."[1]

The history of Indian music, in common with that of other arts and sciences, furnishes us with similar instruction. It first origin seems to have been to convey the idea of our passions to others. In progress of time, when language arrived to a certain degree of intelligibility, its use to began to be restricted to the worship of the Supreme being. All music lovers commonly know that Indian classical music has its origin in the Sama veda. Yet the singing of the Sama veda has practically disappeared from our country, so if we want to explore the details of the origin of Indian classical music from Sama veda, we have to study the philosophy of the word 'Sama'. And for this we have to take the help of research. In other words we can say as history and science are complementary to each other. The science of Indian music (theory) owes its existence to the different stages of development in the course of its evolution and its importance as historical concepts in Indian music. Materials collected from the various sources play, the greatest and in establishing, the validity in Indian music. And for this we go back to research methodology, which guides us to the rules and regulations of the process of research.

"Every research work ought to have a practical impact and evidence beyond intellectual hypothesis" (S.V. Rai, S.N. 45 p. 55) . A History student can write on the social life and culture of Bharata's time because it is valuable for history as a discipline to know what it was likes in those days. The situation of a music research is different. If he is writing about the Natya sastra or the cultural background at that time, he should bring out the relevance of this information to the music and the cultural background of the present.

WHAT IS RESEARCH

Curiosity is a distinctive feature of us and we are always ready to know about ourselves and our universe. Questions are always arising in our mind. Whenever we encounter problems, we try to find solutions to them. Finding answers to various problems has given toe progress to human life. Research is composed of two words 're' and 'search', which means to search again or a careful investigation to re-understand or re-examine the fact or to search them. A systematic search for an answer to a question or a solution to a problem is called 'Research'. Research denotes original investigation leading to new knowledge. "The word research has been derived from the French word 'recherche', 're' and 'cercer' modern 'chercher', to search. These words put together mean a critical examination into a topic or subject to discover new facts for increasing sum total of human knowledge."[2]

The origin of research is curiosity. It, therefore means a continued search for knowledge and understanding. As long as man's inquisitive pursuits do not end, the onward march of human society to more advanced achievements will not stop. It is an organized inquiry.[3] It seeks to find explanation to unexplained phenomenon, to clarify the doubtful facts and to correct the misconceived facts. Karlinger defines research as a "systematic, controlled, empirical and critical investigation of hypothetical proposition about the presumed relation among natural phenomena."[4]

Research does not always call for hypotheses. It may also be carried out for the discovery of hypothesis. Research in common parlance refers to a search for knowledge. One can also define research as a scientific and systematic search for pertinent information on a specific topic. In fact, research is an art of scientific investigation. The Advanced Learners Dictionary of Current English Laydown the meaning of research as, "a careful investigation or inquiry specially through search for new facts in any branch of knowledge."[5] Red men and Mory define research as a "systematized effort to gain new knowledge."[6]

The Websters International Dictionary proposes a very incisive definition of research, "a careful critical inquiry of examination in seeking facts or principles, diligent investigation in order to ascertain something". This definition indicates in a very general way what people mean by research. It is also specific to give us a complete and clear idea of what research involves.

And also Webster's third new international dictionary of the English Language (1981, Vol. 2, 1930) defines research as "a studious inquiry or examination especially. Critical and exhaustive investigation or experimentation having for its aim, the discovery of new facts and their correct interpretation, the revision of accepted conclusions, theories, or laws in the light of newly discovered facts, or practical applications of new or revised conclusions, theories or laws" George A Lund Berg says, ". . . sufficiently objective and systematic to make possible classification, generalisation and verification of the data observed". The New Century Dictionary: "A searching made for something especially with care also, a continued careful enquiry or investigation into a subjects in order to discover facts or principles". "It is essentially a systematic inquiry seeking facts through objective verifiable methods in order to discover the relationship among them and to deduce from them broad principles or Laws".—M.H. Gopal.[7]

This is a definition of research in the general sense. According to Moaly, "Actually research is simply the process of arriving at dependable solutions to problems, through the planned and systematic collection, analysis and interpretation of data." (Mouly 1964, p. 4) Fox says "We must know what we do and why we do, we must also known what ways we have considered and rejected and why" (Fox 1969, p. V). According to John Best, "Research is a more systematic activity directed towards discovery and the development of an organised body of knowledge.[8] In other words "Research is considered to be the more formal systematic intensive process of carrying on the scientific method of analysis. It involves a more systematic structure of investigation usually resulting in some sort of formal record of procedures and a report of results or conclusions.

Research is an honest, exhaustive, intelligent searching for facts and their meanings of implications with reference to given problem. It is the process of arriving at dependable solutions to problems through the planned and systematic collection, analysis and interpretation of data. The best research is that, which is reliable, verifiable and exhaustive so that at provides information in which we have confidence. – P.M Cook.

Research is a systematic and refined technique of thinking, employing specialised tools, instruments and procedures in order to obtain a more adequate solution of a problem them would be possible under ordinary means. It starts with a problem, collects data or facts analysis than critically and reaches decision, based on the actual evidence. – C.C. Crawford.

Clifford Woody defines research as "... research per se constitutes a method for the discovery of truth which is really a method of critical thinking. It comprises defining and redefining problems, formulating hypothesis or suggested solutions, collecting, organizing and evaluating data, making deductions and reaching conclusions and at last, carefully testing the conclusions to determine whether they fit the formulated hypotheses". He further states, "Research..., is a method for the discovery of new knowledge that is, a method by which is . . . mended the existing body of organized facts, ideals and aspiration."[9]

The name of research involves mainly a 're-search' activities undertaken to repeat a search and it may be stated that research refers to "a critical and exhaustive or experimentation having as its aim the revision of accepted conclusions in the light of newly discovered facts."[10] "The obvious function of research is to add new knowledge to the existing store, but its power for cleaning our mind of cliches and removing the rubbish of applicable theory is equally notable."[11]

In short, the search for knowledge through objective and systematic method of finding solution to a problem is research. Thus, re-searching may be effective to turn the construction of new theories to take the place of those are no longer able to fit the data of the empirical world. Research, stated otherwise, is a systematic attempt to push back the bounds of comprehension or a seek beyond the horizon of our knowledge some 'truth', some reality, to keep on extending and also consolidating these horizons without end.

Young defines Research as "a scientific undertaking which, by means of logical and systematic techniques aims to —

(*a*) discover new facts or verify and test old facts,
(*b*) analyse their sequences, inter-relationships and causal explanation,
(*c*) develop new scientific tools, concepts and theories which would facilitate reliable and valid study of human behaviour."[12]

The urge of human brain to re-examine and to understand things may rightly be called 'research' at least to begin with. Research, therefore has been an integral part of academic pursuit in the past. It may not only be for academic interest but for more human enlightenment that one should study history to understand the dimensional development of mankind. The first step, therefore, in the development of the concept of research was to think systematically.

The primary purpose of research is to discover principals that have universal applications. Research is the formal systematic and intensive process of carrying on the scientific method of analysis.

Characteristic of Research

— Research is systematic: It is a structured process. It has carefully designed procedures. Research is rarely a blind, shot gun investigation.
— Research is logical and objective, applying every possible test to validate the procedures employed, the data collected, and the conclusion reached. The emphasis of the researcher is as testing rather than proving the hypothesis.
— Research is empirical. It is the collection of data that identifies research as an empirical process. Research is based upon observable experience or empirical evidence. Research rejects revelation as methods of establishing knowledge. It accepts only what can be verified by empirical observation.
— Research is directed toward the solution of problem. It may attempt to answer or to determine the relation between two or more variables. It discovers the cause and effect relationship variables.
— Research emphasis the development of generalization, principles or theories. Research is more than information, retrieval or the simple gathering of information.
— Research demands accurate observation and description. It uses quantitative measuring devices, the most precise form of description. It requires valid data gathering procedures. It may employ mechanical electronic or psychometric devices to refine observation, description and analysis of data.

— Research is reductive, as a part of the attempts to translate from reality to an abstract or conceptual state. Reductionism enables research to play an explanatory role rather than simply a descriptive role.

— Research requires carefully designed procedures that apply rigorous analysis.

— Research requires expertise: The researcher knows what is already known about the problem and how other has investigated it. This is thoroughly grounded in the terminology concepts and technical skills necessary to understand and analyze the data that gathered.

— Research is replicable and transmittable. Previous important studies are deliberately repeated using identical or similar producers with different subjects, different settings and a different time. Replication is always desirable to confirm or to raise questions about the conclusions of previous study. Research is considerably less transitory in nature then the products of other problem solving processes.

— Research is characterised by patient and unhurried activity. It is rarely spectacular.

— Research sometimes requires courage to face the position.

— Research tells us relationship between cause that one effects. It is directed towards what is the solution of the problem or to answer of a question.

— Research demands accurate investigation and description.

— Research involves gathering of new data from primary or secondary sources.

— Research requires deep knowledge in the subject concerned.

— Research was born out to solve the main problems.

Thus the purpose of the research is to serve human beings. The knowledge gained by research is of the highest order. It is not based on assumptions, beliefs and untested generalization. The term 'research' is used to the more systematic and formal research as the systematic objective, an accurate research for the solution to a well-defined problem.

In a short way we can write:

(*a*) Research is directed towards the solution of a problem.

(*b*) Research is based upon observable experience or empirical evidence.

(*c*) Research demands accurate observation and description.

Mere collection of facts and presenting them in a systematic way, summarizing a book or an article or telling an old thing cannot be considered as 'research', because it provides no original contribution to knowledge. Research is an art, involving appreciation and expression and is an effective form of training in advanced types of reflective compositions. It helps the researcher to acquire a thorough knowledge of the topic under investigation. It also provided an indispensable technique for future research workers to find out, what methods and procedures of particular import have been applied? What literature of selected investigations has been covered, and what contributions have been made to arrive at the solutions of the problem under investigation.

RESEARCH IN MUSIC

Introduction

The Indian word for music 'Sangita',[13] which includes vocal music, instrumental music and dance. Music that evolved on the Indian soil and was cultured all through ages in diverse ways and forms by the Indian people and matured in a religious and spiritual atmosphere is called 'Indian music'. It is commonly believed that it originated from nature. But it has a systematic and chronological history, as it passed through different stages of evolution in order to take shape as a complete system of science and art. "Music is a dual entity—it is a science as a matter of exigency and is an art, by nature. As a science it has to obey certain physical laws, while as an art it creates its own forms and order, so as to make a direct appeal to man's aesthetic instincts and enrich him emotionally"[14]

India music includes music in all its forms, vocal, instrumental, and choral, together with the allied arts of dancing and gesticulating. Music is considered to be a fine art. As such it may be defined as an art, which employ sounds, combined so to be agreeable to the ears, as a medium of expressing one's emotion and perceptions. It is the finest among the fine arts.

Research in initial stages moved on the lines of other humanities department. 'Research' in its contemporary mean have not a long history. The meaning of this word is to collect and analyse facts and information and try to gain new knowledge or new understanding. Research in Indian music should be understood in the light of the uniqueness of Indian thought and values. Recent research works on music are accordingly characterized by critical study, analysis, and comparative study of Vedas, Puranas, Natya Shastra and series of works on ancient musicology.

We also find interesting epigraphic interpretation. While recent research unfolds glorious part of Indian music—its highly developed and rich tradition. Music is essentially a performing art. The area of research having relevance in some way therefore appears equally desirable. If the researcher's concern is the style and structure of the music, the methodological tools, transcription and analysis are used. Transcription is a subjective interpretation of a sounding musical phenomenon and its transformation coded in a graphic form. The methodology helps to study the music in and as culture, instead of separating music as an individual component unrelated to the performer or composer.

In order to carry out the research in the perspective of culture and society, the fieldwork is emphasised. By undertaking the fieldwork, not only the music is learnt directly from the teacher but also the social and cultural background. By using the audio recording devices and motion films besides learning to perform the style of music, the researcher must gather the data and material for further investigation. Music in culture is studied either as a microcosm of the culture, in the sense that the musical culture replicates in detail the total cultural, and social system that people have adopted or the music is considered as a commentary of that particular culture. Not mere coverage of the new era, but change in the fundamental approach, practical impact and evidence might make research work really useful. Actual performance should form the basis of research work. Research on instruments from an historical point of view will have to rely as references in musical texts, general contemporary literature, careful, examination of paintings, sculpture and other fine arts, epigraphic references, folk lore and mythology for arriving at a conclusion The realm of research in this regard is practically virgin, but imperative.

The development of Indian music has not been the work merely of inspired artistes. It was born from the profound wisdom of ancient seers, and from what remains of ancient writings on musical theory, we can see that it was a most elaborate science. To day if the music of India is to be saved, we have to reconstruct the bridge between theory and practice. The decadence of some branches of Indian music came from the fact that the practice became separated from the science. Practical musicians can carry the traditions of music for a certain time. But they are unable to adopt it to new conditions.

There still remain many great performers who are the direct disciples of the musicians of the past and they remains also large literatures, which can allow us to rebuild the basic theory of Indian music. The unity however cannot be re-created through a mere scholarly approach of the ancient books. It requires a true understanding of the principles underlying the whole system of music. This study will have to be carried into three main branches of research, which must be co-ordinated and we might call scriptural, archaeological and ethnological. They will refer to manuscripts and books, then to monuments, paintings and other remnants of the ancient ages and finally to the popular tradition of the various peoples, castes and tribes.

It is generally very difficult to arrive at a proper interpretation of available texts without the other sources of information being explored. For example, we have representations of musical instruments in the sculpture of temples, we have their description in ancient books and often find that they have survived almost unaltered in some tribe of the Himalayas or Nilgiris, and it is only when we co-ordinate these three images the description, the picture and the actual use—that we can come to a proper interpretation of the texts. Similarly, the notations of ancient ragas and talas can only be understood by reference to still existing forms found somewhere in the country. Until these are properly studied, the interpretation of ancient notations will remain uncertain. The ancient books tell us for example that the oldest music had a descending and not on ascending scale.

An efficient work of research should therefore mean the study and photography of monuments and ancient paintings, the collecting and editing of the main treatises on music, the recording of popular tradition music and study of popular instruments and musical technique. There is no other country in the world where these three elements are found together with such abundant richness. Therefore, there is no country in the world more important than India for the study of the history and development of music. Indian music is the key to all the existing systems of music. India is the treasure house of music. If research on all the aspects of ancient and traditional music is undertaken on a sufficient scale, it will be possible and even easy to bring back to light some of the most brilliant treasures of Indian musical, theory and this will be the only sound means of preserving the music itself.

The information regarding the music can be divided into documentary sources and non-documentary sources. The documentary sources may further be classified into primary, secondary and territory sources. The non-documentary sources or non-book materials are gramophone records, audio tapes, audiovisual tapes and computer floppies. Materials from other fields also contain information relevant to the music researchers e.g. paintings, sculptures, architecture and coins. The non-book materials are very important sources of information. These sources contain knowledge that cannot be communicated through published materials.

The findings of research in some areas of science may be truly dramatic but the research findings in the field of performing arts cannot be spectacular. About music research Watanabe writes, "It is characteristic of the artistic field that fresh facts are additive rather than replacive, tending more to increase the body of knowledge than to displace or multify data previously accumulated. Each study, no matter how small should contribute something to the sum of human learning and appreciation. Regardless of the magnitude of the project, research is a logical process, it is the pursuit of facts and ideas, the organization of the data to point to some possible concessions, the evaluation of the results and the presentation of the whole in an intelligible fashion."[15]

VARIETIES OF RESEARCH

Research can be divided under two categories. First, according to the methods and second to the purpose. Research may be broadly classified according to its major intent or the methods. It is just an approach to differentiate the distinctive approaches to research, for the purpose of understanding. The different types of research are not sharply distinguishable from one another. There may be overlapping between one type/method and another depending upon the topic or area to be studied. According to this, research may be classified as :

- *(a)* Pure research
- *(b)* Applied research
- *(c)* Action research
- *(d)* Exploratory or formulative research
- *(e)* Discriptive research
- *(f)* Experimental research
- *(g)* Evaluation research

1. Pure Research: Developing scientific theories or basic principles are called 'pure' or 'basic' or 'fundamental' research. The term basic and applied refers to the extent to which the research is directed towards the solution of the problem. "Basic research is designed to add to an organized body of scientific knowledge and does not necessarily produce results of immediate practical value." Pure research is undertaken out of intellectual curiosity. It is not necessarily problemoriented. It aims to extension of knowledge. It may lead to either discovery of a new theory or refinement of an existing theory. The findings of pure research enrich the storehouse of knowledge that can be drawn upon, in the future to formulate significant practical researches. In the words at Direcy, "natural knowledge pursued for its own sake without any direct view of future. Utility will often lead to results of most unexpected kind and of very high practical importance."[16] "Pure or Basic research is a search for broad principles and synthesis without any immediate utilisation objective."

Fundamental researchers are original and investigative studies of a basic nature. The topic or area of investigation would be new and fresh investigation would be carried out to originate a new theory, making additional contribution to knowledge. It may also throw new light on the existing theory or body of knowledge. This research is also known as Theoretical research because its objective is to discover new but broad principles without aiming at any immediate application. This research may be entirely a new discovery of the knowledge, which has not existed so far. Such discovery may follow the researcher's own idea or imagination.

Basic research is concerned with the formulation of theory or a contribution to the existing body of knowledge. It obtains and uses the empirical data to formulate, expend an evaluate theory. That is, why it is also termed as pure or fundamental research. Pure research —

(*a*) "Helps in developing general principles
(*b*) Helps in to find out the central factors in practical problems
(*c*) Becomes a standard procedure for researcher to find out an answer to the problem."

Pure researches aim is to develop theories by discovering broad generalizations or principles. It is primarily interested in deriving new knowledge. Sometimes pure research is described as research conducted to acquire knowledge for its sake. It has little concern with application of findings to the actual problems. Thus, pure research lays the foundation for applied research.

2. Applied Research: Applied research is meant for testing the known theories. In this research, the problem is identified and the results are expected to be applicable in the improvement of the practice or solution to a problem producing material gains. The purpose of applied research is a process testing theoretical concepts in actual problem situations. It has also most of the characteristics of fundamental research.

Applied research carried into finding solution to a real life problem, so requiring an action or policy decision. It is, thus problem oriented and action directed. It seeks an immediate and practical result. Like pure research, applied research also contributes to the development in the following manner:

(*a*) Applied research uncovers new facts, which enrich the concerned body of knowledge.

(*b*) Applied research can put theory to test. From that knowledge of theory, researchers develop a conceptual framework for there study and formulate hypothesis Thus this study offers an opportunity to test the validity of existing theory.

(*c*) Applied research may aid in conceptual classification. The concept surfaces most sharply when we attempt to operationalise it for dealing with research. Thus, research aids conceptual clarity.

(*d*) Applied research may integrate theory of previous study/studies. A practical problem has many facts. It can not be solved by the application of abstract principles. So this problem may require some integration of the theories and principles of various disciplines.

Though the immediate purpose of an applied research is to find solutions to a practical problem, it may incidentally contribute to the development of theoretical knowledge by leading to the discovery of new facts. Applied research adopts the theories, developed through pure research to the solution of problems. Thus, it is concerned with setting things done.

The major difference between an applied and fundamental research is that fundamental research provides the basis upon which the whole super-structure of applied research is built up.

The term 'pure' and 'applied' just represent the polar ends of a continuum. "Research studies have differing degree of 'purity' and 'applicability'', depending on whether their purpose is solely to advance knowledge in a field or to solve some functions problem."[17]

3. *Action Research:* Action research is a type of evaluation study. It is a study of an action programme launched for solving a problem for improving an existing situation. It is the study undertaken with the goal of immediate application. In this type of research, the researcher appears as a participant rather than observer and therefore is actively and even emotionally involved. Its findings are to be evaluated in terms of local applicability not universal validity.

"Its purpose is to improve school practice and to improve those who try to improve the practices to combine the research processes, habits of thinking, ability to work harmoniously with others, and professional spirit"

(Best and learn 1986). According to Lehmenm and Meherem (1971) Action research is a type of applied or decision oriented research, but with the stipulation that the researcher is the same person as the practitioner who will make and line with the decision. "The success of the action research depends on the cooperation of action implementing people and the beneficiaries of the action programme. To differentiate between the fundamental research and action research it can be stated that while fundamental is usually conducted to establish broad generalizations action research is conducted to improve practices. Fundamental re-search is done by 'outside' specialists while people who want to evaluate that own work situation do action research."

4. Exploratory or Formulative Research: Exploratory research is preliminary study of an unfamiliar problem about which the researcher has little or no knowledge. It usually takes the form of a pilot study. An exploratory study/research is one, which has the purpose of formulating a problem for more precise investigation or for developing hypothesis.[18] This study however, has other functions e.g. increasing the investigator's familiarity with the phenomena.

The exploratory study may be considered an earlier step consisting of problem finding or hypothesis formulation to be followed by other steps consisting of problem solving or hypothesis, testing, on a continuum of research process. The purpose of an exploratory study may be —

(*a*) to generate new ideas or
(*b*) to increase the researcher's familiarity with the problem or
(*c*) to make precise formulation of the problem or
(*d*) together information for clarifying concepts or
(*e*) to determine whether it is possible to attempt the study.

An exploratory research does not aim at testing hypothesis. According to Daniel Katz, it just attempts "to see what is there rather than to predict the relationships that will be founded."[19] He advised that "it is much more effective to take one central set of variables and investigate them as thoroughly as possible than to try to study the universe in one piece of research.[20] The end of an exploratory study comes when the researcher finds that further research is not presently possible on the problem or succeeds in identifying the major dimensions of the problem. In the latter case he/she has to plan the formal research design.

5. Descriptive Research: Descriptive research is a fact-finding investigation with adequate interpretation. It is the simplest type of research. It is more specific than the exploratory study, as it has focus on particular aspects or dimension of the problem studied. This research is often referred to as questionnaire or opinion study. It is designed together descriptive information and provides information for formulating more sophisticated studies. All problems do not lend themselves to descriptive study. This method is applicable to problems, which satisfy certain criteria. A descriptive study identifies relevant variables but does not aim at testing hypothesis. Descriptive information can focus directly on a theoretical point. It may be useful in verifying focal concepts through empirical observation.

6. Experimental Research: There are various phenomena such as motivation productivity, development efficiency, which are influenced by various variables. It may become necessary to assess the effect of one particular variable on phenomena. This need has given rise to experimental research. This is a powerful method and it can be used to establish cause and effect relationships between two or more variables.

It involves procedures for gaining knowledge by collecting new or fresh observations under controlled conditions. It studies observable changes that take place in order to establish a cause and effect relationship. According to Festinger, "The experiment is the proof of a hypothesis which seeks to took up two factors in a casual relationship through the study of contracting situations which have been controlled an all factors excepts the one of interest the later being either by hypothetical case or the hypothetical effect." The experimental method which is considered to be the most objective. The important factor of experimental research is the formulation and testing of the hypothesis. It can be said that the experimental research combines the two processes — induction and deduction. Induction is a type of thinking or reasoning form the specific to the general whereas deduction is reasoning from the general to the specific. It is impossible for any researcher to observe all possible situations and therefore he/she must generalize from what he thinks true of some of his/her observations to what is true for all possible observations. Experimental studies have their purpose to test a hypothesis of a casual relationship between variables.

7. Evaluation Research: Evaluation study is one type of applied research. This type of research is primarily directed to evaluate the performance of the developmental projects and other economic programmes that have already been implemented. Education research is a recent addition to the types of research. It would be appropriate to call this category of research as a product of development programming, which has been adopted on a very large scale.

Suchman defines evaluation as, "determination of the results attained by some activity (whether a programme, a drug or a therapy or an approach) designed to accomplish some valued goal or objective."[21] The evaluation is carried out with respect to the broader changes and major objectives of a programme. It is also concerned with changeover time.

The Evaluation research is of three types mainly:

(*a*) *Co-current evaluation:* The word co-current itself points out to the fact that the evaluation goes on side by side with the implementation of a project. This is a continuous process and takes the nature of an inspection of an ongoing programme.

(*b*) *Phasic or periodic evaluation:* This is made after each distinct phase.

(*c*) *Terminal Evaluation:* Terminal valuation is the evaluation of the find these of the project. This is done after the completion of a programme. In this, overall assessment is made to see how best a project has served the objectives for which it was launched.

It is very essential for the conduct of this type of research that the researcher knows very well the objectives of the programme and the process of its implementation. While carrying out the evaluation research a researcher can scientifically took into the performance of the project in relation to the objective that has been laid out and in line with the processes that had been recommended for its implementation.

Some of the varieties of research have been studied above. We have to decide the type of research according to the problem that we undertake to study. Data depends upon this. Data study is taken in the next chapter.

References

1. Encyclopaedia Britannica, 9th ed. Art, music.
2. Quoted from 'Research Methodology in Social Sciences', Dr. S.P. Dhondyal, p. 12.
3. Emory, C. William, Business Research Methods Home Wood Hlinous, Richard D. Irwin, 1976, p. 8.
4. Karlinger, Fred. W., Foundation of Behaviral Research, N.V. Holt, Rinchart and Winston, 1975, p. 11.
5. The Advanced Learner Dictionary of Current English, Oxford, 1952, p. 1069.
6. Redmen, L.V. and Mary, A.V. H., The Romance of Research, 1923, p. 10.
7. Research Methodology and Statistical Techniques, Santosh Gupta, p. 4.
8. John, W. Best, Research in Education, Prentice Hall, New Delhi, 1977-78.
9. Sangeet Avam Shodh Research.
10. The Encyclopaedia of Social Sciences, Vol. ix, Maxmillan, 1930.

11. Clifford Woody, 'The Value of Educational Research to the Class Room Teacher', (Journal of Educational Research), 1927, pp. 172-73.
12. Yong, Pauline V., Scientific Social Survey and Research, New Delhi, Prentice Hall of India, 1977, p. 30.
13. Shloka : 'Geetam, Vadyam tatha Nrtyam tryam Sangeet Muchchyate' (Sangeet Ratnakar 1/21).
14. Hindustani Music (an outline of its physics and aesthetics) G.H. Ranade, p. 26.
15. Watanabe, R.T., Introduction to Music Research, New Jersey, Prentice Hall, 1967, p. 5.
16. Thompson, J.A., Introduction to Science, Oxford University Press, p. 181.
17. Emory, C. William, *op. cit.*, p. 21.
18. Section 8.4, Pilot Studies and Pretests.
19. Festinger, leena nd Danial Katz (eds) Research Methods in the Behavioural Sciences, New York, Holt Rinchart and Winston, 1966, p. 74.
20. *Ibid.*, p. 77.
21. Suchman Edward, A Evaluation Research, New York, Russell Sage Foundation, 1967, pp. 31-32.

2

Selection of Research Problem

INTRODUCTION

The usual sequence of steps presented on research methodology is likely to give out an over simplified version of what all is involved in doing research. It is well worth remembering that the research process involves a number of interrelated activities that overlap continuously rather then follow a prescribed sequence. Thus the researcher has to be constantly anticipating at each step in the research process, the requirement of any slip that may have accrued previously. The first step in the research process in the choice of a suitable problem for investigation. Research starts with a felt difficulty. It takes place when there is a problematic situation and a need to solve the problem.

The decision in this regard to the general area of interest i.e., the topic hardly puts the researcher in a position to start considering the procedures for data collection, since at this stage he does not know precisely what specific questions within his general area of interest he would want answered. Thus a researcher needs to formulate a specific problem before he can take steps relating to collection and analysis of data obviously, without a problem, the heaps of data would hardly mean anything. The meaningfulness of data collected can be ensured only after organising with a view to finding out how they answer a specific problem.

Research really begins when some difficulty or problem demanding a solution perceived by the researcher within the area covered by the topic selected by him. The general area or topic of a study may be suggested either by some practical concern or by some intellectual interest. The researcher may be interested in specifying more on exact conditions that effect the given phenomena in a particular way. If the researcher is working in a field in which there exists a highly developed theoretical system, he/she may want to test specific prediction or expectations based on that theory.

Topic selection is an area of primary importance for the secret of success in research. It is frequently much matter of selecting an appropriate problem, as it is being able to solve the problem that has been selected. Selection of a suitable research problem requires initiative originality and good judgement. The selection of a topic for research is only half a step forward. This general topic does not help a researcher to see what data are relevant to their purpose, what method they would employ in securing them and how they would have to organize these. Before, considering these aspects, we need to formulate a specific problem. The problem defines the goal of the researcher in clear terms. Thus, without a problem research cannot be proved because there is nothing to proceed from and proceed forward.

The formulation of a topic with a research problem is really a first step. A problem have some difficult experiences by the researcher in a theoretical or practical situation. Solving this difficulty is the task of research. Says John Dewey, "It is familiar and significant saying that a problem well put is half solved to find out what the problem and problems are which a problematic situation presents, ... is to be well along an inquiry. To mistake the problem involved is to cause subsequent inquiry to be irrelevant. Without a problem there is blind grouping in the dark."[1] If we go by appearances, it would seem fairly easy to pose a problem for research. But this is not so in reality.

Merton distinguishes three principle components in the progressive formulation of a problem.

(*a*) The originating questions (What one wants to know?)
(*b*) The rationale (theoretical or practical) (why one wants to have the particular questions answered?)
(*c*) The specifying questions (possible answers to the originating questions in terms that satisfy the rationale).[2]

Researchers should choose a broad field within which he/she will conduct the study and he should have a deep interest in the field. Their enthusiasm and real curiosity enhance their motivation for the successful completion of the study. He should approach this task of selecting the problem with considerable humility. A thorough understanding of the field is the first prerequisite in selecting a problem for study. It should be selected from a field of interest and related to the subject of specialization. In other words, A researcher may select a problem for investigation from a given theory in which he was considerable interest. In such situations the researcher must have thorough knowledge of that theory and should be sufficiently inquisitive to explore some unexplained aspects or assumptions of that theory.

The researcher should bear in mind that the research problem originates from a situation of need, where unsolved difficulties appear. In selecting the problem for the study, weightage should be given to the problem and the solution of which would have a great utilitarian value and which needs priority attention.

A good problem selected by the researcher should conform to the following criteria:

1. The problem should express a relation between two or more variables.
2. The problem should be related clearly and unambiguously in question form.
3. Good research problems stem from a clear understanding of the theoretical, empirical and practical aspects of the subject derived from personal experience.
4. Problem should be sufficiently original so that it does not involve objectionable duplication. Originality is the basic credit point of any research. Ignorance of prior studies may lead a researcher to spend time on a problem already investigated by some other worker. While originality is an important consideration, the fact that a problem has been investigated in the past does not mean that it is no longer fit for study. There is need for the testing of former findings under changed cultural conditions.
5. The problem should be interesting for the investigators themselves. If they are not interested in it, he/she will not able to face and overcome the obstacles, which come at every step in research. A major reason for encouraging a researcher to select his own research problem is that the results should prove better in terms of the growth of the investigator and the quality of his work.

Goode and Hatt give the following criteria for the selection of a problem:

"(*a*) the researcher's interest, intellectual curiosity and drive;
(*b*) practicability;
(*c*) the urgency of the problem;
(*d*) anticipating or expected outcomes. Their importance for the field represented and implementation; and

(*e*) resources, training and personal qualifications of the personal, availability of special equipment, data, methods, time and sponsorship and administrator's cooperation."[3]

FORMULATING THE RESEARCH PROBLEM

The selection of a topic for research does not immediately put the investigator in a position to start considering what data they will collect by what methods and how they will analyze them. Before taking these steps, we need to formulate a specific problem, which can be investigated.

"The word 'problem' is derived from the Greek Word 'proballein' anything thrown forward... A question proposed for solution,"[4] A 'problem', in John Dewey. "Represents the partial. Transformation by inquiry of a problematic situation into a determinate situation."[5] In the opinion of Parsons: "A problem is essentially that aspects of the situation which if modified will correct the difficulty."[6] According to Gibson, "a problem is really a spring board for a leap into the unknown."[7] If the problem has been well conceived in the beginning of on inquiry, the student will have very few difficulties in the investigation of the problem.

According to Whiteny (1964, pp. 180-81), "To define a problem means to put a fence round it, to separate it by careful distinctions from like questions found in related situation of need." John Dewey rightly observes: "It is a familiar and significant saying that a problem well put is half solved. To find out what the problem and problems are which a problematic situation presents to be inquired into, is to be well along in inquiry. To mistake the problem involved is to cause subsequent inquiry to be irrelevant or to go astray Without a problem, there is blind groping in the dark."[8]

The practical usefulness of the problem in majority should play a significant role in guiding a research worker in its selection of data. Formulating the problem is unquestionably the most important initial step in research work. Rummel in his work, "An introduction to research procedures in education" says "that personal interest, personal capabilities value of the topic and availability of data are the important principals to consider in the formulation of a research problem". (p. 29). There are many methods and techniques that can be adopted for research in music. Clear thinking and specificity are the basic requirements for a researcher.

As Cohen and Nagel point out "the ability to perceive in some brute experience the occasion for a problem and especially a problem whose solution has a bearing on the solution of other problems is not a common talent among men...is a mark of scientific genius to be sensitive to difficulties where less gifted people pass by untroubled by doubt."[9]

Research in its largest definition is "a process of enquiry necessitating careful and diligent, investigation with careful examination of the facts aiming at objective interpretation." (Webster 1979). The initial concern of the researcher is the problem to be investigated. It needs to be formulated with a specific statement or hypothesis that is testable with appropriate tests. A clear concept of the initial problem is very essential to begin the research process. After identifying the problem of research, the researcher should take for adequate supervision and whether necessary source material and equipment are available to conduct the research.

The problem should be defined clearly and should be familiar with the literature in the field to find out what has been done and what not has been done. After the selection and definition of a problem situation for the purpose of research, the researcher should determine the level of generalization of reflective thinking with respect to the implication of the work, which they about to begin. This means what they should try to find out what aspects of the problem selected by them, have already been investigated into, what techniques were employed by different research workers, and what progress has been made in the direction of the desired solution.

The researcher should determine the right kind of research plan or methodology but suited to the nature of the chosen research problem. At this point researchers of Indian music have to decide whether their study will be essentially historical, experimental or cultural or combination of these. The musical facts should be recognised in two ways one historical and the other systematical. The first one is concerned with the music of past by epochs, people individual composers, the study of the systems of notation from the past to present. The systematic way aims at various branches such as in playing musical instruments, use of voice in singing rules for various compositional forms and other theoretical branch of music from the present to the future. The researcher in music should first of all assess the problem and should decide under which category the problem belongs, whether historical or systematic, depending upon the category, the right type of methodology should be adopted.

If the researcher selects on absolutely new problem, which has never been tackled before, their research may become a pioneer study. They will take up some aspects of a problem, which has not been completely studied, they may also re-work on a problem situation, finding a more effective solution to the existing problem, and therefore they may proceed along the pathway of previous research workers.

All questions raised must be related to the problem. Each major issue or element should be separated with its subsidiary or secondary elements and these should be arranged in local order under the major division. A good statement of a problem must clarify exactly what is to be determined or solved. The most important step in this direction is to specify the variables involved in the questions and define them in operational terms.

We now know that research begins with a problem or a difficulty. It is advatangeous and desirable that the researcher should propose a set of suggested solutions or explanations of the difficulty and such tentative solutions or explanations formulated as proposition are called hypothesis.

HYPOTHESES

Research means systematic method of innovating principle or discovering new facts on the basis of data. One should collect data or information for or against some point of view or proposition and this is termed as hypothesis. After the definition and statement of the problem, the derivation of hypothesis is the most important step in research process. A hypothesis is a smaller body of proposition and small versions of theories.

The word hypothesis is derived from the Greek word hypo 'under' and 'tithemi' — place i.e. to place under mother words, a theory placed under known facts of the problem to explain them.[10] The research hypothesis is a tentative answer to a question. It is an educated guess, generally based upon prior research or theory and to be subjected to the process of verification or disconfirmation (Best and Kahm 1986).

'The hypothesis is precisely defined as a tentative or working proposition suggested as a solution to a problem and the theory as a final hypothesis, which is defensibly supported by all the evidence. The final hypothesis, which fits all the audience, becomes the chief conclusion inferred from the study (Koul 1984). Lund Berg defines hypothesis as a tentative generalization, the validity of which remains to be tested. In its most elementary stage, the hypothesis may be any hunch guess, imaginative idea that becomes the basis for action or investigation."[11]

Goode and Hatt define it as, "a proposition which can be put to a test to determine its validity."[12] "Webster's New International Dictionary of English Language 1956 defines the word hypothesis as a proposition condition or principle, which is assumed perhaps without belief in order to draw out its logical consequences and by this method to test its order to draw out its basically consequences and by this method to test its accord with facts which are known or may be determined". Cohen and Negal highlight the value of hypothesis thus, "we cannot take a single step forward in any inquiry unless we begin with a suggested explanation or solution of the difficulty which originated it. Such tentative explanations are suggested to us by something in the subject matter and by our previous knowledge. When they are formulated as propositions, they are called hypothesis."[13]

Once a researcher knows what is their question (problem) and is they can make guess (a number of a guesses) as to the possible answers? According to Werkneister, "The guesses he/she makes are the hypotheses which either solve the problem or guide them in further investigation."[14] The role of hypothesis for research in the words of Haddock who summarizes it thus (A hypotheses) in the scientific sense is...an explanation held after careful canvass of known facts, in full knowledge of other explanation that have been offered and with a mind open to change of view, if the facts disclosed by the inquiry warrant a different explanation. It is therefore held with the definite purpose of including in investigation all available and pertinent data either to prove or disprove the hypothesis... (A hypothesis) gives point to the inquiry and if founded on sufficient previous knowledge, guides the lines of investigation. Without it much useless data may be collected in the hope that nothing essential will be omitted or important data may be omitted, which could have been easily included if the purpose of inquiry had been clearly defined."[15] The hypothesis is a powerful tool in research process to achieve dependable knowledge. The hypothesis is firmly rooted in a framework of theory. "The function of a hypothesis is to direct our search for the order among facts. The suggestions formulated in the hypothesis may be solutions to the problem. Whether they are, is the task of the inquiry."[16] It's seems to be an accurate statement of the nature and value of hypothesis in investigation, but we believe it to be too sweeping in its assertion that research cannot begin until a hypothesis has been formulated. In this connection, Jackson observes "when search for data is thus guided there will be a minimum of blind collection of irrelevant facts and a minimum of cluttering of the literature with undigested factual information."[17] "The use of hypothesis, thus prevents a blind research and indiscriminate gathering of data which may later prove irrelevant to the problem under study."[18] The formulation of hypothesis is very crucial and the success or the failure of a research study depends upon how best it has been formulated by the researcher.

Importance of Hypothesis

Hypothesis has a very important place in research although it occupies a very small place in the body of a thesis. It is almost impossible for a research worker not to have one or more hypothesis before proceeding with their work. If they are not capable of formulating a hypothesis about their problem, they may not be ready to undertake the investigation. Thus the hypothesis is the foundation of research, If a clear simple specific hypothesis has been developed, it accounts for one fourth of the research works has come to an end.

The importance of hypothesis can be made specifically stated as under:

(*a*) It provides direction to research. It defines what is relevant and what is irrelevant. Thus it prevents the review of irrelevant literature. It not only prevents wastage in the collection of data, but also ensures the collection of data necessary to answer the question posed in the statement of the problem.
(*b*) It is guide to the thinking process and the process of discovery.
(*c*) Without hypothesis, research would be an aimless wandering.
(*d*) It serves as a framework for drawing conclusions. It provides the outline for setting conclusions in a meaningful way.

The importance of hypotheses in research has been emphasized by Cohen and Nagel, who state, "We cannot take a single step forward in any inquiry unless we begin with a suggested explanation or solution of the difficulty which originated it. Such connotative explanations are suggested to us by something in the subject matter and by our previous knowledge when they are formulated as propositions, they are called hypotheses."[19]

SOURCES OF HYPOTHESIS

The sources of hypothesis provide the basis for investigation and ensure the proper direction in which the study should proceed. It facilitates the collection of adequate facts, and helps one to arrive at appropriate conclusions, suggestions and observations. The task of deriving adequate hypothesis is essentially parallel to that of selecting suitable problems, The derivation of a good hypothesis demands characteristic of experience and creativity. Success in an investigation depends on the considerable time and effort spent in tracing and stating tentative hypothesis. A good investigator must have not only an alert mind capable of deriving relevant hypothesis, but also a critical mind capable of rejecting faulty hypothesis. It can be derived from various sources.

(a) Theory: This is one of the main sources of hypothesis. It gives directions to research by stating what is known logical deduction from theory leads to new hypothesis;

(b) Observation: Hypothesis can be derived from observation. From the observation of the behaviour of an artist, for example, we can find the relationship between him and spectators for an article, is hypothesised.

(c) Personal Experience: This may also contribute to the formulation of hypothesis. Personal life and experiences of persons determine this perception and conception. These may in turn direct a person to certain hypothesis more quickly.

Characteristics of Good Hypothesis

(a) Conceptual Clarity: A hypothesis should be conceptually clear. It should consist of clearly defining and understandable concepts. A good hypothesis does not conflict with any law of nature which known to be true.

(b) Specificity: A hypothesis should be specific and explain the expected relations between variables and the conditions under which these relations will hold.

(c) Testability: A hypothesis should be testable and should not be a moral judgement. It should be possible to collect empirical evidences to test the hypothesis.

(d) Availability of Techniques: Hypothesis should be related to available techniques. Otherwise, they will not be researchable. Therefore, the researcher must make sure that methods are available for testing his/her proposed hypothesis.

(e) Simplicity: A hypothesis should be a simple one requiring fewer conditions or assumption. But simple does not mean obvious. Simplicity demands insight. The simpler will be his/her hypothesis about it.

COLLECTION OF DATA

Meaning

The search for answers to research question calls for collection of data. Data means observation of evidence for research findings. The term data (singular datum) refers to facts from which other facts may be reduced. A datum is what is observed, is manifest or phenotypic.[20] About data, Bernard Russell remarks, "The question of data has been mistakenly, as I think, mixed up with the question of certainty. The essential characteristics of a datum is that, it is not inferred."[21]

Standardized research tools or self-designed instruments may be used for data collection. It is accumulation of specific evidence to enable the researcher to analyze research. His purpose is to verify the research hypothesis. Data is required:

— To provide a solid foundation for research
— To determine the quality of research
— To verify the hypothesis
— To find out the fact through qualitative data and
— To provide solution of the problem.

Data are organized in systematic order and can be interpreted easily and objectively. They are directly linked with research conclusions and are always collected with a sense of purpose. Data served as the basic or raw material for analysis. Without an analysis of factual data, no specific inferences can be drawn on the questions under study. Inferences based on imagination or guesswork cannot provide correct answers to research questions. Data from the basis for testing the hypothesis formulated in a study. The method of collection of data depends mainly upon the nature, purpose and the scope of inquiry. On one hand the availability of researches and the time on the other.

Sources of Data

The process of accounting and the systematic recording of the results obtained after concluding the investigation are called the collection of data. As we have mentioned earlier that collection of data is an essential part of a research proposal. Once the purpose has been defined, the problem is to collect data, which are relevant to that purpose, to analyze these data and to present them in a meaningful manner. These data for research investigations may either be primary or secondary. Datas on the basis of collection can be classified in these categories *(a)* primary sources (*b*) secondary sources (*c*) territory sources. The primary sources are the first to appear. Secondary sources come out next. Territory sources are the last to appear. The use of above terms is not always clear cut in practice, the usage may vary sometimes.

Primary Sources

"The Primary sources are original sources from which the researcher directly collects data that have not been previously collected. They are first hand information that is collected through various methods such as observation, interview, and questionnaires. Availability of time and finance also effect the choice of method for collecting primary data.

Besides these, the bulk of primary sources in literature appear in the form of periodicals. There are many periodicals, which are exclusively devoted to reporting original research. It may be pointed out that an article in a journal would be considered a primary source, if it contains information, representing original thinking or a report on new discovery of something. However, an article in the same journal would not be considered as a primary source of information, if it were to contain summary of findings of others or report produced by other persons. Universities normally require a candidate working towards a doctorate degree to write a thesis, under the supervision of a guide. These are usually expected to show evidence of original research and are supposed to form an important category of documents for researchers in the concerned field; these should be considered primary sources of information. There are certain primary sources of information, which remain unpublished e.g. memoranda, diaries (a diary is a personal record of what interested the diarist, usually it is kept from day-to-day), letters to or from a particular individual, oral history (Oral history memories are records of interview it consists of a systematic attempt to obtain from the lips of lining persons, who led significant lines, a fullest record of their contribution to the cultural life of their nation. It can be both detailed and as intimate as any private correspondence and often more reflective in nature. The interviewer and the subject can also verify the transcript).

Secondary Sources

These sources contain data, which have been collected and compiled by other person. Secondary data are already been analyzed earlier and used by other in their own way. They are usually the data, which have been collected by some one else and made available to others in the form of publishing e.g. newspaper, journals, textbooks, diaries, encyclopedias, bibliographies etc.

While using secondary data for research studies, it is essential that these data be properly edited. As the data have been collected by different peoples, it is not likely that these will be published in a manner as would be required by the researcher. Hence, the researcher has to put it strenuous efforts to change the format of the data to suit his/her own requirements. Many times, secondary data may prove completely useless if these have been collected by untrained eminerator or for entirely different purpose. Due to their very nature, secondary sources are more easily and widely available than primary sources. These not only provide digested information but also serve as bibliographical key to primary sources of information. The primary sources are the first to appear and these are followed by secondary sources. It is difficult to find information from primary sources directly. Therefore, one should consult the secondary sources in the first instance, which will lead to specific primary source e.g. all periodicals do not report original work. There are a number of periodicals, which specialise in interpreting and providing opinions on developments reports in primary sources of information. Such periodicals may be considered secondary sources.[22]

In the words of John Medge "the distinction between primary and secondary sources is of 'record' and report'. Record is primarily concerned with a translation — taking place how, whereas the report is written after the event has taken place."[23] It is observed that the process of assembling primary data is called collection of data is different from the process of 'compiling' data from published sources. Thus, the term 'collection' refers to primary data while 'compilation' to secondary data. The nature, purpose and scope of a research study greatly determine the choice of method to be adopted for collecting data. Data, which are primary at one time, may become secondary at another. Once primary data have been made use of, it loses its original character and becomes secondary.

The degree of reliance on primary or secondary sources of data is usually determined by the nature of inquiry. Usually the use of secondary data in thesis writing is made with a view to supplementing or supporting the primary data. When the primary data are localized, the secondary data provide information from contiguous or remote field, and enables the investigator to compare and contrast. But only a judicious and controlled use of secondary data can strengthen in interference drawn from the primary data.

The following points are noteworthy for the preference of primary source in comparison to the secondary source:

- "The primary source gives data in greater details composed to secondary source. The secondary source often omits part of the information;[24]
- In the secondary source, there is a possibility of mistakes due to errors in transcription made then the figures were copied from the primary source.
- The availability of trained investigators also effects the choice of the method to be employed in data collection. If trained investigators are available, primary method should be adopted

for the collection of data. In case of non-availability of trained investigators, it is recommended to adopt secondary method of data collection.

— The objective and the scope of the inquiry also determine the method to be adopted in the collection of data. The selected method must suit the objective and the scope of the inquiry."[25]

The difference between primary and secondary data is only of the degree of detachment with the original source. The choice between primary and secondary data mainly depends upon the nature, objectives and scope of the inquiry, availability of time and money, degree of accuracy desired and the status of the investigator. The primary data are more reliable on the face, but the secondary data can be relied only by examining the source from which they have been obtained, their true significance, completeness and method of collection. Sometimes in a certain investigation both primary and secondary data are used as supplement to one another. The advantage or disadvantage of a particular technique of data collection cannot be understood unless it is examined against the purpose of the study for which it is employed.

References

1. John Dewey, Logic The Theory of Inquiry, Henry Holt & Co., N.Y., 1938.
2. Robert, K. Merton, et. al., *op. cit.,* pp. ix-x.
3. Research Methodology, P. Saravanaul, p. 65.
4. Research Methodology in Social Sciences, Dr. S.P. Dhoadyal, p. 66.
5. John Dewey, *op. cit.,* p. 108.
6. Kenneth, H. Parsons, the Logical Fundament Economic Research, In. of Form Econ., (vol. xxxi, no. 4, 1949), p. 663.
7. Quoted from Meta, R. Enberger and Marian, H., *op. cit.,* p. 19.
8. Cohen & Nagel : An Introduction to Logic and Scientific Method, p. 51.
9. John Dewey, *op. cit.,* p. 108.
10. Research Methodology in Social Science, Dr. S.P. Dhondyan, p. 79.
11. Lundberg, G.D., Social Research, New York, Longman Green & Co., 1942, p. 119.
12. Goode, William J. and Hatt, Paul K., Methods in Social Research, Mc. Graw Hill, 1952, p. 56.
13. Cohen and Negal, An Introduction to Logic and Scientific Methods, p. 51.
14. Werkneister W.H., Basis and Study of Knowledge, Harper & Sons, New York, 1948, p. 300.
15. Chaddock, R.E., Principle and Methods of Statistics, Houghton Miffilin Co., New York, 1925, p. 372.
16. Cohen & Niger, *op. cit.,* p. 56.
17. L. Jackson, Soil Chemical Analysis, Prentice Hall Inc. Englewood Cliff N.J., 1958.

18. Young P.U., *op. cit.*, p. 104.
19. Cohen & Negal, *op. cit.*, p. 56.
20. Johan Gathing, Theory and Methods of Social Research, N.Y., 1867, 27.
21. Bertrand Russell, An Inquiry into Meaning and Truth, New York, V.W. Nortcn and company, Inc. 1940, p. 155.
22. Reference Service, Krishan Kumar, pp. 115-16.
23. Wilkinson & Bhandarkar, Methodology and Techniques of Social Research, p. 145.
24. Research Methodology and Statistical Techniques, Santosh Gupta, p. 129.
25. *Ibid.*

3
Primary Sources

INTRODUCTION

The process of working out a research design involves, as we have suggested, making decisions (with references to the research problem or purpose) about the techniques to be employed for collection of relevant data, reliability and precision of the instruments of data collection, that would serve as a basis for drawing fairly acceptable inferences about the given problem or given research work. The process of deliberate anticipation goes a long way toward the researcher getting prepared against future hazards. Through these sources the investigator ensures that he will most properly achieve his research objective without having to spend amount of time, money and energy.

The plan of research thus complete, the researcher turns to the implementation part of it. He set himself to the task of formulating the instruments or tool of data collection, such as the questionnaire, interview, observation, case study, surveys, historical methods etc. The task of formulating these measuring instruments is not an easy one by any means. Usually considerable preparation in terms of a deep understanding of the research problem, discussion with experienced and knowledgeable persons, systematic study of pertinent literature etc. has to go under way before the researcher is really in a position to formulate his final work. The choice of techniques to be utilized for data collection and the form in which these are to be preside into service depend on such consideration as: who are to be the respondents, what is to be known from them, when where and how. Some techniques have a distinct advantage over others in certain kind of situation. Certain situations and problems require that not one but two or more techniques be used for obtaining information.

PRIMARY SOURCES

Primary sources of information are the first published records of original research and development or description of new application or new interpretation of an old theme or idea. These are original documents representing unfiltered original ideas. These constitute the latest available information. A researcher producing new information can make it available to the particular community through use primary sources. Often, it may be the only source of information in existence. Primary sources are unorganized sources, which are rather difficult to use by them. The secondary sources help us to use these. These are important sources of information. A subject becomes a discipline in its own right when independent primary sources begin to be produced in that area. Primary sources and the researchers to:

(*a*) Keep themselves up-to-date and well informed of new developments,
(*b*) Avoid duplication in research, and
(*c*) Help other to build on this by means of further work and thus generate more information.[1]

The compilation of primary data is done through various methods. Therefore, it is essential to understand that how these methods are applied while collecting primary data. Some of the methods frequently used in the music research are being studied.

QUESTIONNAIRE

"In general word questionnaire refers to a device for securing answers to questions by using a form which the respondent fill in himself." Goode and Hatt (1952) "By questionnaire is meant a set of question, developed in an organized and ordered manner, for gaining information from the people in relation to a given problem". Questionnaire method of data collection is the tool, which is more frequently used in mail survey research than any other method of data collection.

The questionnaires are usually mailed to the respondents, who are expected to read and understand the questions and reply to them in writing in the given spaces. It is the most flexible tool in collecting data. It serves as a most appropriate and useful information-gathering device.

Types of Questionnaire

Questionnaire can be divided into different types on the basis of the type of response required.

(i) Structured and Non Structured Questionnaire: Structured questionnaires are those in which definite concrete and pre-ordained questions are formed with additional questions. The questions are presented with exactly the same wording and in the same order to all the respondents. The form of the question may be either closed or open. The important point is that they are stated in advance and not constructed during the questioning.

A non-structured questionnaire is often used as the interview guide, which is non-directive. The interviewer possesses only a blue print of the enquires and they are largely free to arrange the form or statement of the questions. Instead of approaching respondents with a fixed list of questions, the interviewer attempts to get respondents to talk freely about the subject of interest. By doing so, the interviewer hopes to put respondents to ease and to encourage them to express any ideas, which they have on the subject. This type of questioning secures more information from the respondent who is not kept in the strait jacket of a set list of questions. This flexibility is a major advantage of the method. The main disadvantage is the difficulty and cost of interpretation.

Although the data collected in the two studies were not directly comparable, the results obtained with the simple structured, questionnaires were similar in nature to those obtained by the non-structured approach. The structured study, however, benefited from having the prior data as a guide to the study design.

(ii) Fixed or Closed Questionnaire: In the fixed or closed response type of questionnaire, not only the questions but also the answers are already given. A respondent is asked to check the answer that fits them the best. These answer may be simply Yes or No, for example:

Do you think the classical music
is understood by everyone? Yes / No

Do you watch classical music
on television? Yes/No/sometimes

No writing is required on the part of the respondent thus, it helps in acquiring answers quickly, but sometimes respondent may be forced to make a choice among alternatives that do not fit them well and this lead to a wrong information.

But where a respondent cannot express himself verbally, the fixed response item is an advantage. One of the major draws back of the closed questionnaire is that it may force a statement of opinion on an issue about which the respondent does not in fact have any opinion. Although the wording of questions is the same for all respondents which may be quite different from those intended by the researcher. And he may be led to choose a response, even when they have no knowledge of it, or limited alternatives may not cover their point of view.

(iii) Open End Questionnaire: The open forms 'open end' or 'unrestricted' or free response type questionnaire call for respondent's own words. This type consists of questions, which are written, in specific language, but the respondents are free to give answer in their own words. No clues are provided. In this type of questionnaire, respondent is not forced to reply in terms of the given choices. It probably provides greater depth of response. The distinguishing characteristic of open-ended questions is that they merely raise an issue but do not provide or suggest any structure for the respondent's reply. The respondent is given the opportunity to answer in their terms and own frame of reference and is not forced to reply in terms of any of the given choices. So it helps in gaining insight into the opinion and behaviour of the people. The main disadvantage of this is that involves difficulties in coding, classifying, grouping and comparing of the responses and persons who cannot express themselves adequately on paper as compared with fluent persons.

(iv) Mixed Type Questionnaire: Many questionnaires are of mixed type. They include open and close type questionnaire. This means that they consist of both fixed and open-ended type of questions. Thus questionnaire may consist of factual inquiries about an individual marital or occupational status and on the other hand many questions are related to mental process and need to be of open end type or descriptive in nature.

(v) Pictorial Questionnaire: In the pictorial questionnaire pictures are used to promote interest in answering questions. It is used extensively for illiterate persons. In this questionnaire, selected alternative answers in the form of picture concerned.

Construction of Questionnaire

Questionnaire construction may apparently seem to be a simple task but in reality is not. A good questionnaire is one that helps the researcher to obtain data related to the objective of the study. The researcher cannot develop a good questionnaire simply by what they think would provide them the type of data for which researcher is looking. Various steps are to be taken for developing a questionnaire.

The development of a questionnaire, whether it is used in a personal interview, is to be self-administered. Developing a suitable questionnaire is the most challenging aspect of research. The researcher must have some insight into the process of human communication and must be intelligent enough to anticipate the type of responses they may get in reply to certain question. A questionnaire is a format, containing a list of questions sequentially ordered to obtain information relevant to the objectives of the study.

It is not only a list of questions used to obtain responses, it is also specifically intended to obtain particular kind of data. The development of a questionnaire as a whole rather than the mere wording of any particular question. It requires a certain amount of technical knowledge and researcher must decide what to ask potential respondents. He must make an outline of the several possible aspects of his investigation topic. At this stage, the researcher should write down every area in which additional facts would be helpful in the proposed research.

When information is gathered by personal interview or mailing the questionnaire, the respondent can read the questions and record without interviewer help, such a questionnaire is called a self-administered questionnaired. This process is not a matter of simply listing questions that comes to his mind, it is a rational process involving much time, effort and thought. As questionnaire is an instrument for gathering data for a specific study, its construction should flow logically from the data, required for the given study and these data can be determined by a deep analysis of the research objectives. When the variables are not known, it becomes difficult to decide as to what information is to be sought.

In determining the contents of the questionnaire, the researcher should consider the problem, which they want to investigate, or the hypothesis to be tested. Once these are specific and clear, the researcher use these contents for the questionnaire. The review of literature helps the researcher to discover the types of questionnaire or data collection procedures that other used under similar conditions. The researcher should make every effort to encourage each participant to build other ideas to develop extensive possible areas in questionnaire content.

In framing of a questionnaire, first of all we have to decide about the general strategy of the questionnaire and should have to decide whether structured or unstructured, direct indirect questions that would help to achieve research objectives. Thereafter, the form of each question has to be decided. Whether they should be open or closed. Similar, structure of answers or form of response has to be decided. Its structure depends upon the nature of quality of information wanted and the type of the respondents.

As the meaning of words differs from persons to person, the question designer should choose words, which carry same meaning to every person. The use of structured questions assumes that all respondents will understand the same thing by the same word. The collection of data is ultimately an exchange of ideas between the investigator and the respondent. The exact understanding between them call for the use of vocabulary common to both parties. Each must understand what the other says and it should be exact or precise reflecting what the question contents. Ambiguous or loaded words and long questions should be avoided, as they are hard to follow. They can be used only when they serve some specific information. Such items that will give rise to confusion should be formulated as two or more questions.

The order, in which questions are arranged in a questionnaire, is an important as question wording. First, an appropriate sequence can ease the respondent's task in answering. Second, the sequence can either create or avoid biases due to context effects. The opening question is important; one should start with easy questions so that the respondent would enjoy answering. Later on one should slowly switch over to more specific and difficult questions. In some special cases one may use closed questions first and open one later on. Questions to which the informant may be sensitive should not be put at the extreme end because this may leave him with wrong impression and make it difficult to question him later.

Advantages of Questionnaire

The questionnaire is an impersonal technique, so its uniformity from one situation to another is provided by its standardized wordings of questions, their sequences and its instruction for recording responses. Since its approach makes it possible to cover a large number of people, it is decidedly more economical in terms of money and time. Another typical merit of the questionnaire is that it ensures anonymity. The respondents have greater confidence that they will not be identified as holding a particular view or opinion. The questionnaire places less pressure on the respondents for immediate response. It gives more time to consider each point carefully before giving their reply in writing. Usually the questionnaire suffers from certain errors with the results that the reactions of questionnaires are often unfavourable and response is slow.

Disadvantages

One of the major limitations of the questionnaire is that it can be administered only on subjects with a considerable amount of education. It is seen that very few have the motivation and patience to write as much as they might speak out. The usefulness of the questionnaire is restricted to issues on which the respondents have more or less clear views that can be simply expressed in words. A significant limitation of the questionnaire is that the researcher is not in a position to vary the stimuli or social atmosphere. John Galting has offered a very apt analogy. He links interview to the musical symphony "Waves after waves of sound impinging upon the audience. The questionnaire on the other hand has been linked to presentation before subjects of stimuli in the manner of a painting, various shades of colour spread over the canvas. In other words, the interview method involves presentation, one after the other of stimuli in the continuum of time whereas in the questionnaire, these are presented in space."[2]

To conclude question designing remains a matter of common sense and experience and of avoiding known pitfalls. Alternative versions of questions must be rigorously tested in pre tests and the pilot study for the absence of the hard and fast rules, test of practicability must play a crucial role in questionnaire construction.

OBSERVATION

Observation means viewing or seeing. We go on observing something or the other while we are awake. Most of such observations are just casual and have no specific purpose. We are almost constantly engaged in observation. It is our basic method of obtaining information about the world around us. "We are all constantly observing and noticing what is going on around us. We look out of the window in the morning to see whether the sun is shining or if it is raining and make our decision about carrying an umbrella accordingly. There is no need to example, as long as we are awake, we are almost constantly engaged in observation. It is our basic method of getting information about the world around us."[3]

In the ancient time, the scientists observed the phenomenon around them and come to conclusions, but observation, as a method of data collection is different from casual viewing. Observation may be defined as a systematic viewing of specific phenomena in its proper setting for the specific purpose of gathering data for a particular study. Observation is a method for both seeing and hearing. It is a primary technique for collecting data on non-verbal behaviour. In this method, one collects the information by directly or indirectly watching and recording the events as they go on.

The term 'observation' sounds to be very simple. From this, one may derive that it is an easy and simple method of data collection. Though observation is one of the most widely applied methods yet it is often criticized as being the most subjective and unreliable method. Even then the observation method is still important. The concise Oxford Dictionary defines it as 'accurate watching and noting of phenomena as they occur in nature with regard to cause and effect or mutual relations.' Observation method is "a data collection method in which a person (usually trained) observes subjects or phenomena and records information about characteristics of the phenomena" (Sprall 1988, p.166).

Although observation most commonly involves sight or visual data collection, it can also include data collection via the other senses, such as hearing. Observations are often conducted as a preliminary to surveys and may also be conducted jointly with documental study or experimentation. "Observation is deliberate study through on eye, may be used as one of the methods for scrutinizing collective behaviour and complex of institutions as well as separate units comparing of totality." (P. V. Young). Observation as a tool of research deals with the external behaviour of persons in appropriate situation controlled or uncontrolled.

Observation is preferred when one wants to study in detail the behaviour, that occurs in some particular setting or situation. Indeed, it is a primary research instrument of gathering data in a more natural way. Observation technique is adopted for testing hypothesis where structured method cannot be employed. Thus observation is a perfect method of investigation and probably most popular one in gaining knowledge of research. In every act of observation, there are two components, the object or what is observed and the subject or the observer. If one may observe one's own immediate experience, it would be subjective observation or introspection and if the observer becomes an entity apart from the thing observed it would be objective observation or extrospection.

Types of Observation

Observation may be of many types. It may take place in the natural or real life setting or in a laboratory. The procedure adopted in observation may vary from one study to another, depending upon the nature of data and purpose of study under investigation. We may classify observation broadly as under :

(*a*) Participant/non-participant observation,
(*b*) Structured/Unstructured observation.

The observational technique to be chosen in a particular study depends on the purpose of study.

(a) Participant Observation: Participant observation is based on the theory that an interpretation of an event can only be approximately correct when it is composite of two points of view, the outside and the inside. Thus, the view of the person who was a participant in the event, and the view of the person who was not a participant but only an observer or analyst. The participant observer is a regular participant in the activities and the other participants do generally not know his dual role. In this, the observer is a part of the phenomenon or group, which is being observed, and he acts both as observer and a participant. He shares the situation as a visiting stranger, an attentive listener, and a eager learner. He gets deeper into the feeling emotions and behaviour of the actors and thus observes and records them more accurately.

Observer not only sees the actions or behaviour, but also able to know why and under what given situation an individual acts or behaves in a given manner. Recording of behaviour in this context increases the richness of data. In sum, to quote John Madge, "When the heart of the observer is made to beat as the heart of any other member of the group under observation, rather them as that of detached emissary from some distant laboratory than he has earned the title of participant observer".[4]

(b) Non-Participant Observation: A non-participant observer does not participate in group activities and does not pretend to be a member of the group to be observed. The observer takes a position at a place, where his presence is the least disturbing to the group but from where he can observe in detail. This type is applied, when the observer collects facts in the most formal manner. In non-participant observation, the observer is unattached with the activities of the group so that he impartially and objectively maintains his observation.

(c) Structured Observation: It is often used to provide systematic description or to test casual hypothesis. While using this method, the researcher should keep in mind things like: What should be observed? Or how the accuracy of observation can be ensured? In structured observation method one makes use of more carefully drawn schedules and questionnaire. He may even use the audio visual aid etc. Being standardized method the structured observation can be easily repeated and the limitations of the study can be easily assessed. Since the situation and the problem are already explicit, the observer is in a position to set up in advance the categories in terms of which he will analyse the situation.

(d) Un-Structured Observation: The unstructured observation is diametrically opposed to the structured observation in its ideal typical formulation. The observation method is said to be simple and unstructured when things to be observed are not prefixed. The observer is more or less in a free situation and he has to decide at the spot of observation about the things to be observed. This give the observer greater opportunities of decision making and this makes the role of his more significant. Since unstructured observation is mostly used as an exploratory of technique, the observers understanding of the situation is likely to change as he goes along.

Advantages of Observation

Observation is decidedly superior to survey research, experimentation or document study for collecting data on non-verbal behaviour. The virtue of observation is its directness.[5] It makes it possible to study behaviour as it occurs. The researcher needs not to ask people about their behaviour and interactions, they can simply watch what they do and say. In observation, generally behaviour takes place in its natural environment. It is less reactive than the other major data collection technique.

However, the observation method has various limitations. Firstly, it is an expensive method and the information provided by this method is very limited. Sometimes unforeseen factors may interfere with the observational task. Observation cannot be used as and when the researcher finds it convenient to use it, they have to wait for the event to occur. For example, an observation of folk dance of a tribal community is possible only when the trebles perform it or if the observer wants to listen a classical raga or watch a classical dance, he will have to wait until the singer or dancer start performing.

In research the three commonly used techniques for gathering data are the questionnaire, the interview and the observational techniques. Observational techniques are considered most suitable for describing behaviour as it occurs. It is desirable that observation should be accurate, valid and reliable. Observation is frequently considered very valuable in research. Thus it is, "widely recognized as a prime requisite of research in general and descriptive research in particular". (Bush and Hater 1980, p. 147.)

INTERVIEW

The different methods of data collection used in research help us to gain accurate knowledge and the important ones are observation, case study questionnaire, schedule and interview. The interview method varies from being most highly qualitative method. The observation method is mainly suited to the study of culture or human behaviour. It cannot be used to gain information about the person's perceptions, feelings, emotions, motivation, anticipation etc. Such type of information can be collected through questionnaire, interview methods. These methods differ among themselves in their directedness and structuredness.

Interviewing is one of the major methods of data collection. It may be defined as a two way systematic conversation between an investigator and an informant initiated for obtaining information relevant to a specific study. The face to face conversation between the researcher and the respondent is called an interview. It is a process of personal interaction. It involves not only conversation but also learning from respondent's gestures, facial expression. Interview as a research tool is, in a sense, an oral type of questionnaire of schedules whereby the subject supplies needed information in a face to face relationship. In simple words, interview can be called as the process of talking in more purposive and more systematic manner than our day to day gossiping with each other.

According to P.V. Young, "Interview may be regarded as a systematic method by which a person enters more or less imaginatively into the life of a complete stranger".[6] In interview method respondent tries to enter into the feelings of the respondent but at the same times tries to maintain the objectivity of research while studying about the individual. The dynamics of interviewing however, involves much more than in oral questionnaire. It is based on the process of communication or interaction between the interviewer and the interviewee or respondent. It is relatively more flexible tool than any written enquiry form and permits of explanation, adjustment and variation according to the situation. Harder and Lindman quote, "Interview consists of dialogue verbal response between two person or between several persons. These responses while verbal in an objective sense are conditioned by a number of other factors some of which are subjective and some objective".[7]

M.N. Basu quote, "An interview can be defined as a meeting of person face to face on some point."[8] According to him it is a way of collecting information by the interviewer from the informant in a face to face relationship on some point. Interviewing may be used either as a main method or as a supplementary one in studies of persons. It is the only suitable method for gathering information from illiterate or less educated respondents. The participant, the interviewer and the respondent are stranger. Hence the investigator has to get him introduced to the respondent in an appropriate manner. Interview is not a mere casual conversational exchange, but a conversation with a specific purpose viz. obtaining information relevant to a study. It is mode of obtaining verbal answers to questions but verbally. The interview is not necessarily being on a face to face basis, it can be conducted over the telephone too. Although it is not a conversation between two persons, it can also be conducted with a group of persons depending on the requirement of the study. G.W. Allport sums up beautifully. He says, "If you want to know how people feel, what they experience and what they remember, their emotions and motives are like, and the reasons for acting as they do, why not ask them?"[9]

During the interview, care should be taken that responses should be interpreted in context and may not be comparable from one social context to another. Steps in an interview are all the same as those of questionnaire. A first step is to write a statement describing the general purpose of the research. Thus a good interview, as a tool of research requires a proper preparation, skilful execution, adequate recording and interpretation.

Interview is an intersectional process and it is between interviewer and the respondent, depends upon how they perceive each other. The respondent reacts to the interviewers appearance, behaviour, gestures, facial expression and his own personal needs, therefore the investigator must become alert to what he/she is bringing to the interview situation though their appearance and behaviour. He should not argue or dispute and should rather maintain an impartial and objective attitude.

Musicians in India are the storehouses of knowledge for Indian classical music. Such knowledge is orally communicated from teachers to pupils. Most of the researchers working in this field have to personally contact the musicians and musicologists for the needed information. Interview method has to be adopted for the topic related with individuals, gharanas, music, education forms and styles in music and trends and traditions in classical music. In India the musicians have their own opinions about various issues and problems related with music and their possible solutions. For eliciting their views on some topic researcher should be advised to personally contact such personalities and ask questions. By observing the mood and response from the interviewee then he should proceed further cautiously.

Structured Interview

The structured interview is the one in which questions are posed in a face to face, situation and the respondent is offered a complete test or some of the potential answers. Questions to be asked are formulated before the interview. In this method, the investigator collects information by directly asking the respondents on the basis of a schedule. In it, not only the type of information sought, but also the specific question to be asked, the language of the question and their order is prefixed. So the interview does not have the freedom to ask extra questions.

Structured interviewers mostly contain closed-ended questions. There are those questions in which the responses are fixed in form of 'yes' or 'No' or series of answers, out of which a respondent can choose the one. Structured interview method is used when data is to be collected from a large number of people. It helps in systematic collection, comparison organization and analysis of data within a limited time period. But it suffers from some limitations. It tends to use the spontaneity of natural conversation and the way in which the interview is structured may be such that the respondents view are minimized.

Unstructured Interview

Unstructured interview is one in which questions are posed in a face to face situation and the respondent is permitted totally free or limited free response. This is the least structured on. In this method the questions are not essentially preplanned structured or ordered. The investigations are given some broad topics upon which they have to collect information. This mode of interview is, therefore known as narrative interview. And the interviewers encourage the respondent to talk freely about a given topic with a minimum guidance. Often the arrangement and wording of the questions are to be determined on the spot by the investigator and he must also be able to analyze quickly what the respondent says so that he can probe for further information. He must know how to deal with different types of respondent.

The type of information that one cannot get through standardized structured interview is gained through this method. The flexibility of the unstructured interview helps in bringing out the spontaneous and revealing responses from the subjects and by this flexibility in unstructured interview, it becomes difficult to compare one interview with other one. Compared with structured interview, this interviewer provides a far greater flexibility with regard to questioning the subjects. It is generally better for studying perceptions, attitudes and motivation but is more difficult to analyse. Unstructured interview provides greater opportunity to explore the problem is an unrestricted manner. As John Galling says, "The advantage of unstructured response is to be unprecise, that they permit the unexpected response".[10]

The Directive Interview

This type of interview is also designed as controlled or guided or structured interview. This interview often takes the form of a questionnaire because questions are presented in this type of interview with the same wording and in the same order to all the respondents so that the respondents are replying to the same questions. There are two types of questions as fixed alternative or closed and open-ended questions. In closed questions the responses of the subject are limited to stated alternatives. The open-ended question is designed to permit a free response from the subject rather than one limited to the stated alternatives. The direct interview has many disadvantages also, as it uses closed questions, which sometimes force the respondents to give some sort of opinions in case about which they do not have any opinion.

Non-Directive Interview

It includes questions of the open-end form and permits much freedom to the interviewer to talk freely about the problem under study. In most, interviews, interviewers are allowed to ask questions about the given topic but they are instructed not to influence or bias or direct the respondents to change the response. In non-directive interviewers does not follow pre-determined structured or guided questions. The respondent is encouraged to talk freely and frankly.

Personal Interview

Personal interview method requires a person known as the interviewer asking questions generally in a face to face contact to the other person or persons. At times, the interviewer may also ask certain questions and the interviewer responds to those, but usually the interviewer initiates the interview and collects the information. This sort of interview may be in the form of direct personal investigation. In the case of direct personal investigation, the interviewer has to collect the information personally from the sources concerned. They have to be on the spot and have to meet people from whom data have to be collected.

For music usually a tape recorder is used for recording the talk. This is done with the permission of the interviewee. If the answer is not clear, supplementary questions may be asked. If the researcher does not like a question or is uneasy to answer it, he may immediately drop or reform the question. Moreover, the interviewer must have a fair knowledge about the persons to be interviewed and the elementary questions as Guru and Gharanas name, style in performing, their first performance, age from which they started to learn music etc., but must not ask about the professional qualifications, this can be hurt their ego.

Telephone Interview

Telephone interviewing is a non-personal method of data collection. It may be used as a major method or supplementary method. This method of collecting information consists in contacting respondents on telephone itself. It is not very widely used method but plays important part in urgent surveys. One chief advantage of the telephone interview is that it is fast. It might be possible to conduct a number of interviewers in short time on telephone. It has lower cost compared to direct interviewing. They are generally much lower then travel costs for interviewers. Quality of responses is good because; interviewer bias is reduced as there is no face to face contact between the intérviewer and the respondent. One disadvantage is that respondents are often less motivated, visual material cannot be used and limited to a persons with listed telephones. Hence this method is not useful in every field, only five or six simple questions can be asked. Hence the telephone cannot be used for a longer questionnaire. A further limitation is that the interviewer is unable to observe the respondent and thus cannot gather non-verbal data. Finally, since the interviewer is not present before the respondent, they cannot persuade the respondent to complete the interview, cannot standardize the surroundings in which the interview takes place.

"The greatest value of interview method is the depth and detail of information than can be secured, when used with a well conceived schedule, an interview can obtain a great deal of information".[11]

Interview is not free from limitations. Its greatest drawbacks are that it is costly in both time and money and its results are often adversely effected by interviewers mode of asking question and interactions, incorrect recording and also by respondents faculty perception, inability to articulate etc. But there is always a possibility to achieve an excellent communication between respondent and an interviewer. An interview is most appropriate for certain types of information, which are personal and confidential in nature. These include personal habits and characteristics, opinions and beliefs etc.

In comparison to other methods of data collection, interview is more useful for music students. It is flexible and any number of questions and counter question may be asked and clarification may be sought. As already said that the musicians in India have much information that is personal to them. By tactful handling such type of information may be documented for future artists.

Pandit Ravishanker — In an Interview

1. What is the life span of an artiste in terms of performance? Seeing the kind of vigor and energy you perform with no one can judge your age.

Thank you, that is a nice compliment. You mean musician? For a musician, it varies with his health. You hear people like Mallikarjun Mansoor. He is almost 74, and singing exactly as he was years ago, which is really an outstanding achievement for a vocalist, because to maintain a voice is difficult with age. Instrumentalists, or course, have an advantage, I have seen that in my own life, since my childhood whether in the west or here. Pablo Casals used to perform till he was in his 80s, and Rubenstein, the pianist who died recently, did the same, to name a few. In our country my Ustad Baba Allauddin Khan, as well as Ustad Hafiz Ali Khan, and a number of musicians perform till very late in their age. It depends upon their health, stamina and all that.

2. Where would you be teaching them?

Mostly wherever I am, I have been doing it for the last three to four years. In Benaras I have my organisation called RIMPA which means Ravi Shankar Institution for Music and Performing Arts. It used to be research but it is changed to Ravi Shankar, and I have this cash course, master classes for two to three weeks where almost 20 to 25 students come from all over India.

3. Who is an advanced student in sitar?

An advanced student is the one who has been playing at least for 10 to 15 year and is already advanced on the verge of performing or already performing, but still hasn't reached the final destination, and whose till needs more instruction in 'Ragas' and the intricacies of "tals' and things like that.

4. You wouldn't like to do that on a permanent basis — like all the year found?

No no, I believe in this old style of person to person teaching — Gurumukhi vidya it is known as, and that's the best apart from teaching, I also have tremendous urge to do a lot of creative things. So it is creative work I am mostly interested in. It's my second love next to playing the sitar, whether it is composing orchestral music, or ballet, or opera, or writing for films.

5. ***Panditji, since Indian music is not written how does one leave behind a tradition of Music? Is there a Ravi Shankar be preserved?***

Yes. That's the whole thing, we can't what I perform on the stage or a regular performance can be preserved only by modern technology — a cassette records, spool recorder or disc recording or video now. This is the only way to hold the music that has been performed. But there is no way to write it down and preserve it. The only thing that we can write and preserve is something which is composed like a music piece which is done in films or for a special occasion (like the Asiad) or for a ballet, an opera or orchestral composition that can be written down, but it is not necessarily pure classical raga music.

6. ***What about your disciples, for instance? They will be your legacy left behind in the world.***

I have a number of students already performing who are recognized. I regard as a performer Gopal Krishna who plays the Vichitra Veena, and some students on the sitar like Jaya Vishwas or Manju Mehta or Uma Sankar or Deepak Chaudhuri. A few others, like Shamim Ahmed are already performing. But overall, on the other side, as composing music following creative pattern, there is only one unique person for whom I have great regard and love, though he is a student of mine in flute, but he has wonderful things as a creative artiste. That is Vijay Raghav Rao. He has worked with me and assisted me from the beginning in whatever I have done in films, in India, mostly. In Indian tradition that means a musician can pass down his knowledge through different musical instruments also.

I have got vocal students, violin students (Satyadev Pawar who is a wonderful performer), flute students like Sachdev and many others santoor students.

7. ***Is that unique and only applicable to you?***

I think most musicians can do that. I have vocal students like Laxmi Shankar, Vinay Bharatram, but it is possible for any musician who has had good 'talim' on different instruments, and voice also.

All our music is based on voice vocal music, and it is their 'ragas' and 'tals' which are the basis. So if one already knows the technique of handling a particular instrument all he has to learn are new ragas, new 'bandish' and how to improvise, elaborate a demonstrative raga, how to proceed, these are the things beyond the technique of the instrument but it is the music itself, and that is where I can help.

8. ***There are two things I want to ask you. One is your haven't mentioned tabla at all. Do you have tabla students also?***

I don't know in the sense whether I can call them students, but I have helped many famous names who have had training in Laya kari which is rhythmic patterns and calculations so I have almost all the younger generation tabla players who have somehow been influenced and directly learnt many things from me.

9. ***Are there any definite number of 'ragas'?***

According to the old Shastra of scriptures there seem to be some 16,000 old 'ragas' but there is no mortal human being who knows all the ragas. But we follow the pattern between 200, 250 or 300 ragas that are popular in a period, and then some new 'ragas' come into vogue, and some of them become obsolete. This is something which has been going on for ages.

10. ***Is there any particular favourite raga of yours?***

Well, they also change from time to time, but my all time favourite raga is Yaman kalyan and it's mostly a raga for beginners. We mostly start withYaman kalyan. It is such a beautiful raga that you feel it never ends, and always discover something new in it. Of course, there are many other ragas that I love, like the Marwa or all the variations of Bhairavs and many early morning 'ragas', which are seldom heard nowadays.

11. ***These legendary stories of Tansen which we hear, that the lights or diyas came as when he sang etc. Have you been motivated or moved audience to these heights of emotionalism?***

Well, I can never compare myself, in my dreams even with Tansen or such great musicians, but I can tell you that I have a lot of miraculous experiences in my life, and fantastic ecstasy which I felt myself, and I have been told by people crying and coming to me.

12. ***Is there any one particular incident you can recall?***

There are so many that I cannot be specific and specially in experiences that had also, spiritual experiences — playing for great in sages, saints like Satya Sai baba or Anand mai or Shankaracharya in Kam koti, the old man, and in certain temples or churches — fantastic experiences. I love their background, and atmosphere of spiritual places.

13. Which is the longest period you have performed continuously?

Ten-and-a half hours, 1 remember I've played once in Jabalpur where I started at about 9 in the evening and ended at 7-30 in the morning with just one short interval of 20 minutes.

14. When was this?

In the middle 50s. I don't remember exactly, may be in 1956 or 57.

15. From 1956 which is when you went abroad till now, is it the first time you will be returning to India to live here?

I have actually been more in the west from the period of 1967. I've been travelling from 1956, but that was going for a tour for two or three months and coming back, but from 1967 onwards I stayed for a longer duration in the west.

HISTORICAL METHOD

The critical examination of past event or happenings in orders to know truth and later on, to generalization is known as historical method. History is a key subject for the study of different subjects and it is worth to mention the famous English dramatist George Bernard Shaw's view that the past is not behind the group. It is within the group. This means a proper study of past will provide key to the present. Pandit Jawaharlal Nehru says that the man's growth from barbarian to civilization is supposed to be the theme of history. Historical study is a study of past records and other information sources with a view to reconstruct the origin and development of a movement or a system. Any research, which makes use of observation based on past events, is known as research in historical approach.

The word history is known from the Greek word 'historia', which originally meant a learning by inquiry research exploration or information. Later it took on the connotative sense of the results of research, a verbal or written account. Now it is used in english in different sheds of meaning like—

(*a*) a narrative of incidents which may be either true or imaginary
(*b*) a written record consisting of narratives arranged in order of time relating to the past, events of a country, people, individual etc.
(*c*) the accounts given of that past based on certain modes of investigation and

(*d*) the branch of knowledge dealing with the past events. Besides these several techniques of investigation were developed for the study and description of the past happenings.

Historical research's aim is to apply reflective thinking to unsolved problems by discovering past trends of events, facts and attitudes, and by tracing lines of development in human thought and action. This research method like all other methods is not merely concerned with collection of data and facts by editing analysis, evaluation and interpretation. This research conducts critical evaluation and interpretation of historical documents and records in such a manner that general laws, trends or hypothesis can be framed. This historical knowledge provides a connected, coherent and intelligible form of knowledge about the past by which the social structure in its entirety can be explained. The researcher should be able to distinguish between legends about '*what happened*' and '*what, really happend*'. The historical truth is always liable for change, depending upon the facts that are brought for consideration. Therefore, the researcher has to strive hard to collect all facts, whatsoever trivial they may be, which can be used as evidences. The sources of facts are literary compositions, diplomatic and donate inscriptions, engraved on stone or copper plates or written on palm leaf and paper. The researcher must consider the most that can be said for and against any hypothesis and relative weight of evidence on either side before drawing conclusions of the truth.

Historical research in education is important for several reasons. The findings of this research enable educators to learn from past discoveries and mistakes to identify needs for educational reform. Different thinkers have reflected in their own way about what is Historical research such as

— A Historical research is a critical investigation of event developments and experiences of the past, the careful weighing of the evidence of the validity of sources of information of weighed evidence (Karlinger 1978).[12]

— Historical research deals with the past experiences ... Its aim is to apply the method of reflective thinking of social problems, still unsolved by means of discovery of past trends of events fact and attitude. It traces lives of developments in human thought and action in order to reach some basis for social activity (Whiteney 1961).[13]

In the simple words, "Historical method seeks to find explanation of questions of current interest by an intensive study of the past. Past always contains elements of the present. Past, present and future are well interlined. In fact every project of research has more or less historical approach. In discussing any problem, we must know the history of the problem and only them the problem can be solved easily, quickly and accurately. To quote P.V. Young, "The part, if it can be located, contains the key to the present, though today is different from yesterday, it was shaped by yesterday. Today and yesterday will probably influence tomorrow.

Historical method seeks to find explanation of questions of current interest by an intensive study of the past. Past always contains elements of the present, and future present and past all these three are interlined. In fact every project of research was more or less historical approach. Historical study helps us in visualizing the society as a dynamic organism and its structures and transformation. Generally, there are the following major sources of historical information before a research

- Books and magazines
- Assessable documents papers, and literature
- Cultural and analytical history material
- Memories, personal letters
- Diaries and confessions
- Autobiographies
- Sacred Archives
- Artistic material, historical paintings, portraits, sculptures, epigraphic records.

Historical research is useful both for theoretical and practical purposes. It has made important contribution to various branches of researches some problems are so typical that they can only be investigated by this approach. Thus this method fills a gap of making the research possible and meaningful. Historical records provide a very useful and important information that helps in a long way towards the solution of a problem. The researcher sometimes has no other alternative, excepts to fall back upon past date since they cannot create these a fresh. It makes possible to study the development of a particular idea, concepts, philosophy or theory. It also helps to make a comparative study for a historical period of time, factors situations etc.

Historical methods are used to study the processes through which music changes. Research made on the history of individual composition as they have unfolded into their many different versions with their cultural contexts. This method in music is valuable in analysing the status of music in the past in preserving artifacts, evolution of musical instruments, musical forms and musical facts and theories and also for providing historical information from the specific situation for possible generalization to other areas. In this connection "a balance must be maintained between history as a body of facts, based solidly upon research and history as an exercise in analysis interpretation and generalization". (Allan Navin, p. 300).[14]

The advantages of historical methods are:

(*a*) Some problems are such, which can be investigated only by this method and may not offer to other methods. Therefore, historical method fills in a big gap of making the research possible and also meaningful on the problems that otherwise would have remained unexplored.

(*b*) Secondly, historical data is not repeatable under any circumstances one therefore, historical method serves as a ready hand method to the researcher whose problems depends on historical observation. Historical method therefore has an advantage to offer the past data under the prevailing conditions and afford an opportunity to the researcher to view these observations in the past setting.

(*c*) Thirdly, historical records provide very useful information that goes a long way toward the solution of a research problem. As already said that the researcher is compelled to fall back upon past data since he cannot create these afresh and hence it is highly advantageous to follow historical method where the use of time series data is unavoidable in any case.

Historical method is not free from the limitation and difficulties. The main drawbacks are :

(*a*) As the historical study is concerned with the past, reliable and adequate data may not be available.

(*b*) It is also difficult to test the geniuses and authenticity of sources and the data that are available from them. Personal biases and private interpretation often enter unconsciously.

(*c*) It is difficult to establish the time order of events.

(*d*) The dispersal of documents is another limitation. The researcher may not succeed in locating all documents.

(*e*) It is difficult to perceive the real significance of the data because of their remote time period.

(*f*) In historical research precise measurements verifications and replications are not possible.

History is not merely a chronicle of events. All happenings have to be studied as manifestation of the human psyche. The major areas to be covered under historical studies can thus be identified:

(*a*) Concepts and forms
(*b*) Attitudes and values
(*c*) Patronage (Shifting of patronage to the middle class in modern times)
(*d*) Social, ritual and cultural of musical performance
(*e*) Musical instruments.

So, several methods are being used in music research. History is the record of past events. It is completely accurate and meaningful records of man's achievements. History helps us to study the society, its structure, functions and processes.

Nevertheless, a thorough and systematic historical study is of immense use in understanding the past and drawing inference for the present and future.

SURVEYS

The word survey has been derived from the word 'sur' and 'veeir' which means 'over' and 'see' respectively.[15] Literally survey means something taken over from a high place but it has come to be used as a term with specific purpose of its own. In other words, survey is used as the method of investigation by direct observation of phenomena or getting information through interview or questionnaire. The survey can define as Herman "a method of analysis in scientific and orderly form for defined purpose of a given social situation and activities." F.L.Whitney — "Survey research is on organised attempt to analyse, interpret and report the present status of a institution, group or area." C.A. Moser — "The research should look upon surveys as a way and a supremely useful one, of exploring the field of collecting data around as well as directly on the subject of the study, so that problems is brought with focus and points worth studying are suggested."[16] The quality of a survey depends upon the thoroughness of the planning, soundness of sampling, adequate and reliability of data, the quality of analysis and the interpretation of the findings. Survey research is approached through the methods of personal interviews, mailed questionnaires and personal discussions, besides indirect oral investigation. A survey will be become a basis for further investigation and supply of information to the needy one. It is the main objective and the needy one, be an institution or an individual. Thus, the survey is meant to provide information regarding the problems.

The purpose of survey is to get information and it is not meant to test any hypothesis, but simply describe the things. Therefore it can be started without any hypothesis. Availability of nature of information is the main source for undertaking a survey. The survey may be classified with following steps:

(a) General or Specific Survey: The general survey concern with collecting general information about population, institutions or phenomena without specific object or hypothesis. Government for providing data mostly takes up this type of surveys. When any survey is undertaken with the specific motive for testing and validity for some theory or hypothesis, it is termed as specific survey. Information collected through the specific survey is generally of a very little value.

(b) Regular and Ad-hoc Survey: Regular survey is regular in nature and repeated after regular intervals. To this, permanent machinery for collecting information is to be set up. Many of such surveys are mainly economic surveys. Ad-hoc survey is undertaken once for all. It may be conducted in phases if the area of investigation is large and due to its largeness, it never entitles as regular survey.

(c) Preliminary and Final Survey: A preliminary survey is one, which is to be undertaken well in advance to get the first hand knowledge of the universe to be surveyed. Further, it help with the nature of the problem and he/she can be able to get rich response. After conducting this survey, the construction of schedule or questionnaire may be taken with the picture. The preliminary survey may also be called 'pilot study' after this, the study has been completed and final survey is made.

The quality of the survey depends on the preparation made before the survey, so the planning of survey is of paramount importance in research. The surveyor has to give careful and conductive thought at the planning of a survey. Its planning in research programme is must for its successful execution. The purpose of the survey should be specified clearly at the very beginning. A clear objective of the problem indicating the interest in determining the type of information is needed. Next to the purpose of survey, scope of it is an important step regarding to the type of information the purpose of surveys however, will determine the scope of survey. In selecting a particular method for a survey, the surveyor should take the consideration of its suitability and their own knowledge of it.

Survey method has some advantages in comparison with other method:

(*a*) In this method, the researcher has to come in close and direct contact of the people, whom he/she wants to study. A survey brings the researcher in a position to come face to face with the realities of life and see things personally.
(*b*) Survey method is very useful in testing the validity of many theories. In several cases, it has been observed that the actual surveys have led to entirely different results.
(*c*) Surveys have proved their usefulness in leading to the formulation of hypothesis. At a more advanced stage, surveys are also helpful in putting the hypothesis to test.
(*d*) Under survey method, a researcher is in a position to observe the activities of a group under study from a much closer distance. It helps the researcher to have a better insight of their doings.
(*e*) The survey method is flexible to use the various methods of collection of data like observation, interviewing and mailing.

Limitations

(*a*) Survey method is primarily meant for collection of data from primary sources individual, households and institutions that it depends upon the willingness and co-operation of the respondent.
(*b*) Survey method is costly, time consuming and wasteful in certain cases, where the objectives are limited.
(*c*) Under this method, it is very difficult to verify the accuracy of the data that has been collected because it is dependent upon the honesty, sincerity, personal qualities and unbiased attitudes of the enumerators and co-operation of the respondents.
(*d*) Survey method is only useful for current problems and is not suitable for the problem that requires the study in the historical retrospect.

CASE STUDY METHOD

Now these days, the case study method is widely adopted in carrying out research in the field. The credit for introducing case study goes to Frederic Le Play.[17] The English social philosopher Herbert Spencer was among the first to adopt case study method in comparative studies of different cultures. Historian have had resorted to this method while portraying historical character of a particular historical period and describing the development. Today, many of the novelist and dramatist have used some semblance of the case study method for presenting a word picture of character. A case study is a deep and intensive study of a particular social unit, thus, the field of study is limited but it aims to study all aspects of the unit. It is also a diagnostic study, oriented towards findings out what is happening and why it is happening and what can be done about it. It is one of the most popular types of the research method and its purpose is to understand the interaction between factors, that explain the present status or the development over a period of time.

The case study method is exploratory. In the words of Pauline V. Young, "A comprehensive study of a social unit of a person, a group, a social institution, a district or a community is called a case-study."[18] Goode Hatt, "Case study is a way of organizing data so as to preserve the unitary character of the object, being studied. Expressed somewhat differently, it is an approach which views any unit as a whole."[19] It is observed that the case study method is a qualitative, inclusive, intensive, insight, stimulating and comprehensive approach. This approach may not be based on given hypothesis or any well-established conclusions, but the study itself may help in formulating a well-founded hypothesis for further investigation. This approach to research is, therefore, an open end and objective. investigation of a particular unit with a view to develop a hypothesis in character, so the researcher has complete freedom in selecting a problem that he/she considers.

The case study is an intensive study through which one can know precisely the factor and cause of a particular phenomena. It is a very good method for collecting information about an individual, a family or a group of persons. It helps to secure the information about the unit to study, which may provide clues and ideas for further research. Thus, case study gives us a total view of a unit or a clear insight picture of a situation. The perspective of a case study is both qualitative and organic. It gives an over-all generic picture of a problem. Berges termed the case study method as "the social microscope."[20] Case study is most valuable for diagnostic, administrative and therapeutic purposes. It develops idea sometimes leading to conclusion and sometimes to hypothesis to be tested. It may also be useful for developing new concepts for testing existing concepts.

Methods in Case Study

The following methods are undertaken in case study:

(a) Determination of Factors: First of all, the collection of materials about each of the units or aspects are very essential. The determination of factors can be of two types — particular factors and general factors.

(b) Statement of the Problem: In this process, the defined problem is studied intensively and the data are classified into various classes.

(c) Analysis and Conclusion: After classifying and studying the factors, an analysis will be made to help in drawing conclusion.

Sources

Case studies are not limited to any single source of data collection. Researcher should employ number of sources. Many have made case studies with preliminary interviews, conferences with specified intervals, conversations, observations etc. Sometimes researcher has to use different techniques and tool to collect data about the different aspects of the cases. In the case study method, the main sources are few:

(a) Personal Documents: Most of the people keep personal records, documents, letters, write their own autobiography or memories. These documents play an important role in the case study, as they contain description of the important events of the life of the writer as well as his relation towards them. These documents may also contain the description of even those events in which the narrator has played his part only as a witness. So the personal documents can be a source of a great deal of information, which is necessary for the study of the problem.

(b) Life History: In the case study method, the life history of a person may be very essential. This can be obtained through interviews with the respondent. In this study 'the entire life of the respondent is taken into account of life history data'. It is generally gathered through prolonged interviews with the respondent. He can use any written material about his life conferences at specified intervals, observations, post-experimental interviews and various lists on the analysis of facts.

Phases

The case study is often termed as a method, sometimes a 'technique' of others 'an approach' to social reality and occasionally a mode of organising data in terms of some chosen units. A researcher, through the case study method, tries to understand the complex of factors that are operative within a social unit as an integrated totality. The technique of gathering and processing data is related to some of the phases (stages).

(a) *Selection of cases and identification of situation:* Before taking up the case study, a researcher has to take some decisions such as which unit has to be taken up for studies? What aspect or what period of life of unit can be studied? What are the situations in which unit exists? All these questions should be answered. Keeping in view this question a researcher has to choose representative and typical data. The selection of such unit highly depends on the ability and skill of the researcher.

(*b*) *Collection and Recording of Data:* A careful collection and recording of data depends on the skill and ability of the researcher. He/She has to use different techniques and tools to collect data about different aspects of the units. Studies of personal documents, life histories, observations, interviews, questionnaires, schedules etc. are the techniques and tools for collection of data. The data should be recorded uniformly, topic wise, accurately and objectively with clarity. While collecting data, the researcher should be constious about Dr. Thomas warning. "Be suspicious of striking cases. They may be as surprising to the people among whom they occur, as they are to you." Unusual or rare cases should not be overlooked but regarded as exception. In practical sense, the wholeness of case can be preserved, as Goode and Hatt stated in four headings namely

(*i*) Breadth of data
(*ii*) Level of data
(*iii*) Formulation of index indues
(*iv*) Interaction in a time dimension.

The breadth of data refers to the fact of data collection. Level of data concern to many facts of life of the unit, that is available. Index relates to the various traits, that are actually used in characterizing the unit and the time dimension emphasis upon the process and the time that provided may be short or long.

To sum up, in phase of case study two essential elements in the choice of cases are first, selection of representative units. The ability of the researcher to recognize the representative case is important and may facilitate selection. Secondly, although the case study has an overall outlook, a well-defined and carefully selected problem is presumed and is being studied.

Case study method has been used extensively in psychology education, sociology etc. It has been regarded as best suited for tracing the evolution and growth of a problem in its different aspects. A stabilised material can be studied by a technique, but the effective study of dynamic and mobile material requires intensive and genetic approach possible only in the case study method. Since in the case study, a researcher undertakes an intensive as well as extensive study of definite unit for a long period, he gains many new insights with human behaviour and become emotionally mature. But the case study method has some limitations and difficulties and due to these, research work cannot be done properly e.g. through this method, proper data collection is very difficult. This is because generally the respondents do not reveal the actual facts to the researchers. So, when it is not possible to collect proper data and information through this method, the generalisations on this basis become defective and faculty. The method is unorganised and unsystematic, because there is no control on the researcher and on the respondent. Thus, verification is not possible. Hence, the data collected by this method is often unreliable and the generalisation drawn from it is also inaccurate.

Adopting one of these sources (method) either historical, surveys etc. to find solution for choosing the research problem, the researcher should present deductions in a systematic, logical and scholarly way. The researcher is challenged to deal with the acquisition of knowledge as a continuous process and seek to integrate the best from the past and present in order to develop capacity for systematic and imaginative inquiry that extracts knowledge from information and wisdom from knowledge.

References

1. Reference Service (Krishan Kumar), pp. 110-111.
2. Galting, *op. cit.*, p. 117.
3. Sellitz and others, *op. cit.*, p. 479.
4. Madge. *op. cit.*, p. 131.
5. Machnuas, David and Nachmids Chana, Research Methods in the Social Science, *op. cit.*, p. 74.
6. P.V. Young, Scientific Social Research, Englewood Hall, N.Y., 1955, p. 149.
7. J. Hardr and Lindman, Dynamic Social Research, p. 129.
8. M.N. Basu, Field Method in Anthropology, p. 129.
9. C.F. Sellitz, et al., *op. cit.*, p. 236.
10. Galting, *op. cit.*, p. 120.
11. Encory, William C., Business Research Method, *op. cit.*, p. 268.
12. Advanced Research Methodology, G.N. Prakash Srivastava, p. 176.
13. *Ibid.*, p. 176.
14. Research Methodology for Music, Dr. S.A.K. Durga, p. 52.
15. Logic and Methods of Sociological Research, Dr. M.M. Lavania, p. 50.
16. Methodology and Techniques, R.K. Varma and Gopal Verma, pp. 35-35.
17. Logic and Methods of Sociological Research, Dr. M.M. Lavania, pp. 105-106.
18. Pauline, V. Young, Scientific Social Surveys and Research, New Delhi, Prentice Hall of India, Private Limited, 1975, p. 247.
19. Methodology and Technique of Research, R.K. Verma & Gopal Verma, p. 25.
20. Burges, 'Research Methods in Sociology', in George Gurnitech and W.S. Moore (eds.) Twentieth Century Sociology, The Philosophical Library, 1949, pp. 25-26.

4
Secondary Sources

INTRODUCTION

Secondary sources of information are those, which are either compiled from or refer to primary sources of information. These contain information regarding primary or original information. The original information having been usually modified selected or reorganised so as to serve a definite purpose or group of users. Such sources contain information, arranged and organised on the basis of some definite plan. These contain organised repackaged knowledge rather than new knowledge. Information given in primary sources is made available in a more convenient form.

In an age, when reading and writing are rare accomplishments, the art of painting and sculpture plays a part in national Indian art which we are reviewing. Art, religion and education had no existence apart from each other as they have in this age of specialization thought and culture. And like all true artists, they were keen observers and lovers of nature. Their art was glowing with spontaneous warmth and fantasy like the nature, which inspired it. The main sources of our knowledge of our Indian music and its history are manuscripts, epigraphs, coins, architecture, sculpture and painting. A proper recognition of the value of these sources provide a counter check to eliminate obscure episode, confirm known events, correct wrong concepts or identification and produce finally a clear and authentic narration.

Secondary sources of information besides sculptures, paintings, musical pillars, stones, manuscripts, inscriptions as they all are our historical sources we are also linked with our oral tradition. Musical compositions of various artists, other advance instruments like tapes, C.D., A.I.R., gramophone records which we put in our non-documentary sources. These sources are very useful in our music research because the non-book materials form a very important part in saving knowledge in this field and they cannot be communicated through book materials for music this has extra importance. One may read a composition or its notation of a particular raag. But listening it give the actual tonal form and it also has is own charm and cannot be equated with reading. Except these journals, articles, books, newspapers play a important role in this connection.

SCULPTURE

Sculpture is almost as old as mankind. For uncounted years, men evolution is marked by false starts and dead-ends. His first significant step forward was a man the tool maker". The second and more significant step marked his emergence as man the 'image maker'. The dark galleries of pre-historic caves show our ancestors preoccupation with the concrete image. In his painting and sculpture, early man was trying not to copy nature but originated in his mind and therefore depicted things not just as they were, but as he desired them to be. Art serves much purpose, but fundamentally it deals not with the actual but with the ideal. For centuries, man had shaped stone and softer materials like wood, bone and horn to serve his practical ends. When he become sure that the image in his mind could be given concrete form, he already possessed the technology to do so.

From stone axe to stone image is a relatively small step. The giant stride came when man first realised that his thoughts and desires could be translated into solid reality. Their approach towards the visual arts was always basically sculptural, meaning that sculpture, architecture and even painting were conceived in terms of palpable volumes. In depicting the human body, the Indian sculptor sought not to produce nature but to create form parallel to nature. The image cult, which is so deeply rooted in our life, must have began before the days of Harappa, when the image had already been stylized. The beginnings of stone sculpture in India go back to very remote age. The earliest evidence of the sculptural art in India is found in the seal engravings. The human figurine and the naturalistic models of the animals of the Indus valley civilization, that existed from the third millennium B.C. to about seventeenth century B.C.

During the Mauryan period stone become the medium of building and from this time onwards, the early sculptures of historical times have come down to us. The chief sculptures surviving from the Mauryan period are the capitals of Ashokas pillars. This contain a persepolitan bell shaped lotus, surmounted with four adored loins which supported a wheel (now lost), the symbol of the first preaching of Buddha that called 'The Wheel of Law' a bull an elephant and a horse. The superb modelling of the figures shows skilful blending of realistic form with idealised signs and dignity. Sculptural art of India occupies the foremost place in the history of world art. The artists in India had attained a high degree of excellence at a very early period and specimens produced by him are truly marvels of human industry and skill, Havell has expressed "The best Indian sculpture touched a note of deeper feeling and finer statements than the best Greek. There is in their art a depth and spirituality which never entered into the soul of Greece."[1]

India occupies an exalted position in the realm of art of the ancient world. If Greeks excelled in the portrayal of the physical charm of the human body, the Egyptians in the grandeur of their pyramids and the Chinese in the beauty of their land scope, the Indian were unsurpassed in transmitting the spiritual contents to their plastic forms embodying the high ideal and the common beliefs of the people. Indian art is deeply rooted in religion. India is the birth place of three of the world's great religions Hinduism, Buddhism and Jainism and these faiths have inspired most of our Indian art. None had actually seen the major Gods like Rama, Krishna, Vishnu and Shiva etc. but according to their description in the scriptures, the Indian artists visualised them in the human form and idealised their image.

The beginning of stone sculpture in India, go back to very remote age. The excavation at the ruins of Mohanjodaro and Harappa, light a highly developed urban civilization archaeologically known as the Indus Valley. Clay was the earliest medium in which man began to mould and we have discovered a large number of terracotta figurines from those sites. Among the few stone figurines a male dancer discovered from Harappa is an important carving showing how music and dance had a great place in life almost 5000 years ago. It amply proves the dexterity with which the sculptor 5000 years ago could catch beautiful movements of dance & poses and express them in stone. The bronze-dancing girl of the same period discovered at Mohanjodaro is perhaps the greatest achievements of the metal work of the Harappa age. This world famous figure show a dancing female standing as if relaxing after a dance number, with right hand on her hip and the left dangling free.

By the efforts of centuries techniques of art were perfected, definite types were evolved and ideals of beauty were formulated with precision Indian art is as real as any other art only the reality has a different meaning for us. The reality consists in the relation of the form of the visible world with the energies and emotions, which belongs to the forms. The study with the help of sculptures properly begins with the sculpture from Bharhut Sanchi and Pitalkhora. (2nd and 1st cent. B.C.) Amaravati and

Nagarjunakonda (Ist and 2nd cent. A.D.) Pawaya (5th cent. A.D.) etc. is studied with references to the early period. The medieval period includes sculptures found during the 11th cent. A.D to 14th cent. A.D. The sculptures found in Jain temples on Mount Abu, Konark, Belur, Holebid, Bhuvaneswar temple, Chidambaram etc. constitute the material for the study.

Music in Indian Sculpture

Sculpture and music have played a prominent part in cultural development. Sculpture illustration may be treated as visual document of the different periods to which, they belong. They portray so much of contemporary life and thereby prove to be good guides and reliable informants. The figures of dancers discovered in Mohanjodaro are full of swing and movement. This miniature creation of art reveals to us that dancing was not unknown say 3000 years back. Even as early as the stone age, a rock drawing portrays a masked dancer dressed in wild beast skin, playing a flute, a crude specimen with a rough and uneven surface. A survey of Indian sculpture found mainly in our temple in large stock and variety will bring our notice to many factors relating to music.

Music has been a hand made to religion through the ages and therefore any place of worship as the temple, the church, the vihara can be objects of our study. From the representation of the dynamic art of music and dancing on stone, it is possible for us to acquire knowledge of the type of music and dance practised at different period, and in the study of the history and evolution of music in general and musical instruments in particular. They give us an idea of the construction and shape of the instrument, the manner in which they are held and played, the type of concert and number of people taking part and instruments used by them. The fact that our artist and philosopher of long ago could give much highly aesthetically and beautiful plastic form to the imagination of a dancing 'Nataraja'. Expressing the highest reaches of human thought and feeling, conclusively proves that dancing as art had fully developed in ancient India and the spiritual significance of dancing had been well realized.

"According to the Hindu tradition, Indra and the other Gods be sought Brahma the creator for a pestune to be heard and seems by all. Brahma these upon distilled the essence of the four Vedas, taking words from the 'Rig', music from the 'Sama', the art of gesticulation from the 'Yajura' and aesthetic elements Rasa from the 'Atharva Veda' and compounded them in masterly was into one. This goes by the popular term the 'Natya or Natya Sastra."[2]

"There are several references to ritualistic dances in the Vedas and Puranas. At the end of 'Aswamedha Yagya' women are mentioned as dancing round the scared fire with water pots on their heads beating the ground with their feet and singing. This is honey."[3] Indian sculpture shows us visibly in plastic form, the exact nature of human movement and the development of stylization dancing during different periods of history. The cave frescoes of Ajanta and Bagh, and the numerous sculptures at Ellora and Elephanta speaks of the important place where dancing held in the cultured life of the nation.

"From the Mohanjodaro figurines and Harappa torse to the bronze Nataraja figure of the 16th century is a long journey. This journey of movement bears testimony to the acute sensitivity of the Indian artists to movement. Like the seer of the Rigveda period, the conductors of Upanishad, the priest of the Brahmans and the dramatists of the sanskrit theatre. The Indian sculptor, whether he was creating sculpture in the round relief or casting in bronze or sculpturing in wood, he was conscious of the human body as a most powerful instrument for the communication of moods, bhavas and rasa. Like the creative poet and dramatist, he was also knowledgeable."[4]

In India aesthetic theory of interrelationship of the arts have been known and recognised not on the level of the aesthetic experience alone but also on the level of technique.

PAINTING

Culturally contemporaneous history of every country offers clear and abundant evidence that man has always aspired to the attainment of concrete vividness of visual presentation of the real and the ideal, depending on the peculiar evolution stage of his civilization at a particular period of time. He came to prefer the two chief visual languages — the language of image making and of drawing and painting, which endowed the creations of sculpture and painting. These two were the media to which the Indian became prefertically with the result that Indian painting and sculpture have perhaps been more naturally expressive of the thoughts and ideas of the nation than any other representational art.

As with sculpture, so with painting in ancient India, it was pursued not for its own sake, but was undertaken to sub-serve a religious purpose so that people might be taught in vivid manner of the truths of religion. The salvage is sufficient to establish the existence of a very rich and colourful creative art of painting in India, characteristic running throughout and in every art style be it frescoes paintings on banners and palm leaves or patras, miniatures or book illustration. Every type and technical detail exhibits a mastery of time and proportion, striking postures and expressions, remarkable adornment of figure and finish, and above all a note of interpretation apart from limitation. Painting is one of the most delicate flowers of human thoughts and feelings, expressed in line and colour. It is so inherent in human hearts that even many thousand years before the dawn of history, when men was only a cave dueler, he painted his rock shelters to satisfy his aesthetic sensitivity and creative nature.

Among Indians, the love of colour and pattern is so deeply ingrained that it is certain that from earliest time, they must have also produced some sort of paintings even during those periods of history for which we have no direct evidence. Recent excavation have shown that even in pre-historic time, cave duelers used to embellish their primitive habitation with paintings which possess remarkable vigour and grace. It is clear that the artistic impulse is one of the most fundamental elements in the human psyche and through the ages, man has expressed his hopes and aspirations, his dreams in most ages through the medium of art. Indian painting at its best has therefore been an expression of the deal. At different time in history and in different regions, people evolved specific styles of drawing and painting by developing certain ideas and objects, certain arrangements of lines and spaces, so that Indian painting has blossomed and decayed reviewing every time in new splendour.

Painting as a way of life, as an integral part of our everyday existence, has infect persisted right through the centuries in our country. It has always been considered and practiced as a polite secular accomplishment. The history of Indian painting may be said to have begun with the wall paintings of Ajanta in the first century of the Christian era. The Ajanta paintings considered to be the best testimony to the qualities of the ancient art bear the profound marks of a background of wealth, splendor and cultural magnificence. The walls of Ajanta show the remarkable perfection of workmanship, expression and harmony accomplished by the anonymous artists trained by centuries of religious and artistic discipline. The Ajanta paintings are unsurpassed as works of art. There is no attempt to depict light and shade, but the figurines are portrayed with such beauty and freedom of brush outlines that they give them amazingly life like attitudes. For the painting, the process employed was usually known in Italy as 'fresco bunono', in which colours mixed with lime waters, are applied to prepare surface of the finest plaster while it is still wet, so that they are chemically visited with the ground. Indian fresco-bunono, when the wall is a suitable one is an exceedingly permanent process for interior decoration and much more durable in the tropical climate then oil painting. The technical process of the frescos is the surface of the hard rock was first covered with a rough layer of a mixture of clay, cow dung, powder rock. Over this, spread ground of fine white lime plaster and on this polished surface, while it was still moist, the paintings were executed in water colour. Brushes were made up from the hair of animals, such as goat, camel, mangoose etc. The first sketch was drawn by an experienced hand and subsequently corrected in many places with a strong black or deep brown lime. The principal colours in use were red, orcher, vivid red, yellow ochre, indigo blue, lamp black (kajjal), Chalk white and green. It is likely that some paintings may have been executed on the wood, clay or brick walls.

After the frescoes had become less popular, there are preferences for miniature paintings as seen in the page of the illuminated manuscripts done by the Pala School in the east (9th-12th cent.) These pala paintings are characterised by subdued tones of colour. It is a naturalistic style, which resembles the ideal forms of contemporary bronze, and stone sculptures and reflects some feeling of the classical art of Ajanta.

Miniature Painting: (Rajput and Mughal)

Like sculpture, the art of fresco had to be abandoned wherever the sway of Islam extended, but it was immediately replaced by miniature paintings. Series of miniatures, generally on paper and surrounded by illuminations, represent the stories of myths and of history, as the frescoes used to do, but with this difference that the miniatures could easily be slipped in a book or an album. The tradition of miniature painting in India is one which spans many centuries, beginning in the 11th centuries and coming right up to the 19th cent and cover large parts of North India from Gujarat and deserts of Rajasthan, up to the snowing mountains of Jammu and Himachal Pradesh. In India, the two religions Mohummedaism and Hinduism did not produce either a unified religion or even a unified culture. It is not, therefore, surprising that a Hindu school of painting flourished at a time when miniature painting was being practiced in the courts of imperial Mughals. The school of painting has been be signalled as Rajput painting born at the same time as the Mughal school.

The term 'Rajput painting' or its variety 'Rajasthani miniature' is a part mention term. Rajput painter who had worked for a time at the Mughal court and learnt some of the science of miniature painting, as developed in Persia, must have returned to their homes and these produced such work as illustration to: Rasikpriya. Indian painting under the Mughal began with different ideologies and an entirely new outlook and technique. In the technique of the Mughal painting, paper was made generally of cotton, jute or bamboo. The drawing was first sketched in outline, usually in red, and corrected with lamp-black. Mughal paintings of the ragas of that time were influenced by Rajasthani paintings. Regarding the Rajput portrait of the indigenous school Prof. O.C. Ganguly has said that "After the development of Mughal School of portrait in the early 16th cent. The two schools, the earlier indigenous Indian and the later Mughal, got entangled and influenced each other. It is now, therefore, difficult from the products of the fusion of the two to recover the outlines of the earlier. Hindu tradition and the few surviving examples seem to prove that the pure Rajasthani idiom has been practiced side by side with the mixed Mughal style."[5]

In the art of painting about the 15lh cent, blossomed the exquisite Hindu art, called the Rajput art. By Coomaraswamy the main centres of whose early phases were Rajputana and the Punjab Hills, where the art flourished in separate groups known as Rajasthan and Pahari. Unilke the Mughal painting which is primarily secular, the art of painting in central India, Rajasthan and the Pahari region etc, is deeply rooted in Indian tradition, taking inspiration from Indian epics, religious text like Puranas, love poems of sanskrit and other Indian languages, Indian folk lore and works on the musical themes. Among these the cult of Krishna was the most popular one which inspired the patrons and artist. So that Rajput painting is really the picturisation of the simple life of the common man. Love, both human and divine, is its central theme. O.C. Ganguly says, "The most observing theme of the Rajput painting are furnished by the cult of Krishna, idealised in a series of religious mysteries, Shiva and Parvati are also popular and Rama and Sita appear occasionally. But love and adoration of Krishna and Radha symbolic of eternal motif of man and woman, are the main theme."[6] (See Plate No. 1)

The differences between Mughal and Rajput painting are largely a difference between court and folk art. The Mughal schools portrait kings, nobles and saints and scenes of hunting, recreation, entertainment and Durbars. The Rajput and Pahari schools generally deal with the myth and legends. Relating to Krishna and Radha or Siva and Parvati, which appealed to all classes and their works illustrating the various nuances of a love which is at once human and divine are saturated with the denotionalism of the entire mystical movement and the vernacular literature. Besides Krishna and Radha, the archetyal lovers, who are symbolic of the eternal destiny of man and woman to seek each other or the supreme fulfilment of life bliss. The pet deer and peacock, the vigil, tryst and abhisara, the dust storm, the serried mass of cloud, torrential rain and flesh of lightening, the wriggling serpent underfoot, the twining creeper, the blossoming kadama tree and the swirling torrent of Jamuna river, are all subtle and deep symbol in the well understood language of folk: poetry and painting. (See Plate No. 2)

The representation of love scenes erotic sentiments of heroes and heroines, ballads and romantic poems, the visualization of the dramatic atmosphere suggested by the ragas and raginis are other subjects of these paintings. For example a charming woman standing in an open landscape under the brilliant noonday sun generally represents 'Todi' ragini. In her hands, she holds the Veena and the deer in the neighbouring postures stand entranced as she plays. Similarly 'Megh' raga is represented by a group of musician playing outside during the rainy season. The clouds hovering overhead and there is joyous expectancy of rain everywhere. It is a raga suggesting hope and new life 'Bilawal' typifies the heroine who gets conscious of the pangs of love by a vision of her own beauty in the mirror. These and similar pictures of visualised music pulsate with life as only a great piece of art could.

The inventors talents of the Greeks never suggested a more charming allegory then the lovely families of the six ragas named in the order of seasons — BHAIRAVA, MALVA, SRI RAG, HINDOLA OR VASANT, DIPAKA and MEGHA. Each of whom is wedded to five raginis or nymphs of harmony presenting wonderfully diversified images for the play of artists genius. Women have been one of the principal motifs of hindu art, but they inspired from the woman of Ajanta. She is an erotic type, charming and sentimental model but the hindu artist depicted her as a heroine, emotional and delicate innocent and proud. The colours of these pictures are bright and pleasing. Sometimes the surface of the painting is divided into several compartments of different colours in order to separate one scene from other. (See Plate No. 3) The text is written in 'Nagri' on the top.

In the ragamala series of Rasika Priya dated 1634 A.D. for example it represent the 'Megh Raja'. This miniature shows the blue complexioned raga dancing with a lady to the tune of music played by three female musicians. The scene is laid against blue background. The sky is over cast with dark clouds with a streak of lightening and rain indicated by white dotted lines. Four swans flying in a row, against dark background of clouds, entrance the pictorial effects of the miniature. (See Plate No. 4)

Painting and poetry moved hand in hand so too did poetry and music. Poems were written on the themes of the principle melodies according to the categories in which they were classified. But sometimes-lyrical poems like Gita Govinda or the various seasonal love poems known as 'Baramasa', their most striking characteristics are symbolism and rhythm.

Regarding the data of the emergence of the raga and ragini pictures, a researcher Manala and Chamen Lal Mehta has further mentioned in the studies in Indian painting. "It is therefore, probable that the ragini picture first came into vogue sometimes in the 16th cent. After the advent of the Mughal, when the entire fabric of the common life of the people was undergoing a subtle transformation which found expression to note that, there are Hindu as well as Mughal version of ragini and baramasi (seasonal) pictures, which can be easily distingue."[7] With its fine and sensitive lines and marvelous colours, the Rajput painting is a finished composition, like the 'doha' or 'chaupai' distilling the delicate emotion of the hero and heroine, who are depicted abstractly in both song and picture. In the entire history of world painting such concentration of feeling and gesture and coincidence of sensuous and spiritual values are hardly to be found. (See Plate No. 5)

Ragamala Paintings

Besides religious miniatures we owe to the Rajput painters, a set of paintings, known as 'Ragamalas' or 'Garlands of musical modes'. Ragamala painting appears to stand at a crossroad of Indian music, poetry and miniature paintings. It labels it individual paintings with the name of musical modes it gathers the single pages into ragamala album, which are arranged in an order similar to the 'garland of raga' of ancient and medieval authorities of musical learning's. In the theory of Indian melodies, there is prevalent a doctrine. The underline principle of which is to enable one to understand the psychic values of ragas, and to apply them to poetry, particularly emotional situations and interpretation. Each 'Raga' and 'Ragini' is believed to have particular psychic form, corresponding to its tonal body over which the former presides as the nymph, deity or the devata of that particular melody. On the basis of these descriptive verse painters have prepared representations of most of the melodies in miniatures sizes, the verse being quoted on the top of each picture. These pictorial diagrams, visualizing the spirit and character of each melody, were prepared for the use and guidance of our music practitioners. It is proved by the fact that at a certain stage, the descriptive verse were composed in the hindi language for the benefit of those who did not understand the sanskrit language. At the time of Akbar these descriptive verse were translated into persian.

Both the musical and the poetic beginnings of Ragamalas are many centuries older than the painted versions. A 'raga' is a selection of notes from the scale of twenty-two combined in certain characteristic progressions, 'ragini' are modes of the ragas in which certain notes are omitted and the progression and emphasis differ. These ragas and raginis are the foundation of every art song to sing. It is also definitely associated with the certain hour of the day and sometimes with a particular season. It may be remarked that the 'raga' and 'ragini' have originated in more than one way, the four sources generally recognized are:

(*a*) folk song
(*b*) poetical works
(*c*) devotional songs of the yogis and
(*d*) the composition of professional musicians.

These origins are often indicated in the raga names such as Pahari (mountain), Hindola (a swing), Todi (ascestic) and Sarang (from Sarangadeva, a musician of 13th cent.). Other names refer to the sentiment of the raga or ragini or to other effects or appropriate hours as Vasanta (spring) and Depaka (lamp).

According to the system of Hanumana, in most general use, there are six fundamental ragas and each has five raginis. Besides the ragas and raginis, there are also hybrid, called 'Putra' or sons, even ragaputris (daughter) and their wives of sons:

(*a*) BHAIRAVA: Bhairavi, Madhumadhavi, Bengali, Varati, Sandhavi
(*b*) MALKOS : Todi, Khambhavati, Gauri, Gunakari, Kukubha
(*c*) HINDOLA : Vilaval Patmanjari, Lalita, Ramakiri, Desakh
(*d*) DIPAK : Kedari, Kanada, Desi, Kamodi, Nat
(*e*) MEGHA : Mallar, Desakari, Bhupali, Gurjari, Tanka
(*f*) SRI : Vasant, Maru or Malavi, Malasri, Dhansika, Asavari.

All these are described in the technical works on music, of which are earliest extent in the Natya-Sastra of Bharta (5th cent.). As miniature painting developed mainly in north India, the ragamala paintings deal essentially with the hindustani tradition and seek to present, through a vide spectrum of highly imaginative form and colours, the varying moods and modes of classical music. 'The pictures does not necessarily represent the raga or ragini as a visible 'devata', it represents the circumstances appropriate to his or her invisible presence. Our song says Rabindranath Tagore, speaks of the early dawn and the embodridered starry midnight sky of India. Our song is the world sundered separation pain of dripping rain and the world less ecstasy of the deep madness of the early spring, as it reaches the utmost limits of the forests. It should be noted that most of the 'ragas' and 'raginis' have for their burdensome phase of love, either in union or separation, in such as in the picture of 'nayakas', the lover represented are always Radha and Krishna and the art is essential religious. According to the older theory of music, each raga is associated with a specific passion or emotion. The very word 'raga', it is essential to know the Svaranam devata or presiding deity of each svara and its emotion value of rasa of raga. For example, the 'Vasanta' raga is a human reaction of the joy of life, in spring 'Megh' raga to the advent of the rains with all desire and opportunity for enjoyment. 'Bhairavi' is the melody of love and devotion. "Lalita' stands for unstated love, and the sorrow of separation at day break. 'Todi' is the surrender of animal life to the magic and enchantment of the beauty of nature. 'Nata' is the symbol of martial spirit is man"[8]

The representation of certain of the best known 'ragas' is fairly constant. The following are easily recognizable.

(a) Megha Mallara: In this painting the melody is visualized as Krishna sporting with Radha and accompanied by gopis with lutes and drum. Keeping time to the music with their hands. In another versions the noble prime 'Megha Mallar' loves to dance in alliance.

(b) Sri Raga: Depicts a mood of happiness. Holding a flower in his hand, he sits in the garden surrounded by beautiful damsels.

(c) Todi Ragini: Beautiful and elegant, superbly dressed she walks about in the garden, her usual trysting place standing in a dancing pose and playing the vina the music of which attract the deers.

(d) Vasanta Ragini: This is a melody of spring, symbolised by the mango plant brought by the dancer, and a young man wearing a yellow garments.

(e) Bhairavi Ragini: The melody is expressed pictorially in the form of Parvati worshipping Siva. (See Plate No. 6)

(f) Bhairava: This is represented by the god Siva attended by a group of worshipping maidens.

(g) Khambhauati: It is Brahma Puja.

(h) Hindola: As indicated in the name is a swinging scene, the swingers are usually Radha and Krishna. (See Plate No. 7)

'Purvi' the evening melody in the lamentation of nature for the parting day. 'Madhumadhavi' be speaks the peace of love and contentment. The earliest example of the Mewar painting of Ragamala series a miniature shows the 'Lalita' ragini. In this the heroine is lying on a bed with her eyes closed, under a painted pavilion with a door, the hero is seen carrying a garland in either hand 'Ramkali' is visualised as a charming girl of dark complexion.

Besides these, there are paintings in which each illustration takes the form, not of a symbol or icon, but of a dramatic situation conceived in the abstract, and expressing the universal, mood or sentiment appropriate to the season and the time of day or night. Only a very small number of paintings are actually dated and signed. Many paintings are inscribed with their title or even a poem. Of the hundreds or even thousands of ragas known in music only a fraction was used in Ragamala painting. The analysis of any relationship between painting and music, has to take into account two facts, first we have no regards of the performance of raga before the 20th cen. to help to reconstruct their exact form and content in the way we can do with Western music. The second fact is the lack of technical knowledge, which the painter has of music, or the musicians of painting.

Descriptions of raga-rupa or raga forms have been the sources of ragamala pictures in North India after the time of Akbar. These have been painted in many parts of upper India. These pictures offer is a clue to the emotions which these ragas have been experienced to evoke. For instance, Raga 'Asavari' is shown as a female ascetic wearing simple grab sitting near a sandal wood tree, while snakes, deer, and birds gather around, her, listening to the music. 'Deepak' the tune of fire is picturised as a handsome young man gorgeously robed in shining red, which sparkles in the darkness. His person is so brilliant that the brightness penetrates the gloom in which he sits. Thus many ragas are represented in similar pattern in painting, a study of which will help us to find out the rasas of these ragas. Some of the miniature paintingof ragas and raginis of various artists show certain differences in details. But in spite of the difference in details of dress, colouring etc. there are some common features in most of them. For example 'Megha' raga is the Lord of the rains. In one picture it represents as a handsome man of formidable appearance holding a sword in his hands. Heavy clouds blacken the heavens and thunder and lightening tear the musky and thick atmosphere creating altogether dreadful environment. In another representation, it is seen as a company of musicians performing outside a beautiful house in the rainy seasons. The sky is covered with cloud and a few drops of rain have fallen. The animals in the field are happy with new hopes and life. The background of this picture is deep blue S.M. Tagore represents 'Megh' as young king seated on an elephant with his pride at his side. Clouds stretch across the sky and the lightening flashes.

Though there are many different details, indications like rain, thunder, lightening are constant features showing the mood of the 'raga'. Again one artist represents 'Todi' as a nymph clothed in white standing in the bright day sunlight, playing on the 'vina'. The deer from the neighborhood frolics round her to hear her music. Another version shows 'Todi' as a decorated woman, green in colour wearing red garments. She is seen in a forest playing on the lute and caressing a deer. Here also features like the 'deer' and 'vina' are common in both, showing beauty calm and sweetness. (See Plate No. 8)

It can be said in conclusion that the pictorial representation of the ragas of Indian music are essential for formulating the imaginative impulse which is responsible for transforming the abstract notes of music into concert a forms or images. The pictorial representation of the ragas is necessary for visualizing the aesthetic or emotive essence of the ragas. In India as well as China painting was a kin to literature and the abstraction that was achieved for Chinese painting by Calligraphy and for India painting by music. In India, there are appropriate melodies for the various seasons, there are Ragarnala or paintings of musical modes and there are also Baramasi or seasonal lyrical poems. Besides these, there are paintings in which each illustration takes the form, not of a symbol or icon, but a dramatic situation conceived in the abstract, With their simplicity of line, skilful organizations of masses by mean of deep colours. Music is essentially an abstract art, allied to painting, it helps the letter to achieve a degree of a abstraction that is normal to music, directing the human soul to being, which is behind all patterns of sounds, shapes and colours.

The descriptive imagery of the lyrical poems the harmony of the 'ragas' or 'ragini' and the representation of natural scenes in the paintings, all alike and collectively symbolise and evoke the eternal and universal sentiment of wholeness. Wonder and associated with experience of the noumenon or being in the realm of nature. Rarely in the history of the worlds culture, there has been such a collaboration of the arts is express the collective vision of a whole people and epoh as there was at time in Northern.

Musical Instruments in Sculpture and Painting

The musical instruments of India have history as old as its music.

References in ancient writings, specimens carved on the temple walls and the large variety used by the musicians even today to the creative genius of the people. We believe that the emotional effect of melody lies entirely in the words of the song, their meaning and vocal intonations. The instruments on the other hand only emit pure vowel sounds wherein lies absolute music, their works in the rise and the fall of pitch and their order are purely intellectual and hence music produced by instruments has been dry instrumentalist.

The ancient had felt the existence of no such thing as pure instrumental music as the music of the instrument had to be felt or rather made intelligible by reference to the, which made it only an extension of vocal music. In early days music was given an important place in the social life of the nation. In feast and festivities, musical instruments have invariably played a greater part then vocal music, which in a way is responsible for the existence. From the ancient times those were rich varieties of musical instruments.

Nothing can better illustrate the continuity of culture in the long history of Indian than the story of Indian music and musical instruments. In the course of her long history India has evolved a wide variety of musical instruments and much ingenuity has been devoted to the invention of these instruments. There are more than 500 varieties of them, each with distinct name, shape, construction, technique of playing and quality of tone colour. In fact, each of the great families of musical instruments of string, wind and percussion used today, is well presented in those instruments which were devised by the primitive man in order to make a kind of music that was different from the sound of his voice.

In fact, we are introduced to a highly cultured and artistic people, who after centuries of hard-work must have been able to attain certain standard of skill in handicraft, specially in making musical instruments. The first and most interesting fact about the instruments of this country is that the extremely primitive to the highly sophisticated once are found rubbing shoulder to shoulder. The earliest evidence of instruments comes from the Indus valley complex. The information that gathered is mainly illustrated in seals. The study of musical instruments depicted in the sculpture in the early Indian art is based on the hypothesis. (See Plate No. 9)

Musical instruments were not invented, they developed slowly and comparatively much later than singing, the relics of Nagarjunakonda, Amaravati and Sanchi seals of Buddhist religion arrest our attention so do the Ajanta Caves. In all these places, many ponds filled with carving and sculptural illustration of musical instruments. The temples of later period provide equally authentic material for our study though the carved instrument took a little different in their appearance. In a niche in the Kailasnatha temple, is carved a stringed instrument whose resonator resembles that of the vina somewhat, but the end of the stem is not carved and bent downwards, but it seem to spread itself into a fan like shape. It has no frets, that why its strike one as a rare instrument. Another peculiar instrument is found in the caves of Aurangabad. This strange stringed instrument has frets nearly 22 and is seen played with a vallet.

The list of temples we have gone through represents many influences and is suitable for a comprehensive study. But each one stands out on its own merits and can make a significant contribution to the nature of our study. Some musical instruments are identified with the Gods, as the vina with Saraswati, the damru with Siva and the venu with Krishna. We refer that some of them must have become absolute or gone out of use when we do not seen them in the sculpture of the later periods. May be the characteristic of few instruments were transferred to a single instrument. Sculptures disclose to us certain facts about the classification of instrument profession wise and regionwise. The water carriers, fisherman, farmers, fruit sellers, snake charmers, hunters all had instruments assigned to them.

The figurines and carving of Indian Sculpture are source of valuable information of particular interest in the classification of instruments. The oldest is that of Bharata who in his Natyasastra gives four groups, the 'tate', 'avanddha', 'ghana' and 'sushira", perhaps considering the simplicity of the structure and the manner of use the 'Ghana vadya' or the solid instrument are the most primitive i.e. a dried fruit with seeds. Musical instruments have been traditionally classified into string, winded and percussion varieties of these the percussion group has the largest pedigree, wind and string appeared on the scene at a little later stage.

The traditions of keeping time by clapping the hands appear to have continued up to 5th cent. A.D. The purpose of this and stamping the fret was gradually intensified by the replacement of musical instrument such as beating sticks and so on.

Stringed Instrument

The idea of the earliest stringed instrument was possibly suggested to man by hunter's bow that while shooting an arrow, the string of the bow produced a humming sound, the musical bow developed from this. In the main line of evolution of stringed instruments says Harrison, 'There can be little doubt that music must be given a prominent position and that this instrument had its origin in the twanging of the string of the hunter's bow".[9] The bow shaped harp is met with in the sculptures of Sanchi, Bharhut, Pittalkhora, Amaravati, Nagarjunakonda and so on. It is seen in one of the Samudragupta's coin. It has angular shape in some sculpture stringed instruments in ancient time, whether bowed plucked or struck were commonly known as 'Vina'. The sound of the archer's bow must have been their source of inspiration of designing and making musical instruments of primitive people.

The shape of the primitive harp was like the body of bow, similar to the primitive Sumarian harp called 'AL' of pre-historic period (3rd million B.C.). The Indus harp was similar to this harp. The strings of the bow were made of vegetable fibre or gut, sometimes-twisted bark and strands of grass root, twisted together were also used as strings. Gradually addition and alternations were made to improve the structure of the harp and to increase the tonal qualities by adding a number of sounding strings of different lengths. The Boat shaped harp were very popular in the Gupta period (5th cent. AD.) as is evident from some of the gold coins belongings to that period. One of the favourite amusements of kings in ancient India, as is understood from literary sources, was music. Some of the Gupta monarchs were specially devoted to music and adopts in playing instrumental music to such an extant that the got themselves depicted on their coins as playing on a vina –- a harp. In one of the coins of Samudragupta, the harp vina is placed on the lap of the king, sitting on a high decked couch, playing the instrument with the right hand fingers. While the left hand usually keeps the instrument in position the fingers position of Samudragupta testified his high skill in Vina (harp) playing.

A beautiful terracotta from Gupta period shows the figurines of a lady sitting cross-legged and playing on a boat shaped harp. The sitting posture of the lady and the manner of placing the instrument on her thigh are highly reminiscent of Samudragupta figurine in similar posture. Later the word 'vina' came to devote the stringed instruments with or without frets. The evolution of vina has different stages viz. the bow with long strings, with plucked chord with different strings and so on. About 6th cent. A.D. a kind of round box or resonator was attached to the stem. Different lengths of strings for producing different notes were established in the vina.

The 'vina' mentioned in the Ramayana and Saptatantri Vina described in the Mahabharata. Laterly Nanyadeva described 'Sarasvati Veena' according to him, "this vina become important as it gave all the notes, 'shruti' and 'murchchana's. It strings was plucked by fingers or 'kona' and then pressing it by fingers and so the various notes were produced"[10] Bharata has described four ways of producing notes in music called 'Varnas'. The vina with frets, for all the notes is described in the musical works of medieval period. The first description of vina having appears in connection with 'kinnari vina'. It is said to be one of the primitive's Indian instruments. Nanyadeva described the use of frets in connection with 'kinnari vina'. A study of the stringed group will bring to tight the many shapes of the resonator square rectangular, circular and so on. (See Plate No. 10)

We follow the history of the stringed instruments, stage by stage and try to fix the landmark in evolution till the emergence of the vina. The frets and strings, their numbers varying in many of the pictures is a matter for research and study. The earliest of the string instruments were the harp and the lyre. The harp spread from the ancient Egypt to China and evidently to prominent string instrument in India. The Stupa of Barhut (2nd Cen. B.C.) is the first document in stone, which has preserved this instrument. It is played with plectrum are called 'Kona'. Almost all the stringed instruments were plucked either with bore fingers or with kona or plectrum. The bow or 'Danuryantram' is regarded as the four runners of all the classes of string instruments of the world. The Vina with one string (ektantri) and the vina with two strings (duitantri) are very ancient and the historians are of opinion that all the kinds of the later developed 'vinas' evolved from them. In the Rigveda, we find mention of the vina, 'vana' with hundred strings, also known as 'Shattatantri Vina'. There is a fine passage in the Ramayana which comparer the bow of the harp and the plectrum (kona) to the arrow. "Rama has never battled with me, he knows not my powers, when I shall play the vina of my bow with the plectrum of my arrow ...them neither Indra Varuna. Yama nor kubera can face the rain of my arrows".[11] Tambura was slowly earning into vogue. In fact, it came into more use after this inversion of the Mughals and in their miniature paintings.

Percussion Instrument

Rhythm is a proportion of time inherent in all aspects of nature. In music, rhythm is not only that which beautifies the melody, it is also the vital force is melodic imagination. Thus it has been said that rhythm is the 'pulsation of melody, say, of the universe'. Rabindranath Tagore in his 'The Religion of an Artist (Visva Bharti Book Shop, Calcutta 1950, p. 18) says: "What is rhythm? It is the movement generated and regulated by harmonious restriction. This is the creative force in the hand of the artist. So long as words remain in unadvanced prose from they do not give any lasting feeling of reality. The moment they are taken and put into rhythm, they vibrate into a radiance". Men on his own body found the oldest percussion instrument. The beat of the heart and the pulse in man must have evoked in him the sense of rhythm and at the wake of this rhythmic consciousness, he must have provided the first instrumental accompaniment to the dance, by stamping his feet and clapping his hands. Thus it was the first manifestation of the plastic art, which is to be seen represented in the sculptures at Bharhut.

The purpose of clapping hands and tapping the feet was gradually intensified by the replacement of the musical instruments such as beating sticks, clappers and so on. The percussion instruments include a large variety of drums, varying in their sound and model. Earliest sources for drum making available to human might have been floated logs and pots. Another perhaps even more ancient method was to dig pits in the grounds, cover then with plants and stem then, such a drum was the bhoomi dundubhi, mentioned in the vedas. It was hollow in the ground covered with skin. The tail of the animals was itself used as the drumstick.

The first stage in the development of drums is marked by the emergence of 'tambattam'. This instrument is of a circular frame covered, with one side of which is stretched a parchment. It was played with both hands. The 'tambourine' or 'tambattam' of Amaravati sculpture is probably the first depiction. In this sculpture instead of keeping the instrument on his body, supports a portion of its frame by the left side of his chest, in such a way that the drum face is conveniently turned to the right while playing. Long drums must have been made of tunnels of trees, scooped out and both sides closed with leather. There was a drum with three heads called the 'Pushkara vadyam'. It has two faces on each side of the drum, and the third one on the centre of the body of the drum. The sculptural of Hampi is the perfect of this drum. (See Plate No. 11)

The sculpture representing Lord Nataraja as the embodiment of Nada Brahman, illustrates the 'Pushkara' drum. In this form of Nataraja shown as perfect example of rhythm, movement and action, depending on the basis of main form of dancing Siva occupies the main portion of this panel. He has eight hands and every hand is engaged in producing some kind of musical sound (tala). On this fourth hand on the right and left beat the upper drum face while each of the third hand beats the sides of the drum. The Pushkara and the cylindrical drum were once again consolidated into a five-faced drum called 'Panchamukhavadyam'. According to Hindu mythology, it is said that 'Banugopan' (Siva sena) accompanied on the

'Panchamukhavadyam' to the 'Tandava' of the Lord Siva. The unique feature of this instrument is that, it has five independent resonators, all in the shape of a pot.

It is large vessel either of copper or brass. On the top there are five tabular, projections and is covered with the skin of Mitch cow. The drumheads are all of the same level. The diameter of the central face is slightly larger than those of the peripheral faces. Both the hands place the instrument. In performance, the sides of this drum places two small pot drums also of metal, the Kudemuzha, so that they are in all seven faces. It is claimed that they are tuned to the reventone of ancient scale known as 'Shadja grama'. It would be of great interest to get acquainted with the characteristic feature of this 'Panchamukhavadyam'. It is huge five-faced drum and each face is named after the five faces of Shiva, 'Sadyajatam', 'Isanam', 'Talpurusham', 'Aghorom' and 'Vamedenam'. It is used in temple music. (See Plate No. 11)

There are so many shapes of drums like flat, barrel, waisted cylindrical etc. we found in the sculptures. In one Badami sculptural, two drums are seen played by a man sitting on a raised seat. The drum to the left had broad face and is about half of the other drum in height. The pair would correspond to modern Daya (the drum usually placed to the right and played by the right hand) and Baya (the drum with broader face usually placed to the left side and played by the left hand). (See Plate No. 12) With the difference that the Daya and Baya are almost similar in height. The only specimen of the new type is to be seen in the fragment of sculpture from Pawaya of the Gutpa period. The 'mridanga' the classical drum of India literally means made of clay presumably therefore its body should have been originally of clay. The 'mridanga' is considered to be fairly ancient among the drum varieties. It is said to have been devised by Brahma to act an accompaniment to the dance of Siva.

The sculpture at Amaravati shows "Ankhaya Mridanga' is being played by women. It is suspended from the left shoulder by means of a strap and is held in position between the left hand and the right hip. Sculptural evidences of the ancient rock cut temples of India disclose the fact that two or three drums 'Pushkara' of different sizes were used in music and dance. Long before the advent of the Persian and Arabs as well as before the Mohammaden rule. Among the drum with two drums heads, the hour-glass shaped drum represented in the figurines from Mohanjodaro. In one of the terracotta figurines of a women, it is to be seen a drum held an under her left hand. It is of the hour glass shape and the right face is exposed for playing the instrument commonly known in our times as 'Udukkai' or 'Damaru'. (See Plate No. 12)

In the absence of pictorial evidences in the seals and reading, some instruments actual use could possibly be known only by referring to other contemporary civilization such as the Mesopotamia and Sumer. Certain curiously curved blades were discovered at 'Ur' on a gold cylinder seal, which dates about 2700 B.C. On this seal, a dancer in action to the strain of the lyre and is flanked by two attendants clapping the carved sticks. The 'kartal' or the clapper which is an extension form of the hands, is an improvement on the beating sticks. Thus instrument is as old as the Indus civilization, the surminates of which could be seen in the hands of wondering medicants and beggars to day. The stone or wooden clappers were further modified into circular discs by removing the handles. The handles were replaced by thick threads of silk, wool or probably of glass in ancient times, which were inserted into a hole in the centre of the discs and the instrument in this shape was came to be called cymbols or 'Jalra'. (See Plate No. 13)

While the cymbal is primarily used to accompany dance performance along with the drum, it is also seen included as a secondary 'talavadya' in concert party as found in one of the panels in the Lakshmana Temple at Khajuraho. The bigger variety of the flat cymbals, which goes by the name 'Brahma Talam' in, Ajanta caves. At Badami, the representation of the 'Braham Talam' consists of a pair of flat disc with handle to hold. In the Thanjavur frescoes, the royal procession is headed by a group of dancing Apsaras or Gandharvas, one of who is playing on the 'Brahamtalam'. The second variety of cymbals in the shape of cups and flowers are found in Ajanta frescoes with on orchestra comprising of drums and cymbals. The cup-shaped cymbals are depicted in Cave I and XVII. In the painting of Indra and his groups of musicians are included two celestial nymphs holding a pair of cymbals each. The cups are detached from one another and are held separately. (See Plate No. 13)

There were drums, which had more than two faces. They are called 'Tripushkara alias the mridanga, the panavas and the dardura' There are many opinions about these drums. Some news are that the tree position of the mridanga — 'urdhuaka' (the vertical) ankya (held in the lap) and the alingya (the embraced) were included in this. Some opinions that drum with three faces were called 'tripushkara'. A mridanga with three heads has been noticed in the sculptures of Hampi. At Amaravati, a sculpture shows this instrument which is named as Ankhya Mridanga is being played by means of a strap and is held in position between the left hand and the left hip. (See Plate No. 14)

Wind Instrument

The principal of the whistle head facilitated the production of sound from the vertical column of tube, and the ancient Indian must have known this principal, for several types of whistles. Towards the close pre-historic period, wind instrument developed into simple vertical tube. Among the wind instruments (sushira Vadya) Bharta gives 'flute' only as the major one and 'Sankha' and 'Judekini' as secondary one. 'Flute' which is the earliest musical instrument to he depicted in sculpture and painting appears as early as 1st cent. A.D. It was the major wind instrument. As the flute was made of bamboo or seed, it was called 'Vamsa' or 'Venu'. It gave very sweet notes. The numbers of holes are four in the classical period, which was increased later. There are horizontal and vertical flutes also. In a relief, a double flute is also seen. The right pipe played the melody and the other accompanied it a higher note. 'Vamsa' was made of bamboo wood, elephant task, and sandal wood, silver and gold. The hole through which the air was blown called 'Mukharandhra'. (See Plate No. 15)

Decorated flutes piece like the face of Yati or a lion or an elephant are rarely portrayed in the plastic art. In the beginning of the Buddhist art, the flute was mainly played along with conch and drums in processions. Sankha or conch was another wind instrument, which was blown by mouth. It is used in procession along with the drum and other wind instruments. Generally, the sound of the conch is always described as deep and noble and perhaps the addition of the long pipe made it shrill. The process of blowing, it was known as dhamana (blowing) or 'purana' (filing). Sometimes, the conch was attached to a metal piece. The excavations of the many early historical sites have yielded conches both from secular and religious establishment, these by indicating the popular use of wind instrument. In the epic age, conches were largely employed as a war signal. It was generally associated with the bheri or dundubhi and was blown at intervals. The warriors always carried the conches along with them in the battle-field. (See Plate No. 15)

The conch has always a sacred association for the Hindu. Its religious use in India has been continuous for several millennia. It is very surprising to know that these exists even today conch with an additional tube and with a decorative piece at the other end, the tube has no finger holes. By breath control sound is produced. The trumpets and horns are popular in the Buddhist art as they appear for the first time in the sculptured pillars and Sanchi. They are invariably blown in procession along with the drums of different kind. The Gomukha mentioned in the Mahabharata must have been somewhat similar to the trumpet, but with the face of a cow. The straight trumpet seems to have been very popular in the art of Ajanta. The 'Bukara' mentioned in the Rigveda was probably a shell trumpet that used in battle to terrify the enemy. The significance of the Vedic name 'Bakura' is pointed out from the fact that the shell trumpet after words called 'Sanka' also meant to frighten the enemy in the battle. It gives a deep dangerous sound. Trumpet occur both in the earlier and later group of Ajanta paintings.

The 'horns' as opposed to the trumpets are comparatively small instrument with curved tubes with lesser dimensions. Hence they are named 'kona bomba' curved horn. The horn is represented for the first time in the primitive rock paintings. The horn seems to be very rare in Indian sculpture 'Sranga'(horn) was fashioned out of buffalo horn. At its mouth, a piece of bull-horn was attached to increase the volume of the sound 'Pungi' is a favourite instrument of the snake charmers. It is made of two parallel canes glued together. The mouthpieces are connected in a gourd. It can see in the sculptures of Konark. It is also known as 'Nadhaswaram'. Wind instruments with more than one air columns was not unknown in ancient India. Instrument with double pipes is the earliest manifestation in Indian art. The double pipes preserved at Sanchi in small in size with a common mouth hole.

In one of the Gandhara school, is to be seen a panpipe and a lyre. In this scene, to the left of a couple holding drinking cups, is seated a woman playing on panpipes. The panpipes numbering approximately about ten, including the blowing pipe, are kept in a rectangular box which has three holes or outlets are in the center on top and the other two on one of the sides. For all appearance the instrument look like a reed 'sruti box'. (See Plate No. 15)

Orchestration Sculpture and Painting

It will be difficult to place the exact date of orchestration in the history of music, since musical instruments have been in use from the dawn of civilization. It is in the nature of musical instruments that reproduce, what the human voice sings or the mind and intellect want to compose and express. So even the earliest man used his own variety of musical instruments for his emotional expression. 4th cent. B.C. period has revealed a leap forward in cultural development in general and in music as well. The Greeks playing the instruments together and their aesthetic sense promoted them when needed to produce a pleasing melody. They did not confine the grouped, instrumental music to religious rituals but gave it prominence in their secular entertainment also.

Orcher's meant the art of dancing or rhythmical movement of the body and orchestric referred to anything related to the dance. Indian orchestra popularly termed as 'Vadya kathupa' in Bharata's 'Natya sastra' and as Vadya vrinda in modern terminology has a long tradition from the past. The Natya sastra gives us different types of 'kuthupa' such as 'tala kuthupa', 'anandha kuthupa' and so on. According to this view, there never seem to have been enough provocation for group forms to develop, which was the chief reason for the disintegration of a tradition of Indian orchestra. Sources offer us valuable material in the study of orchestral practice through the ages.

In this matter, a noteworthy feature in that ancient Indian sculptures both of north and south India, depict a group of musicians playing a variety of musical instruments on festive and religious occasions. In India music also we say the orchestra is in evidence. Long ago if we take it just a mean sounding many musical instruments together. The vedic literature, which constitutes our earliest literary source gives us an encyclopedic view of some of the instruments that were used in particular rites and rituals. The nature of the instrument to be used is described, string, wind or percussion, its character viz. soft, loud, moving whether played by man or woman, whether solo or in group. We get a pond of information from the Rig vedic hymns, Satapatas brahmans, the Upanishada and other texts. Vishnu dharmothra puranas besides mentioning the musical instruments and its place in the orchestral set up.

We must remember that vedic orchestra which has been the earliest in India, perhaps though popular has served only a accompaniment to vedic chanting. The limited range of the musical scale it was easier to follow the main stream of music. The three varieties of musical instruments, string, wind and percussions were in plenty and combination and grouping of instrument suitable to specific hymns. The classification of orchestral music, as temple orchestra, dance orchestra, prayer orchestra etc. came into existence. The first representation of Indian orchestra is in the sculptured pillars of the stupa of Bharhut (2nd cent. B.C.) where in the three constituents of a typical musical performance. Later geeta, vadya and nritya are depicted. In a representation of a lower panel gives us an impression that the effect of the prayer of the deities is conveyed through the symphony of the music of the nymphs, to the right of four dancers, vocalists and instrumentalist are seated. The song or vocal music is only to be represented by certain gestures and postures mainly including those of hands. The instrumentalist consisting of two harpists and two drummers are sitting close to the songsters.

The concepts of dance concerts in Ancient India with orchestral accompaniment seems to have developed to an advance stage under the patronage of the Gupta King. The first representation of orchestra party is from the frescoes of Ajanta, where more than 12 musicians with various musical instruments can be seen. In the fresco of Ajanta, a king is seen sitting with a princess, to the right of the royal pavilion is painted a dance performance, there are two ladies plying on flutes, remaining five artists, two of them are playing cymbals, one playing an Tripol drum, another on a long drum, and the fifth apparently a guitar like instrument. The formation of the orchestra is in the shape of trapezoid. All these are facing the audience. (See Plate No. 16)

This arrangement of the orchestra reminds us at once of the one presides by the Bharta. He says that on one side of the 'Ranjapithe', the loading drum should be placed, facing east along with the other drums on its sides. On the other side, the vocalists should sit with other instrumentalists (wind and stringed). This arrangements or the sitting up is called 'Pratyahara'. Another reference to orchestra is met with in the temptation scene in Ajanta cave XXVI. The courtesan dancers to the accompaniment of music, in order to divert the Buddha from meditation. The orchestra consists of two drummers seated on either side left is playing on a small drum and the other one on triple drum (two vertical and one horizontal) and one cymbal player seated. Between the dancer a vocalist clapping her hand, who apparently directs the dancer on the stage.

At Aurangabad, cave VI is carved a dance scene. The whole party consists of a dancer with musical accompaniment by three drummers, two cymbal players and one flutist. The pose of the dancer in the middle is very typical of the 'Bharat natyam' style. (See Plate No. 16) An orchestral party in Pandya caves at Tirumayyam, is highly unique that in all these orchestral representation the flute is given more importance since the flutist occupies the key position in the figurines. Thus the archeological evidence of the ancient Indian orchestra with several instruments in one group is noteworthy in all there representation. However the best reproduction of Indian orchestra is that in a panel depicting dance scene from pawaya. It is the only one of its kind in which the triple aspect of Indian music viz. Geeta, Vadya and Nritya, as well as the representation of the three main families of musical instruments is well delineated. In arrangement it is highly significant that the stringed instruments are given the front seat. This accounted for two reasons. In the first instance, from the acoustics point of view, the timber of the stringed instrument is more feeble and soft then those of the wind and percussion instrument. Secondly, 'vina' among the 'tata vadya' is hailed us the national instrument of India.

The definite reference to orchestral party as we see today is found in the Indo Mughal paintings and later in the Marathe paintings. To quote one instance in one painting representing a palace life, a king and queen are enjoying the pleasure of music. Musicians are eight in number and all are women. They held tamburas drums. The party also includes a player on the 'Rudra veena'. (See Plate No. 17) We notice a continuous development and especially usage of all the musical instruments can be noticed throughout the ages from the 4th cent. B.C. to the present period. They includes various instruments like flute, vina, yazh, violin, nagaswaram, various kinds of drums, janjira, tambattam, ghatam, tambura and lastly a combination of all these instruments in orchestra parties. In literature, ancient Tamil classics carry a lot of references to prove the presence of the orchestra in their cultural heritage. Orchestral music for dance for instance is described as follows: The Yazh (harp) followed the flute the louder drum followed, the softer drum and the entire instrument together produced the music of orchestra.

Ancient literature in Indian music mentions various kinds of orchestra called 'kuthupa' or 'vadyavrindas'. According to the number of performers that constituted it, they have been classified into 'uttama', 'madhyama' and 'kaneshtika vrindas'. There were take kuthupas or stringed bands vamsaka vrindas or bands of performers playing on wind instruments and Avanadha kuthupas or bands of performers on drums. These kuthupas provided accompaniment when dramas were staged and dance performed. The archaeological evidences of the ancient Indian orchestra, mark a define to stage in the development of vadya-vrinda, in which instead of depicting group performances of musical instruments of one and the same category, they show an ideal form of orchestra which includes representatives of different types of musical instruments. (See Plate No. 18) The selection of the instrument being different in each representation. In the history of Indian music, the recognition and use of quarter-tones within a octave have played a vital role, especially in the development of the musical scales. This is more or less fixed the nature of Indian music to run on a solo melodic line.

The expression of music as a separate entity, independent of dancing became conspicuous from about the 13th cent. onwards. In the earlier period from the time of Bharta (4th cent. B.C.) music was thought of as consisting of vocal music, instrumental and dancing. The literature beginning with that of Bharta treated all those three aspects of music. With the great strides made in the development of Indian music and with the invention of improved musical instruments gradually both vocal and instrumental and became independent of drama and dance. The realization of the separate entity of music especially instrumental from that of dance is elicited vividly.

MUSICAL PILLARS AND STONES

Generally, the musical pillars or musical pianos are a group of columns of stone being distributed along the periphery with the residual, central massive pillar serving to give stability to the entire structure. They are always seen in clusters. South India is justly famous for her mighty achievements in the realm of music. In the marvelous musical stone, stands without a parallel. Anything even remotely approximating to these pillars can be seen neither in North India nor in the west. The architects who came cross the resonant variety of granite stones, made capital out of them. A thin lining of this resonant stone, when examined under a microscope will reveal interesting features. These stones were made use in carving figures whose limbs gives notes of different frequencies.

It was in the days of the Vijayanagar kings, that the human fancy was drown to make the fullest use of the resonant variety of granite stone. The colour of the stone pillars are white, grey, or black and occasionally of sandalwood. They are different in shape, namely cylindrical, twisted, square hexagonal or octagonal. The heights of the pillar ranges from three to six feet. These pillars have no ornamental base or decorated top. The pillars support the roof like the other ordinary pillars, contributing to the artistic appearance of temples. When a musical pillar is struck with a piece of wood or thin smooth stone, preferably with the latter, one can hear the note given by it and also feel with one's fingers the vibrating state of the pillar. The brilliance of the tone differs according to the manner of striking either a downward stroke or a direct one. In the temple of Drasuram near Kumbakonam the stone steps in the southern face of the Balipitam give notes of varying pitch. One of the stone slabs in the Sanji hill at Tirukalikundram also gives musical notes. Madurai, Tirunelveli and at many other places are just marvels of architecture. The earliest pillars to be carved out were these at Hampi. The height of the pillars range from 6 to 7 feet. In Pasupatisvara temple of Hampi, the ancient capital of Vijayanagar, the musical pillars are built along the 'prakara' These pillars must have been played by four of five musicians at a time, which were able to produce loud notes to serve as accompaniment to the tunes sung by musicians. The numbers of pillars in a structure varies from one to sixteen.

In one of the specimens at Tirunelveli, a group of pillars to the left of the main shrine, we could hear the swaras when struck in the clockwise order. Each is about 6 to 8 feet at the height. It has integral annex, which seems to be cut and carved out of one solid black stone. Here the note 'panchama' is heard only in the square pillars and 'madhyama' is heard only in octagonal pillars alone. It is noted that these notes, when separated and sung result in 'Navaroj' and 'Sankarabharanam'. It is so complex and huge that no musician can play on it single-handed. To tone of the pillar are analogues to that of the 'Jalataranga'. Again there are two similar pillars and a gentle tap at these pillars evokes loud notes with vibration. The pillars in the Minakshi temple at Madurai, which are mostly in damaged condition. But there are four group's still produce 'kaklinishada', 'shadja', 'chatusruti rishabha' and 'antragandhara'. Another group, which is a 'laya' or 'tala' stambha, produces tone like jati and tala mnemenous.

Perhaps these were used for accompaniment to the recital of Tevaram humns. There are also eight pillars of bigger size and they produce the note 'shadja' 'chaturuti rishabha', 'sudha rishabha', 'sudha madhyama'. Chatusruti rishabha, antar gandharva, 'Shudha rishabha' and 'Chatusruti rishabha'. The musical stone pillars in our temples are a standing testimony to the artistic genius of the south. In these pillars, the entire group of pillars is carved out of a single monolith. The notes of some pillars are dull white those of others are rich. In some cases the notes are bright and clear as of metal gongs. In the Sunder Raja Perumal temple at Todikkambu, there are two clusters of musical pillars at the entrance. Both are similar in size and notes they produce are identical. They have different tones at different parts in their height.

The best specimen of a musical pipe scooped out of a granite stone pillar is seen in the temple at Tirunelveli. The pipe is conical in shape and is in the central part of a pillar. The interior of the pipe is smooth and polished. The two ends of the pipes are circular in shape when blown from one end, the tone of the 'ekkalam' is heard and blown from the other end, the tone of the conch is heard. These holes are named 'Ekkalarandra' and 'Sankarandra'. Thus is really a marvelous phenomenon. The length of the pipe is one foot. The pipe has two small folds in the interior and this probably accounts for the differences in tone colour when blown from the two ends. The frequencies of the notes heard from the two ends bear the 'samvadi' relationship. In other temple, there are holes drilled into the granite pillar, which when blown through produce notes of wind instruments like 'conch' and 'ekkalam'.

In the Vardhamana temple at Tirupparuttikuram at Kancheepuram, there is a 'Sangeet mantapa' built during the time of Vijayanagar period. This is a rectangular shaped hall and formed by four rows of pillars planted parallel to the verandah in front of the main shrine. The pillars are all in hexagonal design and circular in form. The first two rows have seven pillars, each indicating the use of seven notes and post to each pillar is evident from the fact that each pillar has tiny sculptures of musicians and dancers. The music of all these musicians must have reverberated in this fantastic Sangeet mantapa when they performed under the order of the king. It is possible at the same time 120 musicians used to sing since there are thirty pillars with four sides. It is also suggested that these thirty pillars might also produce musical notes as in other musical pillars in various temples if struck at the proper level.

The musical stone pillars could be classified under four heads:

(a) ***Sruti Sthambhas*** or drone pillars providing sound which could be used for sruti. There were used for sounding the drone notes. With the tonic notes given by the pillars, the sacred choir gave recitals of sacred music. Vedic hymns or the Tevaram or both.

(b) ***Gana Sthambhas*** or musical pillars which could be used while singing notes. These were used for providing musical accompaniment. In this case two players with thin bamboo sticks stood at opposite end and played in a concerted manner, solo performances also were given with these Gana Sthambha.

(c) ***Laya Sthambhas*** or rhythmic pillars used for rhythmic accompaniment while singing. These were used for providing a cross-rhythmical accompaniment while singing. Rhythmic accompaniment was provided to sacred music with these pillars. These pillars were also found in the Nritta mantapa. In some cases, jatis were played on them for the guidance of dancers.

(d) ***Pradarsana Sthambara*** or experimental pillars used to measure and verify various tones and notes. The pillars here in illustrated acoustical laws and phenomena. The opposite corner pillars are so accurately tuned that when one pillar is just tapped the pillar at the opposite corner which is tuned to the note of the same frequency, immediately vibrates. The vibration can be clearly heard and also felt by the fingers.

The musical icons figuring in some temples offered interesting study. These are seen projecting from big pillars. The various limbs of these figures when tapped give notes of different pitch. By skillfully striking one can play a simple piece of music. In the Venkatachapti temple in

Krishnapuram there are the best specimens of musical icons of huge size. One of the images speaks out the note Sa Pa and Ga. In another sculpture of a main holding an 'Ektantri Vina', the lower part of the instrument produces the note 'Sa' and the dandi gives the note 'Ri'. There is another unique musical icon and it is a 'Saptasvara mahavision', when its limbs are struck, they give out all the seven notes. 'Sa' from the middle of the face, 'Ri' from the middle of the conch, 'Ga' from the middle of the discuss from the region of the heart, 'Ma', 'Pa' from the palm of the hand or the waist, 'Dha' from the middle of the abhayahasta, 'Ni' from both the legs near the calf muscles and the lower 'Sa' from the space between the two feet on the pedestal. This is a peculiar but interesting feature seen in many Vishnu icons, but this is only one where in all sapta svara's are heard.

In the temple of Darasuram near Kumbakonam, the stone steps leading to the balipitham are musical. They are seven steps. In some steps the left side produces one note and the right another. For example the first step produces 'kaklinishada' at the left side and 'shadja' at the right side. The most astonishing feature of these stone pianos is that they are uninfluenced by climate changes and always give forth the same note. These pillars and icons do not need any repair. They are therefore all ages to come, to give forth their beautiful clear notes if men could only use them. These pillars which weather cannot wrap-nor time destroy, should certainly be preserved unaffected with the standards of note as accepted in those glorious days of music.

COINS

A noteworthy feature of India's musical history is the large number of members of the ruling class who have played a notable part in the development of the art from early times. India can just boast of her Royal patrons, Royal musicians, Royal composers and Royal musicologists. Kings of India have always valued the presence of poets, musicians and composers in their courts. Of the royal musicians of the epic period, mention may be made of Sri Rama and Krishna. Valmiki in the Ramayana frequently refers to Rama's attainment in music, Valmiki incidentally happens to be the earliest composer in the history of world music. Sri Krishna took to the flute, because it is the instrument of humanity. It is an instrument upon which one could play all types of music ranging from the highest type of classical music down to the simplest folk music, Ravana, the king of Lanka was also a great musician. How he pleased Siva with his recital of sama gana is well known.

Coming to historic period, we have Emerpor Samudragupta, who has represented himself on one of his coins as playing on a stringed instrument (harp). The subject of musical numismatics begins from him. In his coin, the emperor is seated on a cushioned couch. The left foot is resting on a footstool. The long boat shaped resonator of the harp is lying on his lap. The instrument is held vertical and the strings are plucked with his left-hand fingers. The arm of the harp is being held by the right hand. (See Plate No. 19)

There are also coins of Kumaragupta (C. 414-455 A.D.).) where the king is shown as playing the harp. The strings of the harp are seen clearly in these coins (The instrument depicted in the coins of both kings, is only a harp and not a lyreo as mentioned by some historians). Yoga Narendra Malla of Palem had the title 'Sangitarana Paraga' inscribed on his coins. Kind Udayaman was an illustrious performer on the instrument Ghoshauati. He once soothed a mad elephant by performing on his instrument.

EPIGRAPHY AND INSCRIPTION

Epigraphically and inscriptional records are sources of highest value in the research in music. Their value as contemporary records thus remains permanent. Mostly kings, who helped the country to preserve the records through the medium of stone and other epigraphically all due to the patronage, extended it, resources. The earliest known historical scripts in India are 'khorashti' and 'Brahmi' and varieties of letters are found throughout the country. Epigraphic source is of the highest value in the re-construction of the history of Indian music. Unlike books or other documents written on perishable materials, these inscriptions being engraved on stone and on metal are free from the process of decay and deterioration. Their value as contemporary records thus remains permanent.

These stone records are the static representation of the dynamic art in as much as they contain valuable information regarding the visual demonstration of music, dance and drama. In the re-construction of the history of Indian music, we entirely depend on the extent of literature in Sanskrit, Tamil and Telugu language, for the evidence to the development of the art in the early period. With the help of the dates given in these stone documents and with the aid of the paleographic evidence of the same, it is possible for us to some extent to maintain a chronology of history concepts and landmarks in evolution of music. Many of the kings of ancient India had gained mastery over the fine arts. In fact, it was considered a specially privilege to study the fine art which included music, dancing and painting. The kings of India gave all facilities and encouraged their citizens to acquire a high standard of knowledge in arts and sciences and made necessary provision for them to enjoy the demonstration of music and dance.

The 'Bharat varsha' as country was known the seat of the art like music and dance. It was a country where the beating hearts of lovers sounded like the drum called 'Dakka'. 'The hum of swaram of bees, like the song, the gentle breeze causing leaves to clap together. Like the cymbals (or constonets) truly it seemed as if Manmatha (the God of love) was secretly making Rati dance and so was the Bharta land named from 'Bharata' (the art of music and dance').

Inscription and their Evidence

Epigraphy is the study of inscription and inscription literally means any writing engraved on some object. In India, rocks as well as lithic, earthern or wooden pillar, plates and pots, as also bricks, shells ivory and other objects were generally used for incising inscription. For the ancient and medieval periods of Indian history, the study of inscription has a special importance. India contributed to the civilization of the world in all periods of history, but no more significant contributions to world culture were made in the early period of all sources for the reconstruction of early Indian history. Epigraphic records are the most important as they provided materials for the major part of what we now know about the achievements of the Indians of old. The great importance of inscription lies in the fact that they generally offer information about personages and events of Indian history, about which nothing is known from any other sources.

Materials for Writing

(a) ***Palmyra leaves:*** Palmyra leaves separated from the length-wise joint in the middle were used for writing letters as well as manuscripts of literary work in sanskrit and other languages. For writing, first leaves were dried than rubbed from the both sides, then it was ready for writing.

(b) ***Wood:*** Wooden slabs or plates were used before the introduction of slates. Some mud or chalk was applied to the surface of the wooden states on which brick powder was evenly spread. Figures or sums then written with the help of blunt stick.

(c) ***Stone:*** Stone was used from the earliest times for engraving writing for the purpose of making it cira-sthitika or ever lasting.

Inscriptions were often engraved on rocks stone, pillars or slabs. First the stone was carefully dressed and made very smooth by chiseling than written with ink or chalk on the surface of the stone by a calligraphist.

(d) ***Copper:*** Among metals copper was the most popular writing material in ancient and medieval India. The plates which were in every size and generally a long in shape. The royal seals were also of bronze and gold.

The first references to the musical proficiency of the rulers of India, is that king of Jamamijaya found in 12th cent. It states the king as an adept in the 'Chahaputa' and 'Chachatpuda talas (two varieties of talas from 100 talas). The king was a player of the pure salaja ragas and on the 'Brahma vina'. In short, the king was skilled in the science of music and proficiency in many other sciences also. The Hathigumpha inscription of king Kharavela patronized in the first half of the second cent. B.C. described how the king patronized the art of music and dance. It records that the king who was himself versed in the science of the Gandharas i.e. music. He entertained his citizens with the exhibitions of dancing, singing and instrumental music and also caused to be held festivities and assemblies.

In an inscription of the Pratichara Queen Chitralekha, dated Vikrame year 1012, we have a reference to the prosperity of the country in the region of king Rajajika. In the genelogy, it is stated that his subjects adorned with beautiful ornaments, perfumes and cloths and decked with flowers festivities, songs and sounds of drums (more appropriately sounds of musical instrumental).

Sarunatras—Otsava—Gitaturya—Rasitair amanda sandrab brajah

While such was the encouragement given to the development of Indian music by the kings of North India, the ruler of the south, however, were not lagging behind in their efforts to promote this art. They maintained a happy balance in the steady progress of the art. Epigraphical records disclose that king Rajaraja-I portioned off parts of his country as 'District of Music'. From an inscription of Rajaraja-I. we learn that there was a street in Thanjavur named as gandharvaleru i.e 'the street of the musicians'. The kings inscription portray him as an active man, who spent the later portion of his life in works of devotion. He made enormous endowments in the form of lands and gold to the temple, skilled musicians for singing the devaram hymns, dancing girls The epigraphical records collected from the different parts of India provide ample evidences to the scholarship of the venerable acharyas and saints of the past. The most interesting account registered is the one from the temple as Belgani dated 1193 A.D.

This record belongs to the region of the Chalukya king. His rajaguru is spoken of as a master of all arts and sciences. He was skilled in vocal music, flute playing and mridangam playing he was the most skilled in the world in performing pleasing dances. He took the first place among those who played flutes, with singing women who gave forth enchanting songs, with clear seven notes i.e. sa, ri, ga, etc. and with those, who play sweet sounds on the drum, mridangam. The unique trait of his was that he occupied himself alone in composing, analysing and commenting and even interesting those who did not understand. Coming to the educational system and the institution, we observe that the temples of worship. Invariably they were the seats of learning attracting students from all parts of the country. Students learnt the vedas and other sacred literature in the institution and patha scales maintained by the temple authorities.

In the developments of music and dance, music teachers and dance masters were employed. Besides singing and dancing before the deities, their duties also included the training of the musicians and dancers appointed in the temple service. The idea was to enable these singers to increase their vocabulary of songs. An inscription of the Kulottinga Chola's time informing us that in the temple at Tiruvidaimarudur, one musician (Panam) was appointed to say before the principle deity the temple as to teach the temple 'Devadasis'. During Mahandravarman Sundra Pandyas region serves modes if music flourished along with Tamil literature. In the region of king Bijjana of Kalachari dynasty, the high priest of the temple is said to have been a master of art and letters and as adopt in the science of music and called the 'Bhartamuni'.

Among the musical inscriptions there are two most important inscriptions they being the Arichchalur rock edict and the other is Kudumiyamalai:

(a) ***The Arichchalur Inscription on Music and Dance:*** In the list of inscription that are of technical value, those published by the Ramachandran are chronologically the earliest available records, pertaining to the sphere of dance and music. They are to be found in a cave of Arichchalur. There is a phrase 'Elultum punarttam' means one who taught music by letters, i.e. notation. This is corroborated by the repletion of the syllables like 'ta tai ta tai' which are called 'jatis' in a dance referred to was proficient us much as in accounts as he was in art and the teaching of music and dance. Thus in the history of musicography the notation of rhythm preceded those of musical sounds and musical composition. And in this respect the Arichchalur inscription provides the second stage of musical notation.

(b) ***Kudumiyamalai Inscription of Mahendravarman Pallava-I:*** Music, which had always played an important part in the social life of the people of India was natured with utmost care and attention and received the royal patronage in the Pallava period of South Indian history. The royal artist of Mahendravarman I has left a legacy to the music lovers of India a permanent record with rock of Kudmiyamalai a musical inscription. It stands as a testimony to the inventive landmark in the history of both the practice and theory of Indian music. This inscription has a great interest to the student of Indian music. Their existence of the inscription was discovered in 1904 that kudumiyamalai literally means the hill of the Lord who has the Sikha.

Grama and Murchchana are interchangeable terms in the sense that one grama is nothing else, but a particular murchchana of the other. This is the main theme of the Kudumiyamalai inscription. The body of the inscription is divided into seven sub-sections. This inscription commences with an auspicious term 'Siddham' which is followed by 'Namahsvaya', which means solution or homage to Siva. The seven sub-section in the inscription has sixteen sets of four notes, each under a heading individually ascribed as:

(*a*) Madhyama grama chatusprakara svargramah
(*b*) Shadja grama chatusprahara svara grama and so on.

The other sessions bear the names such as:

(*c*) Shadaba
(*d*) Sadharira
(*e*) Panchama
(*f*) Kaisika madhyma
(*g*) Kaisika.

The reference to 'Gandharava sastram the science of Gadharvas i.e. music, give our conclusion that the king was an adept in music. It can be said, that the king wanted to achieve that was not achieved before in the realm of music. Seeing the various intonation of sounds that stringed musical instrument like the 'vina' alone could produce and actuated by a zeal and determination to produce the same results in vocal music. He designed by dint of uncommon and superior resources probably a successful notation of musical sounds to be produced in vocal music. The instrument referred to the vina since it has been given the title 'chatusprahara svargramah or produced by the four strings of the instrument. The name of this instrument is 'Parivadhini'. It is a big vina and has strings made of gold.

Since the Kudumiyamalai treatise has seven sections and mention 'Parvadini' as the main communicative instrument, the sculpture in relation also must indicate that Lord Siva singing the seven section of the Kudumiyamalai treatise to the accompaniment of 'Parivadini'. This stands that this inscription does indicate a compositional format like that of a 'kriti' or 'kirtana' because no one before or after this particular inscription has sued all the notes of the 22 shrutis in the same composition. The tala has not been indicated the seven sections have been assigned to seven different melas and to ragas deriving from each. The first section is in kharharpriya mela itself, the second in Harikambodhi and so on. (See Table 4.1 & 4.2)

Miscellaneous

1. This inscription is divided into 7 sections, each subdivided into a number of aksiptikas. Each aksiptika is in a horizontal line. Each aksiptika concludes with an end sign. 15 of these are lost.
2. Each section contains a heading and a colophon.
3. The total usage of musical notes in the inscription is 2432.
4. The frequency of usage of the musical notes in the inscription is in the following order:
   (*a*) Sadja — Sa, Se, Su, Si
   (*b*) Madhyama — Mu, Mi, Me, Ma
   (*c*) Dhaivata — Dhe, Dhu, Dhi, Dha
   (*d*) Risabha — Ra, Ru, Ri, Re
   (*e*) Pancama — Pu, Pe, Pi, Pa
   (*f*) Nisada — Ne, Na (Nu, Ni)
   (*g*) Gandhara — Gi, Ga, Ge, Gu
   (*h*) Antara — u.a.e. -
   (*i*) Kakali — Ke, Ku, Ka, -
5. In the order of frequency, the musical notes are dotted as follows:- Madhyama, Panchama, Risabha, Sadaja, Antara, Gandhara, Dhaivata, Nisada, Kakali.
6. The dots on some 38 musical notes are doubtfully determined. Their distribution is as follows:-
   Sa-11, ri-5, a-3, ma-10, pa-5, dha-1, ni-1, ka-2.

Table I
Showing Details of Distribution of Musical Notes in Each Aksiptika of Each Section of the Kudumiyamalai Inscription

Section	*'Aksip-tikā*	*Sa*	*Si*	*Su*	*Se*	*Ra*	*Ri*	*Ru*	*Re*	*Ga*	*Gi*	*Gu*	*Ge*	*Ma*	*Mi*	*Mu*	*Me*	*Pa*	*Pi*	*Pu*	*Pe*	*Dha*	*Dhi*	*Dhu*	*Dhe*	*Na*	*Ni*	*Nu*	*Ne*	*A*	*I*	*U*	*E*	*Ka*	*Ki*	*Ku*	*Ke*	*Total*
	1	13	–	2	2	2	–	1	–	3	5	–	1	1	3	4	–	–	2	4	2	–	–	3	–	–	–	1	14									63
	2	4	–	1	1	9	–	3	3	7	9	1	6	–	3	2	–	–	2	1	3	–	–	1	–	1	–	1	6									64
I. Madhyamagrāma	3	8	–	1	–	–	–	–	1	1	3	1	–	3	1	7	–	1	1	9	7	–	–	5	–	–	3	–	12									64
	4	6	–	1	4	1	–	–	–	3	4	1	–	2	2	4	–	1	–	2	1	–	–	9	1	1	3	2	16									64
	5	9	–	2	3	2	–	1	–	1	5	1	1	3	5	11	2	–	2	–	4	–	–	2	1	–	1	–	8									64
Total		**40**	**–**	**7**	**10**	**14**	**–**	**5**	**4**	**15**	**26**	**4**	**8**	**9**	**14**	**28**	**2**	**2**	**7**	**16**	**17**	**–**	**–**	**20**	**2**	**2**	**7**	**4**	**56**									**319**
	6	13	–	7	3	1	–	2	–	1	6	–	3	1	1	1	–	–	–	5	4	–	2	3	5	1	–	–	5									64
	7	3	–	2	3	12	1	6	1	1	11	–	3	1	–	–	–	–	1	3	1	–	1	2	7	1	–	–	4									64
	8	4	–	3	4	8	–	3	–	4	11	1	6	–	4	1	–	1	1	1	3	–	1	2	5	–	–	–	1									64
II. Ṣaḍjagrāma	9	5	–	–	2	6	–	–	–	2	5	5	–	–	–	1	–	1	5	8	8	–	–	3	3	3	–	–	7									64
	10	3	–	4	2	3	–	1	–	5	6	1	4	–	2	–	–	–	3	4	2	–	–	8	10	2	–	–	4									64
	11	6	–	–	3	1	–	–	1	4	8	–	–	–	–	–	–	–	2	6	1	–	–	9	5	3	–	3	12									64
	12	5	–	1	1	1	–	3	3	6	4	3	1	1	5	11	3	–	1	1	–	–	–	1	10	1	–	–	2									64
Total		**39**	**–**	**17**	**18**	**32**	**1**	**15**	**5**	**23**	**51**	**10**	**17**	**3**	**12**	**14**	**3**	**2**	**13**	**28**	**19**	**–**	**4**	**28**	**45**	**11**	**–**	**3**	**35**									**448**
	13	9	–	4	7	4	5	1	1					–	3	4	2	1	–	–	1	–	–	4	9	1	–	–	6	1	–	1	–					64
	14	5	–	2	3	7	5	10	1					1	5	2	4	–	–	–	–	–	1	3	10	1	–	–	2	1	–	–	1					64
III. Ṣāḍava	15	5	–	2	2	3	2	2	1					–	2	9	3	–	–	–	–	–	–	7	13	5	–	–	7	–	–	1	–					64
	16	–	–	2	5	–	1	2	1					5	4	5	6	1	–	1	–	–	3	5	4	3	–	–	4	4	–	5	3					64
Total		**19**	**–**	**10**	**17**	**14**	**13**	**15**	**4**					**6**	**14**	**20**	**15**	**2**	**–**	**1**	**1**	**–**	**4**	**19**	**36**	**10**	**–**	**–**	**19**	**6**	**–**	**7**	**4**					**256**

IV. Sādhārita	17	11 1 4 5	6 2 3 –		– 3 1 3	– – 7 5	– – 1 5		1 – – –	– – 1 4	64
	18	6 1 4 2	6 3 6 4		1 5 – 3	– – 6 –	1 1 1 13		– – 1 –	– – – –	64
	19	10 – 1 3	4 3 2 1		– 2 1 –	2 – 11 –	– 2 2 16		– – – –	– – – 4	64
	20	8 – – –	1 1 5 2		3 2 2 –	1 2 11 4	– 2 1 13		1 – 1 2	– – – 1	63
	21	6 – 2 5	1 1 – 2		3 6 9 2	– 1 5 –	– 2 1 8		2 – 1 1	– – – 1	59
Total		**41 2 11 15**	**18 10 16 9**		**7 18 13 8**	**3 3 40 9**	**1 7 6 55**		**4 – 3 3**	**1 – 1 10**	**314**
V. Pañcama	22	7 – 6 8	5 3 1 –		1 5 3 3	– 3 3 3	– 1 3 1	1 – – 6	2 – 1 –		64
	23	4 – – 2	7 3 8 2		4 1 2 4	– 4 1 4	– – 3 3	4 – – 5	1 – 2 –		64
	24	– – 1 7	8 – 4 –		3 6 6 6	– 5 1 5	1 – 1 –	2 – – 3	2 – 3 –		64
	25	5 – – 2	5 3 1 –		– 3 6 1	– 2 5 1	– 1 7 12	1 – – 8	1 – – –		64
	26	3 – – 1	4 4 4 –		– 2 3 1	– – 4 1	– 1 5 11	10 – – 8	– – 2 –		64
	27	1 – 1 –	3 3 4 1		5 2 4 1	1 5 5 9	– 1 1 2	3 – – 5	1 – 4 2		64
Total		**20 – 8 20**	**32 16 22 3**		**13 19 22 16**	**1 19 19 23**	**1 4 20 29**	**21 – – 35**	**7 – 12 2**		**314**
VI. Ḳaisikamadhyama	28	15 3 3 2	3 4 1 1		– 6 4 2		2 – 1 4		1 – – –	1 – – 10	62
	29	13 – 1 1	4 11 5 2		2 4 1 1		1 1 1 6		– – – 1	– – – 7	62
	30	12 – 1 3	– 1 1 1		4 1 7 –		– 6 3 15		– – 2 1	– – 1 3	62
	31	9 1 1 1	– 2 5 1		4 1 7 10		1 2 4 6		– – 1 1	1 – – 4	62
Total		**49 4 6 7**	**7 18 12 5**		**10 11 19 13**		**4 9 9 31**		**1 – 3 3**	**2 – 1 24**	**248**
VII. Kaisika	32	13 3 5 1	– 7 1 –		– 1 3 6	– – – –	3 1 3 3		1 – 2 –	1 – – 8	62
	33	2 – 3 4	11 1 4 2		2 7 2 4	1 3 1 2	– 2 – 3		3 – 2 –	– – – 3	62
	34	1 1 1 3	2 – 4 –		5 5 – 9	1 1 – –	2 1 1 1		5 – 10 2	– – 1 2	58
	35	1 – 3 3	2 2 4 2		5 1 5 7	1 5 – 4	1 1 – 2		2 – 3 4	– – 1 –	59
	36	4 1 1 –	6 1 3 –		3 5 2 2	1 1 2 1	2 4 1 10		3 – 1 1	– – – 1	56
	37	7 – 2 8	4 2 2 –		4 3 1 –	– – – –	– 2 3 –		1 – – 1	2 – 6 8	56
	38	11 – – 3	1 3 2 1		2 2 5 –	1 2 5 6	– – 2 1		– – 1 1	– – 1 6	56
Total		**39 5 15 22**	**26 16 20 5**		**21 24 18 28**	**5 12 8 13**	**8 11 10 20**		**15 – 19 9**	**3 – 9 28**	**409**
		217 11 74 109	**143 74 105 35**	**38 77 14 25**	**69 112 131 85**	**15 54 112 82**	**14 39 112 218**	**44 7 7 145**	**33 – 44 21**	**6 – 11 62**	**2378**

Table II
Showing Details of Distribution of the Dotted Musical Notes in Each Aksiptika of Each Section of the Kudumiyamalai Inscription

Section	'Aksip-tikā	Sa	Si	Su	Se	Ra	Ri	Ru	Re	Ga	Gi	Gu	Ge	Ma	Mi	Mu	Me	Pa	Pi	Pu	Pe	Dha	Dhi	Dhu	Dhe	Na	Ni	Nu	Ne	A	I	U	E	Ka	Ki	Ku	Ke	Total
	1	1	–	2	–	–	–	1	–	–	–	–	1	–	–	4	–	–	–	3	1	–	–	–	–	–	–	1	–									14
	2	–	–	1	–	1	–	3	–	–	–	1	5	–	–	2	–	–	–	1	3	–	–	–	–	–	–	1	–									18
I. Madhyamagrāma	3	2	–	–	–	–	–	–	–	–	–	1	–	–	–	7	–	–	–	9	7	–	–	–	–	–	–	–	1									27
	4	–	–	1	–	–	–	–	–	–	–	–	–	–	–	4	–	–	–	2	1	–	–	–	–	–	–	–	1									9
	5	1	–	2	–	–	–	1	–	–	–	1	1	2	–	11	1	–	–	–	4	–	–	–	1	–	–	–	1									26
Total		**4**	**–**	**6**	**–**	**1**	**–**	**5**	**–**	**–**	**–**	**3**	**7**	**2**	**–**	**28**	**1**	**–**	**–**	**15**	**16**	**–**	**–**	**–**	**1**	**–**	**–**	**2**	**3**									**94**
	6	–	–	6	1	–	–	2	–	–	–	–	3	–	–	1	–	–	–	5	4	–	–	1	–	–	–	–	–									23
	7	–	–	2	–	–	–	6	1	–	–	–	3	–	–	–	–	–	–	3	1	–	–	1	–	–	–	–	–									17
	8	–	–	3	–	–	–	3	–	–	–	1	6	–	–	1	–	–	–	1	3	–	–	–	–	–	–	–	–									18
II. Ṣaḍjagrāma	9	1	–	–	–	1	–	–	–	–	–	4	–	–	–	1	–	–	–	8	8	–	–	–	–	–	–	–	–									23
	10	–	–	4	–	–	–	1	–	–	–	1	4	–	–	–	–	–	–	4	2	–	–	4	–	–	–	–	–									20
	11	–	–	–	–	–	–	–	–	–	–	–	–	–	–	–	–	–	–	6	1	–	–	–	–	–	–	–	–									7
	12	–	–	1	–	–	–	3	–	1	–	3	1	–	–	11	3	–	–	1	–	–	–	–	–	–	–	–	–									24
Total		**1**	**–**	**16**	**1**	**1**	**–**	**15**	**1**	**1**	**–**	**9**	**17**	**–**	**–**	**14**	**3**	**–**	**–**	**28**	**19**	**–**	**–**	**6**	**–**	**–**	**–**	**–**	**–**									**132**
	13	1	–	4	1	–	–	1	1					–	–	4	2	1	–	–	1	–	–	1	–	–	–	–	–	–	–	1	–					18
	14	–	–	2	–	–	–	10	–					–	–	2	3	–	–	–	–	–	–	1	1	–	–	–	–	–	–	–	–					19
III. Ṣāḍava	15	–	–	2	–	–	–	2	1					–	–	9	3	–	–	–	–	–	–	1	1	1	–	–	–	–	–	1	–					21
	16	–	–	–	–	–	–	2	–					–	–	5	6	–	–	1	–	–	–	–	–	–	–	–	–	–	–	5	–					19
Total		1	–	8	1	–	–	15	2					–	–	20	4	1	–	1	1	–	–	3	2	1	–	–	–	–	–	7	–					77

	17	– – 4 1	1 – 3 –		– – 1 3	– – 7 5	– – – –		– – – –	– – – –	25
	18	– – 4 –	– – 6 3		– – – 3	– – 6 –	– – – –		– – 1 –	– – – –	23
IV. Sādhārita	19	1 – 1 –	– – 2 –		– – 1 –	1 – 11 –	– – – 1		– – – –	– – – –	18
	20	1 – – –	– – 5 –		– – 2 –	– – 11 4	– – – –		– – 1 –	– – – –	24
	21	– – 1 –	– – – –		– – 8 2	– – 5 –	– – – 1		– – 1 –	– – – –	18
Total		**2 – 10 1**	**1 – 16 3**		**– – 12 8**	**1 – 40 9**	**– – – 2**		**– – 3 –**		**108**
	22	1 – 6 –	– – 1 –		– – 1 3	– – 3 3	– – – –		– – 1 –	– – – –	19
	23	– – – –	1 – 8 –		– – 2 4	– – 1 4	– – – –		– – 2 –	– – – –	22
V. Pañcama	24	– – 1 1	– – 4 –		– – 6 6	– – 1 4	– – – –		– – 3 –	– – – –	26
	25	– – – –	– – 1 –		– – 6 1	– – 5 1	– – – –		– – – –	– – – –	14
	26	– – – –	– – 3 –		– – 3 1	– – 4 1	– – – –		– – 2 –	– – – –	14
	27	– – – –	– – 3 –		– – 4 1	– – 5 8	– – – –		– – 4 –	– – – –	25
Total		**1 – 7 1**	**1 – 20 –**		**– – 22 16**	**– – 19 21**	**– – – –**		**– – 12 –**	**– – – –**	**120**
	28	1 – 3 1	– – 1 1		– – 4 2		1 – 1 –		– – – –	– – – –	15
VI. Kaiśikamadhyama	29	1 – 1 –	– – 4 2		1 – 1 1		1 – – –		– – – 1	– – – –	13
	30	1 – 1 –	– – 1 –		– – 7 –		– – – –		– – 2 –	– – – –	12
	31	1 – 1 –	– – 5 1		– – 7 10		– – 2 –		– – 1 –	– – – –	28
Total		**4 – 6 1**	**– – 11 4**		**1 – 19 13**		**2 – 3 –**		**– – 3 1**	**– – – –**	**68**
	32	1 – 6 –	– – 1 –		– – 3 6	– – – –	– – – –		– – 2 –	– – – –	18
	33	– – 3 –	1 – 4 –		– – 2 4	1 – 1 2	– – – –		– – 2 –	– – – –	20
	34	– – 1 –	– – 4 –		– – – 9	– – – –	– – – –		– – 10 –	– – 1 –	25
VII. Kaiśika	35	– – 3 –	– – 4 1		– – 4 7	– – – 4	– – – –		– – 3 –	– – 1 –	27
	36	1 – 1 –	– – 3 –		– – 2 2	– – 1 –	– – – 1		– – 1 –	– – – –	12
	37	– – 2 –	– – 2 –		1 – 1 –	– – – –	– – – –		– – – –	– – – –	6
	38	– – – –	– – 1 –		– – 5 –	1 – 5 6	– – – –		– – 1 –	– – 1 2	22
Total		**2 – 16 –**	**1 – 19 1**		**1 – 17 28**	**2 – 7 12**	**– – – 1**		**– – 19 –**	**– – 3 2**	**130**
Grand Total		**15 – 68 5**	**5 – 101 11**	**1 – 12 24**	**4 – 132 83**	**4 – 110 78**	**2 – 12 6**	**1 – 2 3**	**– – 44 1**	**– – 3 2**	**729**

7. The seven sections of the inscription respectively consist of 5, 7, 4, 5, 6, 4 and 7 aksiptikas.
8. Musical notes a. i. u. and e are never used together with the musical notes ga, gi, gu, ge in any section of the inscription. Similarly, the notes ka, ki, ku and ke are not employed in any section containing the notes na, ni, nu, ne and vice versa.
9. The notes i and ki are not used anywhere in the inscription.

This inscription was carved at the time, when the Indian music divided into two independent system viz. Karnatic and Hindustani had not come into being. Prava and Murchchana are interchangeable terms in the sense that are grama is nothing else but a particular murchchana of the other. This is the main theme of the Kudumiyamalai inscription. Thus the inscription amply bears out the fact that Mahendravarman was a great creative genius and a man of imagination. This is unique in the world and certainly the only primary evidence of contemporary musical practice in ancient India.

There are three epigraphical records in stone enumerating the tala system in Karnatic music. In the history of musicography the earliest records of musical composition are those belonging to the tallapakkam composers. They are inscribed an copper plates and stone slabs. While the Arichalur inscription is based on the notation of rhythm in terms tala mnemonics and the kudumiyamalai inscription on the notation of absolute music in the form of 'alankaras'. The inscription of the Tallapakkam composers stand out as the one and the only example of epigraphical records of a system of notation of musical compositions with specification of raga. In addition to the above inscriptions, there are more epigraphical evidences of technical importance. These are based on the tala system of Indian music. Of these, few records illustrate scheme of the 35 talas with their angas marked in archair character.

Ritual Music and Temple Establishment

Music has always been intimately connected with temples and religions from the very early times. It has always gone hand in hand with religion helping to propagate religious and moral truths. All writers and musicians of the ancient and early medieval periods dealt only with music used in religious worship. The epigraphical records are full of references to ritual music, ritual dance and also to temple institution and their contribution to the development of the art.

The inscription belonging to the Vijayanagra dynasty is important from the point of view of the history of Indian music. A record incised in the region of Vijaynagara dynasty refers to the 'nagaswaram' players. The inscription is dated A.D.1552. The records, registered of a village to the paper for playing on two nagaswaram and two drums (tavil or dholak) in the temple. In some inscriptions, there was an instrument called 'Panchamahasabda'. Only certain kings and chiefs were entitled to listen to the sounds of this instrument. They refer to as entitled of 'fine big drums' a band of fine chief instruments', a band of five musical instruments' and so on. The fine musical instruments are 'trumpet' 'conch' shell, kettledrum and gong.

Other interesting references in many inscriptions are the occurrence of the phrases 'Anga bhoja', 'Anga rangabhoga' etc. These services invariably referred to the main deity for whom the services for the body anga and entertainment of music and dance 'ranga',

A Rare Copper Plate Inscription

The contribution of the Marathas to the development of Karnataka music has never been underestimated. The title 'Abhinava bhoja', that the great musician, musicologist and composer King Shahaji earned. Another landmark is the magnum 'Sangita saramritha' Tulaja Maharaja equally important where the several copper plates inscriptions of the Maratha rulers are concerned. Recently the Department of Eipgraphy of Tamil University came across a rare copper plate inscription, which bears testimony to the high degree of technique and the science of music that the Maratha had developed. The language of this inscription is Tamil and this rectangular shaped (vertical) copper plate has both the sides inscribed.

On one side of the plate are engraved figures of gods and goddesses and instruments and on other grants of king made. In the rows more than 40 musical instruments of that period are beautifully inscribed could be found. This has a prominent Nataraja figure devoting the significance of the dancing lord. This inscription gives information about King Tukkoji ordering construction of Mutts at the Nageswaraswamy temple and granting them as gift. This is the only copperplate so far discovered inscribing figures of musical instruments. The form and the shape of the instrument are highly artistic and excellent. Some of the instruments are that of hindustani origin, which indicates the patronage extended by King Tukkoji to hindustani music.

It is apparently evident from the above discussion that epigraphical and other records subscribed in the growth and development of musical systems through the ages, under the ardent patronage of kings. Musicians and instrumentalists were highly respected and liberally gifted with grants and endourments. These stone and metal records purport to be the most authentic records for the study of the development of music.

MANUSCRIPTS

The sanskritest is pre-eminently concerned with manuscripts. The information collected from the manuscripts forms the basic material for further research based on other sources like epigraphs. To produce a critical authentic and purposive research document, the sanskritist has to know the nature and value of manuscripts, the scripts and materials used therein. Today we find the sanskrit manuscripts written in (l) Sarada (2) Devanagari (3) Nandanagari (4) Nepali (5) Bengali (6) Maithili (7) Oriya (8) Grantha (9) Malayalam (l0) Telugu and (l1) Kannada.

The tone, earthen objects, shells and other non-metallic aspects like ivory plaques, metals like copper, bronze and iron, palm leaf, birch bark and paper are the known materials of writing in ancient India. The palm leaf is the oldest material put to use for writing. The writings engraved on stone, metal and other hard substances for public inspection are called 'inscriptions' and the writing on any soft material like palm-leaf clothes and paper with the hand are called 'manuscripts'. The word 'manuscripti' is derived from the Latin word 'manuscriptum' in which manus devotes 'the hand' and 'scriptum to write.[12]

Palm-leaf, birch bark, cotton and paper are the common materials for writing long texts of literature. Even in the case of short texts like grants inscribed on stone and metals, they were written first on palm leaf or birch bark before engraved. The earliest known manuscripts of palm-leaf date back to circa first century A.D. The fragments of palm leaf manuscripts representing parts of two plays ascribed to Aswaghosa of Indian literature found in Turfan by a German expedition led by Gruendwedei and Hurth are the earliest. We have numerous palm-leaf manuscripts of the 7th and later centuries from Nepal, Bengal, Rajasthan, Gujarati. e.g we have from Nepal the 'Skandapurana (supposed to have been copied about the 7th cen. A.D) the Parameswara-tantra (C.A.D. 859) and the Lankavatara (A.D. 906-07).[13]

Our old and valuable manuscripts in Indian music are not only available in India but are also preserved around the world Such as:

			No.
1.	Balmiki Ramayan	Adayar Library	
2.	Geet Govind	Prince of Wales Musum	
3.	Sahas Ras	B Library	313

4.	Raag Darpan	Central Public Library	448
5.	Dawaj-deh-maqam	British Museum (London)	578
6.	Misbah-al-Saroor	Asiatic Society of Bengal (Calcutta)	611
7.	Nauras	Prince of Wales Musum	680
8.	Risab-al-Zkre Mugniyane Hindustan	Oriental Public Library Bakipur, Patna.	718
9.	Risal-al-ekalim khani	Bodlin Library	747
10.	Risal-a-Mausiki	Bodlin Library	746
11.	Geet Prakash	Orissa State Museum	941
12.	Risal-e-Raagmala	University of Madras Library	1175
13.	Raagmala	Jaiswal Research Inst. Patna	1901
14.	Parijatak	British Museum, London	1922
15.	Mazmutie Rangeen	India office, London	1557

Tanjavour (South) Saraswati Palace

1.	Bharatiya Natya Sastram	Bharat Muni	Bhartiya Natya Sastra	Telugu	7223&24
2.	Arjun Bhartam	Arjun	Dev Nagari		7229-31
3.	Narttam Nirnay	Pundrik Vitthal	Narttan Nirnay		7242-44
4.	Abhiney Lakshnam	Srinagar Sehkhar	Abhinay Lakshan	Telugu	7247
5.	Hast Lakshman	Hast Lakshan	Dev Nagari		7248-59
6.	Sangeet Sudhakar	Haripal Dev	Sangeet Sudhar	Telugu	7293-94
7.	Swar-mela-Kala Nidhi	Rama-matya	Swar Mel Kal Nidhi		7294-7302
8.	Raag Lakshnam		Raag Laksham		7304-7036
9.	Geetam	Geet Narpar	Devper		7222-24
10.	Padam Pad				7327-28

Bhandarkar Oriental Research Institute Poona

1.	Om Pattam,	Umapati,	309
2.	Geetalankar		310
3.	Dakshini Raagmala		311
4.	Bharat Bhashya	Saraswati hridyalankar	312
5.	Raag Mala	Pundrik Vithal	313
6.	Sadraag Chandrodaya	–do–	318
7.	Sangeet Darpan	Chatur Damoder	320
8.	Sangeet Parijat	Pt. Ahobal	324
9.	Sangeet Raaj	Kumbhakonam Mahimahender	331
10.	Natya Darpan Sutra	Ramchander	333

Sanskrit Sangeet Scriptures Available in Jaipur's Museum (पोथीखाना)

1.	Anoop Sangeet Ratnakar	Bhav Bhatt	—	75,66,73or 668
2.	Anoop Sangeet Vilaas	–do–	1752	7339
3.	Anupankush	–do–	—	7564-61
4.	Geet prakash	Krishna Das Mahapatra	1730	7427
5.	Nartak Prakarnam	Pundrik Vithal	1701	1889,6858
6.	Nritya Prakarnam	Bharat Muni	—	6882
7.	Nritya Nirnaya	Sarangdev	—	5632
8.	Nritya Vinod		1828	4689
9.	Mridang Bhed	Pundrik Bithal	—	6645
10.	Raag tatav Vibhod	Sri Niwas	—	6887
11.	Raag Mela	—	—	6731

12.	Raag Sanket	—	—	6883
13.	Raganupadhiti	Mukund	—	2700
14.	Sankrin Raag	—	—	2137
15.	Sangeet Kalptaru	Ashook Maal	1551	7026
16.	Sangeet Darpan	Sarangdev	—	6585,6586
17.	Sangeet Parijat	Krishna Pandit	1708	6649,6650, 6733,6885
18.	Sangeet Mimansa	Kumbhakarna Maharaja		6652

Bikaner Anup Singh Sanskrit Library

1.	Anup Sangeet Ratnakar	Janardan Bhatt	37
2.	Nrityadhyay	"	38
3.	Anup Sangeet Vilas (Nrityadhyay)	"	241
4.	–do–	"	650
5.	–do–	"	180
6.	Anup Sangeet Vilas (Nritydhyay)	Janardan Bhatt	107
7.	Nartan Nirnay	Pundrik Vithal	53
8.	Sangeet Darpan	Damodar	53
9.	Sangeet Parijat	Ahobal	63
10.	Sangeet Makrand	Ved	83
11.	Sangeet Muktawali	Chintamani Davender	55
12.	Sangeet Ratnakar	Singh Bhupal	42
13.	Sangeet Ratnakar	Sarangdev	108
14.	Sangeet Raj	Kumbhkaran	144
15.	Sangeet Vinod	Anup Singh	31

Some Important Manuscript Collections

S. No.	*Name of the discovery & discoverer*	*Place and year of discovery*	*MS material*	*Script*	*Title of the work/ contents*	*Date of the MS*	*Remarks*
1.	Bakshāli Manuscript	1881, Bakshali near Mardan (Now in Pakistan, 30 m. NE of Peshawar)	Birch-bark (70 leaves)	Sāradā	Mathematical work	12th C. A.D.	Kaye edited in 1927 and published by Archaeological Survey of India as New Imperial Series, vol, XL III, pts. I-II, 1927, pt. iii, 1933 Now in Bodelin Library, Oxford.
2.	Bower Manuscript by Lt. Bower	Kuchar, Kashgaria (also called Chinese Turkistan)	Birch-bark (56 leaves)	North Western Gupta characters	Medical treatises, proverbial sayings, Buddhist story	5th C. A.D.	Ed. By Hoernle and pub. In Archaeological Survey of India series
3.	(Fragments of) Buddhist dramas by Le Coq	Cave temple at Mingai near Turfan, 1904-7 (Chinese Turkistan)	Palm-leaf (144 pieces)	Identical with Northern Ksatrapas and Kusanas	Two plays ascribed to Aśvaghoṣa	Ist C. A.D.	Earliest palm-leaf documents, Ed. By Lueders in 1911 under the title 'Buechstuke Buddhist-iseher Dramen'
4.	Dhar Praśasti of Arjuna-	Dhar (West of Mhow), M.P.	Slab of black stone	Early variety of Nagari	First two acts of the	11th C. (Bhoja's	It is a drama with the poet's Patron King Arjunavarman as

	varman by E. Hultzsch	1903	5'8"x5' (76 verses)		4 act play 'Pārijāta - mañjarī or Vijayasri by Madana	time)	hero in Sanskrit and Prakrit.
5.	Gilgit MSS by Sir Aurel Stein	In a stupa near Gilgit (in NW Himalayas under Pakistani control)	Leaves		Buddhist Sanskrit	Not later than 7th C. A.D.	Now in the custody of the Kashmir Govt. and these MSS were ed. & pub. by the Govt. of Kashmir under the title 'Gilgit MSS' in 1939.
6.	Godfrey MSS by Capt. S.H. Godfrey	Kuchar (North China) 1895	Paper (71 pieces)	–	–		Partly reproduced by Hoernle in JASB, 1897
7.	Horiuzi MS	Horiuzi, province of Yamatọ, Japan	Palm-leaf	Gupta variety	'Prajñara-mitāhṛday-asūtra and Uṣṇiṣadh-āriṇi	1st half of 6th C. A.D.	This is an evidence to show that so late as 1727 palm leaves containing Sanskrit sutras were preserved in the Monas-try of Horiuzi, Japan. These MSS are from China to Japan in 609 AD.

(*Contd.*)

S. No.	Name of the discovery & discoverer	Place and year of discovery	MS material	Script	Title of the work/ contents	Date of the MS	Remarks
8.	Kharosthī Dhammapada by M.Dutreuil de Rhins	Khotan (Western China 1892)	Birch-bark	–	'Kharosthī Dhamma-pada' also called 'prak-rita Dhamm-pada'.	C. 200 AD	This MS is now in Paris and the large portion of this MS is in St. Peters-burg. Russia, ed. By Stein in JA, 1898.
9.	Kurud Plates of Narendra	Kurud, 27 miles Copper (3) from North-East of Raipur, M.P.	Central Indian Nāgarī	Copper plate grant		5th C. AD.	Now preserved in the Mahant Ghasidas Memorial Museum at Raipur, Ep. Ind. 31, pp. 263-267-68
10.	Macartney MSS by G. Macartney	Set I, Ib Kuchar Soft paper Set II Aksufil NE of Khotan Set III Jabu Kum (50 miles NE of Khotan) Set IV Karakul Mazan Khojan (50 miles east of Gunia, North-West Frontier of Pakistan) Set V desert at Kuk Gumbaz (5 days march East of Gunia Set VI Kuk Gumbaj)	–	–	–	2nd C. AD	There are six sets of MSS; set 1b is of importance to us. Several folios of these MSS have been published in JASB, 1987.

11.	Paippalāda MS of the 'Atharvaveda'		Birch-bark (275 leaves; 25 × 20 cm)	Sāradā	Kashmīrī recension of the 'Atharvaveda'		It is now preserved in the Library of Tuebingen University. This unique MS was reproduced by chromophotography by Bloomfield and Garbe and pub. In Baltimore in 1901.
12.	Petrowsky MS		'Kharoṣthī Dhammapada' (in fragments)				This is a complementary codex to the 'Dutreuil de Rhins' MS. This collection is preserved in St. Petersburg.
13.	Texila Copper plate of patika by A. Cunningham	Thupkia in the middle of the ruins of Sir Sukhs. North-East of Taxila (=Ruins of ancient town, lying SW of Rawalpindi, Pakistan	Copper plates 14" × 3"	Kharosthi of the Saka period	Record of the solemn deposition of a relic of Sakyamauni and the erection of a monastry	Not later than 1st C. A.D.	Preserved in the Library of the Royal Asiatic society. Notice by G. Buehler in Ep. Ind. 4,54.

(*Contd.*)

S. No.	*Name of the discovery & discoverer*	*Place and year of discovery*	*MS material*	*Script*	*Title of the work/ contents*	*Date of the MS*	*Remarks*
14.	Two Prakrit poems at Dhar by R. Pischel	Dhar 1903	Stone	Early Variety of Nāgarī	Two Prakrit poems, each with 109 verses. The 1st one is called 'Kumrasa-taka,	11th c. A.D.	In Maharastri Prakrit.pub in Ep. Ind. vol. VIII, pp. 243 ff.
15.	Rajaprasati	Mewar, Rajasthan	Stone slabs(24)		Rajaprasasti in 24 Cantos by Rana-coda		Ep. Ind.Vol.XXIX-XXX, Appendix, pp. 1-123.
16.	Rānākumbha's inscription by G.S. Ojha 1925	Kumbhalgadh, Rajasthan	Stone Slabs 5 (3' 10" broad 3' 7" high)	Nāgarī	Descrip-tion of geograp-hical places of Mewar & praise of many a god	1460 A.D.	Ep. Ind. Vol. XXIV, pp. 304 ff.
17.	Weber MSS by F. Weber	Kuigar (60 miles South of Yark-hand within the borders of western China)	Paper	North-Western Gupta central Asian Nāgarī	Indian Group1-4 Central Asian Group (5-9)	C. 500 A.D.	There are nine manu-scripts.

(Copied from: Methodology in methodological Research by M. Sriramanarayanamurti Delhi. Bhartiya Vidya Prakashan 1991 p. 99.)

TEXT BOOKS

A text-book is a book of instruction. Its primary aim is not to impart information about a specific subject but to enable one to develop proper understanding of the subject. Presentation is extremely important and it is prepared to serve a particular level of readership. A good textbook takes into consideration the method of teaching and it is revised keeping in view new developments and changing methodology of teaching. The most important component in our Indian music tradition is couched in Sanskrit, but there are quite a few texts in Persian, old Hindi and regional languages like Tamil, Telugu, Kannada, Gujarati etc. Indira Gandhi National Center for Arts New Delhi has undertaken the publication of major texts of Sangita sastra viz. Natya sastra, Dattilam, Brhaddasi, Bharata bhasya of Nanyadeva, Sangita samayasara, Sangita makaranda, Sangita parijata, Ragavibodha, works of Pundarika vithal etc. with english translation, textual notes and annotations.

Our knowledge and experience of current practice, which is directly, linked with the oral tradition, naturally condition our understanding of the textual traditions. The notable point is that the text has been composed with a presumption that the oral tradition would supplement the written one. There is a huge corpus of song texts handed down in both the written and oral tradition. A serious study of this valuable material has not yet been undertaken. It is high time that this neglected field is traversed with recognition of its high potential as a major source for retrieving the oral tradition of the respective time and space. Apart from providing insights with the implications of the usage of technical terminology, this body of material has very rich potential for studies from historical and social points of view in respect of patrons, attitudes, centers of musical activity etc.[14]

Text Book	Writer	Pages	Publication
Raag Chandrika Saar	Pt. Vishnu Sharma	16(120 Done)	IInd Pub. 1919
Raag Chiter	Sh. Raghunath Pushti	44 photos	1713
Raag Tatva Vibodh (sanskrit)	Shri Niwas	62(8 chapters)	1650 or 1680
Raag Mala (Hindi)	Yashoda Nandan Shukel	417 Done	1758
Lubzal-e-Sikendershahi	Umar Yahiya	7 chapter	1489
Victoria Samarajaya	Shorender Mohan Thakur	155	1876
Vanshi Manjari	Lala Bhregu Nath Verma		1911
Shri MaJ Lakshya Sangeetam (Sanskrit)	V.N. Bhatkhande (Chatur Pandit)	1026 Shalok	1981
Shankari Sangeetam (Sanskrit)	Jai Narayan	16(12 Patal)	Vikram Samvat 1917
Sahas Ras	(Collection of Nayak Bakshu's Pad)	293(1004 Pad)	
Psychology of Music	H.P Krishna Rao	71 (12 chapter)	1916
Sudhakalash Sangeetonishad Sar	Jain	6 chapter	1324
Sur Tarangini	Maharaja Lakhpat Singh	3 chapters (1380 chhand)	1749
Sangrah Chudamani	Govind	472	18th Cen.
Sangeet Darpan	Pt. Damodar	171 Shalok	
Sangeet Parijat (Sanskrit)	Pt. Ahobal	500 shalok	1665
Sangeet Bhav	YijayDeji	218	1933
Sangeet Makrand	Narad	506 shalok	
Sangeet Mandan	Mandam	4 chapters	1447-1449
Sangeet Ratnakar (Sanskrit)	Pt. Sarangdev	1000(7 chapters)	13th Cen.
Sangeet Samay Saar	Parshav Dev	9 chapters	13th Cen.
Sangeet Sar	Tansen	82 (334 Dohas)	Samvat 1888

Sangeet Saar Sangrah (Sanskrit)	Ghanshyam Das	6 chapters	18th Cen.
Sangeet Sudhakar	Haripal	5 chapters	
Swar Mela Kala Nidhi	Ramamatya	51(5 chapters)	1550
Sangeet Saar Amrit	Tulez	14 chapters	1728-1736
Sangeet Sudhakar	Singh Bhupal	7 chapters	
Brihaddeshi (Sanskrit)	Matang Muni	154(511sholok)	7th Cen.
Raag Tarangini	Pt. Lochan		1082
Hridayakautuk Hridya Prakash	Hridaya Narayan Dev		15th Cen.
Raag Vibodh (Sanskrit)	Pt. Som Nath		1610
Chaturdandi Prakashika	Pt. Vyankat Mukhi		1560
Natya Shastra	Bharat	36 chapter	1st Cen. A.D.
Abhinav Taal Manjari (Sanskrit)	Appa tulsi Kashinath	130 Chhend	1834
Ashotoottar Taal Lakshnam	Pt. Vishu Sharma	17 (108 Taals)	1991 Published
Indian Music	Begum Faizi Rehman	96 (5 chapters)	1914
Introduction to the Study of Indian Music	E. Clements	104 (5 chapters)	1912
A short Historical Survey of the music of Upper India Uttar Bhartiya Sangeet ka Sanskrit Itihaas	Pt. Bhatkhande's English speech translation by Dr. Arun Kumar in Hindi	56	1916
Kitab-e-Nauraas	Ibrahim Idilshah II		1597-1599
Geet Sutra Saar (bengali)	Krishan dhan Banerjee	152	1885-86
419 Illustrations of Indian music and dance in Western Indian style	Vidya Sarabhai Nawab Editor	419 photos	1964
Taal Paintings	Usha Ranade & Kamal Chawan	35 (1200 photos)	
Dattilam	Dattil	244 (Shalok)	

(*Contd.*)

Text Book	*Writer*	*Pages*	*Publication*
The Music of India	Attiya begum Faizi Rehman	95 (8 chapters)	Published 1925
The Music of Hindustan	A.H.Fox Strangeways	364 (12 chapters)	Published 1914
Pancham Saar Saḥita (Sanskrit)	Narad	5 chapters	1440
Bharat Kosh (Sanskrit)	M. Krishna Rao	984	
Bharat Bhashyam(II parts)	Nanya Bhupal		1097-1133
Mansollahs	Someshwar	16,17,18 chapters related to music)	1130
Maarifuraegmat (Urdu)	Nawab Ali	3 chapters	1911-1916
Mridang Mohra (Gujarati)	Maharaj Lakhpat singh		1741-1761
Universal History of Music (English)	S.M.Tagore	355	1896
Raas kaumudi	Shri Kanth	10 chapters	1575
Raag Kalpdrum	Sh. Krishna Nand Vyas	2500	1899

ORAL TRADITION

As the words cannot convey the experience, similarly we can not verbalise why a piece of music was poignant or why we experience a feeling of ecscasty while listening to vedic chanting. This is the case with all real life experience. The performing arts are all experimental and music is more intangible than the other performing arts, so it is more difficult to desirable in language. However, a description in words will be meaningful to some one, who has had an experience of the music and shares a common cultural outlook. In the oral tradition of transmitting knowledge, there was a close interaction between the teacher and the student. Our music is rooted in our culture and this is a matter not only of observation but also of experience. By comparing the western word 'study' to the Indian 'abhyas', we find that in a 'study', we look at something from the outside from a distance and in 'abhyas' we go closer and participate in it with a strong sense of carrying a valuable tradition of music. Daily repetition is common in the oral tradition and the art and its associated values are internalized by the student. The oral tradition forced the students (shihyas) to sharpen their memories, as they could not depend on written or audio aids. Today with all these aids, learning directly from the teacher (Guru) still the best method in our music.

Indian classical music's learners, right from the beginning, tended with care and groomed individually by a guru or master. This tradition of oral personal teaching was mostly confined to the direct or nearest members of their family and only close ones. The guru had neither books of references nor any prescribed curriculum to follow. Every teacher had his own individual method of imparting instruction. He followed the same process through which he had been taught. This was maintained a sort of continuity, in the method of teaching and learning from generation to generation, and this we all known as gharana. The history of these gharanas is hardly 150 years old at the most with three or four generation carrying on their distinctive traditional styles. Notable among these gharanas, are those of Gwalior, Jaipur, Agra, Kirana Patiala, etc., all deriving their names from the names of the respective capitals of the princely states. Hereditary musicianship is not confined to only vocal music, one finds gharana in instrumental music too. i.e. Delhi, Ajrada, Punjab, Banaras and Farrukhabad are mentioned in connection with the tabla.

Each founder of an established gharana had a particular stamp of distinction by which he was known and recognised. Each has its own style of exposition, its own laws, and its own norms. While the student was being groomed in the fashion and style of the established basic norms, he was also expected to enrich the fame of the school further by making his individual contribution to it. The daily practice of several hours in the initial stage, help in the cultivation of the voice in the style fashioned by his guru. In this context few definitions taken from various sources can be considered:

— [15]Tradition, which is the cumulative social heritage in the form of habits, customs, attitudes and ways of life, is transmitted from generation to generation either through written scriptures or through word of mouth. The tradition transmitted through word of mouth is called the oral tradition —S.L.Srivastava[16]

— Oral tradition is now defined as verbal testimony transmitted from one generation to the next one or a later one — Jan Vansina[17]

— Oral poetry is poetry composed in oral performance by people who cannot read or write. It is synonymous with traditional and folk poetry.. All oral poetry is sing or at the very least chanted. — Alex Preminger[18]

— ....for it is strange phenomenon in India, from the oldest times, up till the present day, the spoken word and not writing has been the basis of the whole of the literary and scientific activity. ...the written text can at most be used as an aid to learning, as a support to the memory, but no authority is attributed to it. Authority is possessed only by the spoken word of the teacher ...the works of the poets too, were in India never intended for readers but always for hearers. Even the modern poets do not desire to be read. But their wish is that their poetry may become an adornment for the throats of the experts —M. Wimernitz[19]

— The Vedic system of oral teaching was the only authoritative system to be pursued through the subsequent ages in spite of all material facilities they might bring in their course. There was a traditional opinion absolutely condemning the acquisition of knowledge from written sources —R.K.Mookerji[20]

The definitions cited above are illustrative of representative positions, concerning the scope and nature of the oral tradition. It is a fundamental premise that the final authority in everything "musical" is of the guru. It is assumed that every musician corpus is in fact determined solely by what his guru has taught him. The hard core of a musician's total learning is made up of his guru's teachings. At this stage it is worthwhile to know something about the important factors that go to determine the style of a particular gharana. Every recognised gharana becomes an institution, having an independent tradition peculiarly its own. It is known to have its own mannerisms, voice culture and style of presentation by which a discriminating listener is able at once to recognize the gharana. We have certain specified types of voices, which are often found amongst the recognized gharanas.

(*a*) [21]Broad and low pitched resonator voice (male) within the scale,
(*b*) Voices about two and half tones higher but sounding high pitched, edgy and fast in movement,
(*c*) Broad and low pitched female voices,
(*d*) Sharp and flexible voices having a range of two and half octaves or even longer, and
(*e*) Extra sharp and extremely flexible voices having an unusually long range of three octave.

Gwalior Gharana

Most authorities agree that this is the oldest of the khyal gharanas. This gharana is well known for its full repertoire as the followers of this school are taught and know a rich collection of composition, types, bada and chota khyal, thumri, tappa, tarana, bhajan have been enumerated. Many illustration names we can find among the galaxy of artistes who belonged to this gharana like Shankar Pandit, Krishnarao Pandit, Balakrishnabua Ichalkaranjikar, Pandit Vishnu Digambar Paluskar, Mushtaq Hussain. Most of these artists had a voice raga full three octave and they always sang in an open throated voice. The taans and bol taans were very picturesque.

Agra Gharana

The gharana adopts a kind of voice production, which relies on a flatter variation of the vowel sound 'a'. Many rare ragas are sung in this gharana and the treatment is always as detailed as that of any known raga. As one of the dhrupad influenced gharanas in khyal music, Agra is profuse in 'bol taans' and 'tans' of rhythmic variety, including effective use of 'tihais'. By this Agra, music appears to be more suitable to male voices than female. Founded more than a hundred years ago, laid all emphasis on the importance of rhythm. The performers have mostly broad low-pitched voices, voluminous like loud thunder. Ghagge Khuda Bux initially received training in Gwalior style and founded Agra Gharana. The Agra style, as

Mr. Arvind Mangsulkar, noted musicologist, aptly describes it, is 'Robust and aggressive'. He says, "its successive taans remind us of speedily advancing armies, striking hard at their target, it bol taans of rapid gunfire, nor is the style devoid of a certain measure of guerilla tactics of tones and well planned dodges of rhythm. It captivates rather than delight and extracts an appreciative tribute from the vanquished listener."[22]

Patiala Gharana

The gharana owes its creation to the extra-ordinary talents of Fateh Ali and Ali Hussain. They were known for their incredible speed in the rendition of their compositions. The exponents of this gharana specialised in the cultivation of their voice to full three octaves. In the 'mandra saptak' (lower octave) their tone would sound organ like, voluminous and rich, in the 'madhya saptak' (middle octave) it would be naturally sweet, and in the 'tar saptak' (higher octave) is sounded celestially sonorous. Along side a variety of complex taan patterns, the followers of this gharana exhibited an uncanny skill in weaving very attractive and thrilling 'murkis' and 'harkats', which embellished their presentation. The most noted celebrities of this school were Bade Ghulam Ali Khan and his brother Barkat Ali Khan. "The Patiala gharana, though of comparatively recent origin, has made its mark on the musical scene early and in many ways. The chief feature of the 'thumri'in the school is its incorporation of the 'tappa ang' (tappa apect) from the Punjab region. Thus, the gharana immediately makes its presence felt as a fresh departure from the 'khayal' dominated Benaras and the dance oriented Lucknow 'thumris'. These 'thumris' dazzle on account of their imaginative and extremely swift movements. Of equal importance is the intricacy of tonal patterns — a special mark of 'tappa'. "The Patiala 'thumri' is also influenced by folk tunes of the region, which are in 'Pahadi', and its multiple varieties. The descending and lyrical tonal patterns associated with the Heer songs of the region are known for their moving quality and Patiala 'thumri' has certainly benefited from this regional source."[23]

Kirana Gharana

In contrast to the Agra Gharana, directed all their attention to the cultivation and production of a voice, which is sweet and pleasant to a degree, to give this extra smooth, soft texture to their voice. They deliberately gave a special treatment by contracting their vocal chords while singing, so that their rendering would sound extremely tender, sweet and soothing.

The main feature it exhibits is a melodious use of voice, with a kind of 'o' vowel sound imposed on it, throughout the alap. To sustain resonance in singing, the gharana falls back on a profuse of 'bol-alaps', that is, it uses words for elaborating melodic ideas. "The leisurely development of ragas as well as the premium placed an emotional coloring in music narrows the choice of ragas available to the gharana. This brought out by the relatively small number of ragas favoured by the musician of the school. For example standard kirana fare would rely on Kalyan, Pooriya, Lalit, Darbari, Miyan ki todi, Abhogikananda, and the like. Most of the ragas projected by the gharana are aptly described as 'alap yogya ragas', that is, those primarily conductive to the making of alaps (as apposed to tans)."[24]

Gharanas in Instruments (Sitar)

Sitar enjoys the honour of being the dominant instrument in Indian music today. One of the most commonly stated views is that the descendants of the legendary Tansen led to the formation of three 'senia' gharanas between 16th and 18th cen. Tansen's youngest son Bilas Khan followed 'Gobarhar Bani' while those of Tantarang followed 'Dagur Bani'. It is seen that every major statement on 'sitar' and its 'gharanas', makes an attempt to trace its lineage from Tansen. Instrumental music in the past Tansen period was bifurcated on the lines of two dominant instruments 'rabab' and 'been', these two instruments enjoying different idioms on account of specific constructional features made their own distinctive music for example 'rabab' was more rhythm oriented while 'been' (veena) was melodically inclined. In the later years, when the sitar came with vogue, beenkars took to 'surbahar' and 'sitar' to present their music.

Jaipur Gharana

Followers of this gharana claim their musical lineage from Tansens son Tantarang. A major contributor from the gharana was Ustad Masit Khan. Their followers prefer short taan passages when elaboration with 'tala' accompaniment commences. It takes to playing a medium tempo 'gat' composition after the masitkhani composition in rendering raga music.

Rampur/Mahiyar Gharana

The Rampur gharana, more popularly known as the Mahiyar gharana, also interacted with the style of been, but it followed khyal singing instead of'dhrupad'. On account of many historic musical factors, the gharana makes music influenced by 'dhrupad' and 'been' and thus, creates music of a graver import. It has formulated a methodical approach towards the teaching of sitar.

Imdad Khan Gharana

The other name in the sitar gharana is the Imdad Khan gharana, well known by Ustad Vilayat Khan. This gharana is distinguished by the importance it gave to the left hand, that is, the hand mainly responsible for the melodic tune and its continuity. This school is forefront in making technical innovations in the instrument, includes strengthened 'tabli', modified bridge, new arrangement of strings as also their tuning and changes in the fret-work and their manufacture.

Academies

The Academies also play a vital role in preserving and propagating our classical music. The Government is also aware of the importance, being played by these academies. The following academies are also playing a very important role in preserving our musical heritage. Here are the some of the academies.

1. Bihar Sangeet Natak Academy, Rajinder Nagar, Patna.
2. Sahitya Kala Parishad, New Delhi.
3. Kala Academy, Panaji, Goa.
4. Himachal Academy of Culture and Language, Shimla.
5. Kerala Sangeet Natak Academy, Trichur.
6. Gujarat Sangeet Nritya Natya Academy, S.M Road, Ahmedabad.
7. Karnatak Sangeet Nritya Academy, F.C. Complex, Bangalore.
8. Madhya Pradesh Lalit Kala Parishad, Ravinder Nath Thakur Road, Bhopal.
9. State Academy of Dance, Nagaland.
10. State Academy of Music Dance and Drama (Literature &fine Arts) Imphal.
11. Orissa Sangeet Natak Academy, Music Building, Bhubaneshwar
12. Punjab Sangeet Natak Academy, Sec. 10, Chandigarh.
13. Rajasthan Sangeet Natak Academy, Pauta, Jodhpur.
14. UP Sangeet Natak Academy, Kesar Bagh, Lucknow.
15. West Bengal State Natak Academy, Bagh Bazar, Calcutta.
16. Sangeet Natak Academy, Mandi House, New Delhi.

COMPOSITION AND NOTATION

Music is a progressive art. At a time when all literature consisted of only poetry, the sahityas of musical composition were written after the style of poetry. The sahitya in most cases was conceived first and was set to music later on. When the centre of gravity in a musical composition got shifted to music and it came to realised that what mattered in a musical composition was more its musical setting rather than its sahitya, prose came to be freely used. The sahitya came to be regarded as a mere aid to remember the music. Musicography is 'sangita lipi' or musical notation. It deals with the various symbols used in representing music on paper. It is the translation of music in a visible form. The original music of many of the compositions have been lost since they were not recorded in notation because no notation worth the name had been developed at that time. "Word of mouth is revered in Hindustani music. Therefore notation is employed only in respect of composition skeletons. In view of the reliance of improvisation (elaboration of the basic musical material) notation becomes a virtual impossibility. It is of course simplistic to maintain that notation becomes irrelevant because Hindustani music is too complicated to be reduced to the notation activity. With greater validity it could be held that trying to write down musical nuances, is likely to hamper the spontaneous element which breathes through Hindustani music. It is of interest to note that all attempts to subject Hindustani musical elaboration to notation were made only after the advent of British Rule."[25]

MUSIC NOTATION SYSTEM IN VEDIC PERIOD

In Vedic period, the ved mantras were recited in Epic form and the ascent and descent of those mantras was done on the directions of special signs. Three types of music notation signs were used in that time. These signs were:

(1) Udat
(2) Anudat
(3) Swarit

Udat: A note recited in high pitch is called the ***Udat.*** It is symbolized by a small vertical line marked over the word, which is to be pronounced in high pitch as:

अंहं यशस्विंनों यंशों विंश्वा रुपांव्यां वदे।

ऋ० खल १। १।१।।

Anudat: A note recited in a low pitch is called ***Anudat***. It is symbolized by a horizontal line marked under the word to be pronounced in low pitch. The horizontal line has been shown as the sign of Anudat in Rig veda (kashmiri Lesson), Yajur veda and Atharva veda.

अग्नि मींले (ऋ १ । १ । १) इषे त्वोर्जे त्वां (१ । १ । १)

ये त्रिषप्रा: (अ. शो. १ । १ । १)

Swarit: Swarit note denotes the combination of Udat and Anudat. It is expressed without any sign. In Sam veda udat etc. are expressed by writing the figures over the words instead of above signs of vertical and horizontal lines.

२ ३ १ २
अग्न आ याहि (पू० १ । १ । १)

Note : Some scholars of Vedas differ in opinion about the use of horizontal lines over the words. To avoid this matter of difference in opinion we have used signs on the basis of sound.

MUSIC NOTATION IN SANGEET RATNAKAR

Author — Pt. Sharang Dev
Publishers — C. Subbarayudu
Printed at — Vasant Press, Adyar, Madras.
Year —1930
Language — Sanskrit

It is the only available book which clearly describes Gram, Murchhana, Nad, Shruti, Swaras along with Ragas and their Lakshana. The signs of notation system have been described as follows:

Medium Octave — No sign over the notes.
S R G M P D N

Lower Octave — Sign of dot (.) Over the notes.
S̊ R̊ G̊ M̊ P̊ D̊ N̊

Upper Octave — Vertical line over the notes.
S̍ R̍ G̍ M̍ P̍ D̍ N̍

A Song of Gandhari Jati

1.	गा	गा	सा	नी	सा	गा	गा	गा
	ए				तं			
2.	गा	गम	पा	पा	धप	म	निध	निंसं
	र	ज	नि	व	धू		मु	स
3.	निध	पनि	मा	मपरि	गा	गा	गा	गा
	वि			भ्र	म		दं	
4.	गा	गम	पा	पा	धप	मा	निध	निंसं
	नि	शा	म	य	व	रो	रु	

(Sangeet Ratnakar, Vol. I, Page 207)

MUSIC NOTATION IN SARMAYE ISHRAT

Author — Sadiq Ali Khan
Printed at — Narayani Press, Delhi.
Year — 1874
Language — Urdu

This book deals with Nada, Shruti, Swaras, Saptaka, Gram, Murchhana, Thatas and old system of Raga-Raginis in details along with the description of the Indian musical instruments with illustrations. As the language of this book is Urdu, the notations is from right to left.

The bols of Sitar — Da-Dir-Da-Da, have been given on the top. Below it are the numbers of frets of Sitar for notes. The numbers of Tali and Khali have been written over Dir-Da.

Notation of Gat Rag Kalingara (Bhairav Thata)

Number of Tali	1 Tali					2 Ta[illegible]		
Bols of Sitar	Dir	Da	Dir	Da	Ra	D[illegible]	[illegible]	Ra
Fret Numbers	12	11	9	8	[illegible]	[illegible]	9	9
Khali Tali	Tali						3 Tali	
Bols of Sitar	Dir	Da	Dir	Da	Ra	Da	Da	Ra
Fret Numbers	8	7	6	7	5	6-7	5	6

(Sharmaye Ishrat pages 187, 204)

MUSIC NOTATION OF NAGMA-E-SITAR AND TEHSIL-UL-SITAR

Author — Mirza Rahimbeg Khan Delhi
Year — 1891
Language — Urdu.

In these books the measurements of frets have been given. The gats have been written on the basis of numbers. The method of tuning the Sitar strings and the introduction of Thatas have also been mentioned. The notations have been given from top to downwards as shown ahead:

Gats of Nagma-e-Sitar

Fret Numbers	*Bols of Sitar*	*Tali-Khati*	*Sam*
11	Dir	1 Tali	
10	Da Ra		
9	Da Ra		
6	Da	2 Tali	
5	Da		
9	Ra		
7	Dir		
8	Da-Ra		
7	Da		
9	Da		
10	Ra	Khali	
11	Dir		

Tehsil-Ul-Sitar

The gats in this book have been written as in Nagama-e-Sitar. The distances of frets have been shown as follows:

Fret Numbers	*Notation*	*Distance of Frets*
3	Dha	3.5 fingers
7	Re	2.5 fingers
12	Dha	2.0 fingers
13	Nee	1.5 fingers
15	Re	2.0 fingers
16	Ga	2.0 fingers

NOTATION SYSTEM IN NAD VINOD GRANTHA

Author	—	Gusai Pannalal, Gusai Chunnilal, Mohallah.
Publishers	—	Narain Das, Jangali Mal, Tajur Kutub, Delhi.
Printed at	—	Iftkhar, Maliwara, Delhi.
Year	—	1895.
Language	—	Urdu.

In this book Nad, Shruti, Swaras, Saptakas, Thata and Raga-Ragini systems have been explained in details. Gats of Sitar have also been given.

Notation System for Ragas **Rag Bhairava**

No. of Shruti	2	4	1	2	2	1	2	2	1	2	2	4	4	2	2	2
Notes	Dha	Nee	Sa	Re	Re	Sa	Re	Re	Sa	Ga	Ma	Ga	Ga	Re	Re	Re

Notation System for Sitar Gats **(Gat Raga Yaman)**

Bols	Da	Da	Ra	Da	Dir	Ra	Da	Dir	Ra	Dir	Ra	Dir	Ra	Da	Da	Ra
No. of shruits	4	4	4	4	5	5	5	4	5	5	4	4	4	4	4	4
Notes	Re	Ga	Re	Ma	Pa	Pa	Pa	Ma	Pa	Pa	Dha	Dha	Nee	Nee	Dha	Dha

Gat Raga Bhero (Nad Vindo Grantha)

استھائی بھیروں راگ کی

۲	۲	۲	۴	۲	۴	۴	۴	۲	۲	۲	۴	۴	۲	۲	۱	۲	۲	۱	۲	۲	۱	۴	۲
سم	رے	رے	گا	ما	گا	گا	گا	رے	رے	رے	گا	گا	ما	ما	سا	رے	رے	سا	رے	رے	سا	نی	دھا
۵	۳	۴	۱	۳	۲	۱	۲	۲	۱	۴	۳	۱	۱	۲	۲	۲	۵	۵	۵	۰	۱	۱	۱
پا	دھا	نی	سا	رے	رے	سا	رے	رے	سا	نی	دھا	سا	سا	دھا	دھا	دھا	پا	پا	پا	انترا	سا	سا	سا
							۰	۱	۱	۱	۲	۲	۲	۴	۲	۵	۲	۴	۱	۲	۴	۴	۲
							۰	سا	سا	سا	رے	رے	رے	گا	ما	پا	دھا	نی	سا	رے	گا	گا	ما

NOTATION SYSTEM IN SANGEET SAR

By Sri Krishetra Mohan Goswami

The author of this book has explained the Notation System in a new style:

	P	P	P	P	P	P	P
Sharp Notes	S	R	G	M	P	D	N
	Δ	Δ	Δ	Δ	Δ	Δ	Δ
Half Tone Notes	S	R	G	M	P	D	N
Lower Octave	S	R	G	M	P	D	N
Medium Octave	S	R	G	M	P	D	N
Upper Octave	S	R	G	M	P	D	N

NOTATION SYSTEM OF PT. VISHNU DIGAMBAR PULASKAR

Pt. Vishnu Digamber Ji Pulaskar is one of the reformers of music notation system. In his books Bharatiya sangeet notation system, Bal Udaya Sangeet printed in 1909 and Sangeet Bal Prakash, he has described the notation systems of many Raga Raginis. He established Gandharva Mahavidyalaya in Lahore in 1901. He started instructions of music through Music notation system. He wrote a number of books on this subject. Now-a-days the modified notation system used in the vidyalaya is as follows:

This system has been recognised by the Government.

	नाम	निशाणी
Full Tone Note	शुद्ध	ϕ
Half Tone Note	कोमल	⋎
Double Tone Note	अति कोमल	Y
Sharp Note	तीव्र	Δ
Double Sharp Note	तीव्रतर	Δ
D.D. Sharp Note	तीव्रतम	$\bar{\Delta}$

	तार	
Upper Octave Note	मध्य	स ɪ रि I ग ʓ म प ध ɪ नि ɪ ϱ
Medium Octave	मध्य	

Lower Octave	तार	
	मध्य	स़ I नि़ I ध़ प़ I प़ म़ ग़ • प़
	मध्य	

नाम	निशाणी	गिनती	मात्रा
उच्चारण चतस्त्रा.	✠	१	४
उच्चारण गुरु.	♉	१	२
उच्चारण लघु.	I	१	१
उच्चारण द्रुत.	♀	२	१
उच्चारण अणु द्रुत.	♈	४	१
उच्चारण अणु अणु द्रुत.	♈	८	१
उच्चारण अणु अणु अणु द्रुत.	♈	१६	१

NEW NOTATION SYSTEM

Full Tone Note — No sign.
Half Tone & Sharp Note — Oblique line under the notes

R G M D N
\ \ \ \ \

Medium Octave — No Sign.

S R G M P D N

Lower Octave — A dot on the notes.

Ṅ Ḋ Ṗ Ṁ

Upper Octave notes - A vertical line on the notes.

| | | |
S R G M

Sam 1 — Under the note
Tali 2 3 4 — Under the note
Khali + Under the note
Division of Matras — different signs are used.

NOTATION SYSTEM IN SANGEET PRAVESH

This book, written by Pandit Krishna Rao Shankar, Principal Shankar Gandharva Vidyalaya, Gwalior, was first published in 1927 and the second edition came out in 1932.

Notation system is as follows:

Full Tone Notes — S R G M P D N

Half Tone Notes — R G D N
/ / / /

Sharp Note — M
/

Lower Octave S R G M P D N

MediuM Octave S R G M P D M

Upper Octave S̄ R̄ Ḡ M̄ P̄ D̄ M̄

Talis First Tali I S

Second Tali II S

Third Tali III S

Fourth Tali X S

Khali o S

NOTATION SYSTEM OF FIROZ FRAMJI

Sri Firoz Framji wrote several books on music in his own publication from 322, Main Street, Poona in 1930.

He has used his own signs in these books. His notations are as follows:

Full Tone Notes — S P

Sharp Notes — R G M D N

Half Tone Notes — R G M D N

Double Lower octave – - Two vertical lines below the note.

N D P
II II II

Lower Octave — One vertical line below the notes.

N D P M
I I I I

Upper Octave — One vertical line on the note.

I I I I
S R G M

Medium octave — No sign.

S R G M P D N S

NOTATION SYSTEM OF PV. VISHNU NARAIN BHATKHANDE

Pt. Vishnu narain Bhatkhande has given a very clear and easy notation system. He invented a number of new notations and brought a drastic change in Indian music notation system. In his book 'Hindustani Sangeet Kramik Pustak' written in 6 volumes, is a sound proof of the fact that he has done a marvelous work in musical world. In Indian University education his notation system has been made a base for the musical instruction in higher education of the subject.

Full Tone Note — No sign.

S R G M P D N

Halftone Note — A horizontal line under the notes.

R̲ G̲ D̲ N̲

Sharp Note — A vertical line on the note.

|
M

Medium Octave — No sign.

S R G M P D N

Lower Octave — A (.) under the note.

Ṇ Ḍ P̣ Ṃ

Upper Octave — Dot (.) over the note.

Ṡ Ṙ Ġ Ṁ

Sam	+
Tali	1-2-3-4
Khali	0

NOTATION SYSTEM IN VIVEK DARPAN

Author — Khan Sahib Bande Khan.

Printed at — Sarangi Niwas, Delhi. Language — Urdu.

This book is written on Sarangi instrument in Urdu. In this book the author has explained the method of tuning and system of bowing. The notation system is as follows:

(*i*) O has been used for Khali

(*ii*) 1, 2, 3, etc. are used for Talis. Bols and Swaras have been given below them.

ی	ی	ی	٣ میں		ے	ے	ے	١٢ گا		ے	کیو	سن	١ ی		لو	ل	ی	ا
سا	پ	سا	م		—	گ	—	سا	نمبر١	پ	دیم	پ	سا		گ	سا	م	گ
سا	پ	سا	م		—	گ	—	سا	نمبر٢	پ	نیم	پ	سا		گ	سا	م	گم

ا	تمو	نِ	تَر		مو	رِج	ی	پِنَ		بِ	گ	تِ	جَ		پر	قو	پا	رے
سا	پ	سا	گ		م	گ	م	ن	نمبر١	ن	ن	م	گ		م	م	م	م
سا	سن	سا	سگ		م	گم	م	نم	نمبر٢	ن	نم	م	گم		م	م	م	م

सदारंग कृत ख्याल, राग रामकली
झूमरा (विलम्बित)
स्थायी

				नि								नि	
म	गम	प	प	ध	–	प	मं	प	पध	पधनि	ध	ध	प
मा	ऽऽ	छ	रि	याँ	ऽ	ऽ	ऽ	ऽ	मेंऽ	ऽऽऽ	दी	ला	गी
३							२				0		
मं				म			स		ग		ग		
प	ग	म	(म)	रे	–	सा	नि	सा	रे	सा	म	–	गम
मे	ऽ	ऽ	रे	ला	ऽ	ल	हा	ऽ	थ	न	की	ऽ	ऽऽ
३				x			२				0		
ग				नि			प		प		म		
म	–	गमप	प	ध	–	प	नि	ध	प	गम	रे	रे	सा
हाँ	ऽ	ऽऽऽ	रे	कै	ऽ	सि	ब	नी	रे	ऽऽ	लो	ग	वा
३				x			२				0		

अन्तरा

		नि		ध			नि						
प	प	ध	ध	सां	सां	सां	ध	ध	सां	सां	रें	–	सां
सा	दा	रं	ग	मि	लि	या	रं	ग	धु	लि	या	ऽ	ऽ
३				x			२				0		
सां													
नि	–	सां	–	ध	ध	प	मं	प	प	प	पध	पधनि	ध
ऽ	ऽ	ऽ	ऽ	ऽ	मा	ई	ई	छ	ऽ	रि	याऽ	ऽऽऽ	ऽ
३				x			२				0		
नि							नि			प	म	ग	
ध	–	प	मंप	ग	–	म	ध	--	प	गम	रे	रे	सा
पू	ऽ	जी	ऽऽ	मो	ऽ	ऽ	रे	ऽ	ऽ	ऽऽ	म	न	की
३				x			२				0		

क्रमिक पुस्तक मालिका, भाग - ४

अदारंग कृत ख़याल, राग मियांमल्लर-एकताल
(विलम्बित)
स्थायी

											–रे
											ऽक
		ध़		ध़				ध़			नि़
स	नि़सा	नि़	प़,म़प़	नि़	नि़ध़	नि़	सा	नि़	सा़	सा	सा
री	ऽऽ	ऽ	म,ऽऽ	ना	ऽऽ	म	ते	ऽ	ऽ	रो	तू
३		४		x		0		२		0	
				स	म	म					
–	सा	रे़	सा	प	ग	ग	म	रे	–	सा,नि़सा	–रे
ऽ	सा	हे	ब	स	त्ता	ऽ	ऽ	ऽ	ऽ	र,ऽऽ	ऽक
३		४		x		0		२		0	

अन्तरा

							नि			ध	
मप	प,निध	निध	नि	सां	–	सां	सां	रें	सां	निध	निध
दुख	द,लिड	ऽऽ	द्र	दू	ऽ	र	की	ऽ	जे	सुऽ	खऽ
३		४		x		0		२		0	
							सं				
निध	नि	सां	सां	रें	सां	(सां)	ध	नि	प	म	प
ऽऽ	दे	ऽ	हो	सं	व	न	को	ऽ	ऽ	अ	दा
३		४		x		0		२		0	
	प	ध		म	म			सा			
मप	नि	नि	प	ग	ग	म	रे	रे	सा	म	प
ऽऽ	रं	ऽ	ग	बि	न	ति	क	र	त	सु	न
३		४		x		0		२		0	
				म	म	म					
मप	निध	सां	सां	प	ग	ग	म	रे	–	सा,नि़सा	–रे
ऽऽ	लेऽ	ऽ	हो	स	त्ता	ऽ	ऽ	ऽ	ऽ	र,ऽऽ	ऽक
३		४		x		0		२		0	

क्रमिक पुस्तक मालिका, भाग - ४

A new method of collective education in music Bhatkande invented a formulated notation system. All his textbooks have the ragas movement and salient points written in notation. Bhatkande strongly advocated the cause of a universal notation system for the reason that it would create a common understanding in the artistic field and would build up emotional integration among musicians and music lovers. It would prevent distortions, which inevitably result from an exclusively oral method of teaching. It would also keep a correct record of present day music for posterity. It is true that all the subtle nuances of music and balances of rendering could not expressed and recorded through notations and not possible to express a particular shade of a note in a particular raga. Bhatkande's opinion in this connection is that "his notation system was a basic skeleton which helped a learner to be well versed in the grammar of classical music and only a sound knowledge of the grammar could create well qualified performers, teachers, critics and listeners."[26]

JOURNALS AND ARTICLES

In the modern world of research, the results are communicated through articles, monographs, books and handbooks of these the journals are the major vehicles, where in the articles containing the results of research are published. The articles published in a journal is characterized by the following features:

1. It attempts to answer a question by examination of relevant evidences;
2. It deals with question which are specific narrowly defined and fit to be encompassed in a single investigation;
3. It is started with a brief introductory account of the current state of research on the problem;
4. It interprets the observed facts in relation to the problem; and
5. It draws conclusions on the basis of the interpretation.

List of the more journals mentioned here

1. *Chhayanat* (Hindi quarterly) UP Sangeet Natak Academy, Qaiser Bagh, Lucknow-226001.
2. *Indian Music Journal* (Quarterly) Tyaga Bharti Music Educational Society, 24, Bank Street, Malekote-571431.
3. *Journal of Indian Musicological Society* (Annual) Jambu Bet, Dandia Bazar, Baroda-390001.
4. *Journal of Music Academy* (Annual) 306, T.T.K. Road, Madras-600014.

5. *Sangeet* (Hindi monthly) Sangeet Karyalaya, Hathras-204101.
6. *Sangeet Kala Vihar* (Hindi monthly) Brahmin Puri, Miraj-416410.
7. *Sangeet Natak* (Quarterly) Sangeet Natak Academy, 35, Feroze Shah Road, New Delhi-110001.
8. *Shanmukha* (English and Tamil Quarterly) Plot No. 292, J.Y. Mary, Bombay-400022.
9. *Vageeshwari* (English and Hindi Annual) Music Department, Delhi University, Delhi-110007.
10. *Visva Beena* (Bengali Monthly) 1, Richie Road, Calcutta-700019.

The journals also include besides research articles depending upon their objectives, books reviews notices of articles, current bibliographies to report the current research in the field of specialization.

(i) ***Jitendra Pratap:*** Classification of Tagore's songs Indian Express, New Delhi, 15th Feb. 1989,12.

(ii) ***Sehgal, Rashme:*** Prabha Atre singer par excellence. Statesman (New Delhi) 26th April 1989, 5.

(iii) ***Moudgalya V.C.:*** Pannalal Ghosh Indian Music Journal 8-10(15-20) 1972-74, 30-32.

(iv) ***Moti Chandra:*** Portrait of Tansen. National Centre for the performing Arts : Quarterly Journal 3(1) Mar. 1974, 1-3.

(v) ***Mayor Geeta:*** Homage to Bhatkhande National Centre for Performing Arts, Quarterly Journal 11(3) Sep. 1980, 31-40.

(vi) ***Jayakumar, E.:*** Yesudas: Rafi was his guiding star Illustrated Weekly of India, 1982, 8 Aug. 42.

(vii) ***Raghu Rai:*** The beats of ecstasy (Zakir Hussain) India Today 15 March 1988, 156-166.

(viii) ***Sharma, Premlata and V.V. Sadagopan:*** Music and Musicology. Indian Music Journal 6(1-2) Spring 1970. 59-64.

(ix) ***Sankar Vidya:*** Notation and teaching of Gamakas, Journal of the Music Academy 55, 1984, 182-186.

(x) ***Ahluwalia, Kishwar:*** Ghazal singing is big business Femina 8 Feb. 1981. p. 9.

(xi) ***Das, Prafullakumar:*** Some salient point of Rabindra Sangeet. Journal of Indian Musicological Society 3(4) Oct. 1972, 19-20.

(xii) ***Ray Sitanusu:*** Tagore's thoughts on music, dimensions of appreciation. Sangeet Natak, 40 April 1976, 15-22.

(xiii) ***Amarnath, Pandit:*** Teaching of classical music today. Sangeet Natak 31, July 1975, 25-28.

(xiv) ***Chaudhuri, Debu:*** Teaching of Indian Music. Vageeshwari 2(1) Jan. 1988, 28-32.

(xv) ***Kumaraguru:*** Music as a factor in education Vivekananda Kendra Patrika 7(1) Feb. 1978, 342-343.

(xvi) ***Mukherjee, Sharbari:*** Scientific training in music. Link 26th Jan. 1982, 131.

(xvii) ***Jitendra Pratap:*** Revival of Guru shishya tradition. Indian Express (New Delhi) 16th Oct. 1988, 12.

(xviii) ***Sarvesh Chandra:*** Gharana system of teaching in Hindustani Music; a critical analysis. Journal of the Indian Musicological Society, 10 (3-4) Sep. 1979, 31-33.

(xix) ***Chakravarti, Indarani:*** Modes of music teaching in higher education, Sangeet Natak. 74, Oct. 1984, 27-31.

(xx) ***Chaudhuri, Debu:*** Music research today. Vageeshwari 1(1) Jan. 1987, 20-22.

(xxi) ***Deva, B. Chaitanya:*** Music Academies in India Sangeet Kala Vihar 1 (1) Jan. 1970, 13-14.

(xxii) ***Case for Searate Hindustani Festival:*** (Music Academy, Madras) Hindu (New Delhi) 6th Jan. 1989, 18.

(xxiii) ***A Spiritual Art without Barriers*** (Spic-Macy) Hindu (New Delhi) 12th Feb. 1987, 10.

(xxiv) ***Kothari, Sunil:*** Sangeet Natak Akademi Reaching out to people. Statesman (New Delhi) 31th Jan. 1988, 1-5 (magazine).

(xxv) ***Menon, Raghava R.:*** On preserving the age old paramapara (Sangeet Research Academy) Times of India (New Delhi) 21th Jan. 1988, (metro ad).

(xxvi) ***Karnani, Chetan:*** Pandit Jasraj an appreciation of the famed exponent of the Mewati Gharana Illustrated Weekly of India 21st Oct. 1979, 47.

(xxvii) ***Verma, R.N.:*** Music for peace (Debu Chaudhuri) Hindustan Times. 1st May 1988, 13.

(xxviii) ***Chawla, Hindu:*** The journey of the Gharanas. Hindustan times 30th Oct. 1988, 9-10 (Magazine).

(xxix) ***Jitendra Pratap:*** Mixed fare at Shankar Lal festival. Indian Express (New Delhi) 9th Mar. 1988, 14.

(xxx) ***Menon, Raghava R.:*** Notes fluid and luminous. (Vishnu Digambar Sangeet Samaroh) Times of India (New Delhi) 29th Aug. 1988, 1 (Metro).

DICTIONARIES

A dictionary is a book, which deals with words of a language or of some special subjects, authors etc. Thus a dictionary is a wordbook. Although a dictionary is supposed to deal with words but often it may go beyond this e.g.

(*a*) Encyclopaedic dictionary of Sanskrit on historical principles. Poona, Deccan College of Postgraduate and Research Institute, 1976 vol.1

(*b*) Random House dictionary of the English language. Edited by Jess Stein, Una bridge edition, New York, Random house, 1966.

(*c*) Webster's third new International dictionary of the English language. Un-bridge with seven languages dictionary Springfield. Mass, Merriam, 1961.

Subject dictionaries are important for research as well as development of the subject. For Indian music some dictionaries are available as:

1. ***Amarnath, Pandit:*** Living idioms in Hindustani Music : A dictionary, Delhi. Vikas Publishing House, 1989, 146p.
2. ***Bandopadhya, S.:*** Sangeet Bhashya, Delhi. B.R Publishing. 1985, 479p. (Hindi)
3. ***Kavi M. Rama Krishna:*** Comp. Bharat Kosh New Delhi; Munshiram Manohar Lal, 1985, 984. p. (Hindi).
4. ***Khanna, J.S.:*** Sangeet Ki Paribhashik Shabadavali. Chandigarh, Abhisekh Publications 1991, 194p. (Hindi)
5. ***Nirmala Devi:*** Dictionary of Music. New Delhi; Anmol Pub. 1990. 250p.
6. ***Roy Chaudhary:*** Vimal Kant, Bhartiya Sangeet Kosh. Bombay, Bharatiya Jananpith, 1975, 228p. (Hindi)

Biogrpahical Dictionaries

Biographical Dictionaries contain life sketches of many musicians and the persons related with the field. In such books information varies from a single paragraph to many pages. For Indian music the following biographical sources are available.

1. ***Deshpande, Vasant Rao, H.:*** Between two tanpuras. Bombay, Popular Prakashan, 1989, 216p.
2. ***Kuppuswamy, Gowry and Hariharan, M.:*** Glimpses of Indian Music. New Delhi, Sandeep Prakashan, 1982, 250p.

3. ***Mishra, Susheeia:*** Great Masters of Hindustani Music. New Delhi, Hem Publishers, 1981, 180p.
4. ***Mishra, Susheela:*** Music makers of Bhatkhande College of Hindustani Music. Calcutta, Sangeet Research Academy, 1985, 83p.
5. ***Mishra, Susheela:*** Music Profiles Lucknow. Bhatkhande Music College 1955, 122p.
6. ***Parthasarathy, T.S.:*** Music composers of India. Madras; Ayyar foundation 1982, 84p.
7. ***Raghava, V.:*** Great integrators, the saint singers of India. Delhi, Publication Division, 1966, 184p.
8. ***Rajagopalan, N.:*** Another garland. Madras. Carnatic Classicals. 1992, 520p.
9. ***Rajagopalan, N.:*** Biographical dictionary of Carnatic composers and musicians. Bombay Bhartiya Vidya Bhavan, 1990, 540p.
10. ***Rajagopalan, N.:*** Yet another Garland. Madras. Carnatic Classicals. 1994, 442p.
11. ***Rizvi, Dolly:*** Great musicians of India. Bombay, IBH Publications, 1987, 80p.
12. ***Sambamoorthy, P.:*** Great composers. 2 vol. Madras. Indian Book Publishing House. 1978, 166+354p.
13. ***Who's who of Indian Musician:*** 2nd ed. New Delhi, Sangeet Natak Academy. 1984, 160p.

BIBLIOGRAPHIES

Bibliographies help the researchers in their literature surveys. For Indian music only three bibliographies are available. For Hindi literature in music there is none.

1. ***Kendanath, G.C.:*** Indian music and dance. A select bibliography Varanasi, Indian Bibliographic Centre, 1986, 261p.
2. ***Kuppusamy, G. and Hariharan. M.:*** Indian dance and music literature. New Delhi. Biblia Impex. 1981, 156p.
3. ***Mohammed Haroon:*** Indian music literature. Delhi. Indian bibliography Bureau. 1991, 144p.

Current information about music literature can be obtained from Indian Books in Print, Index India and Guide to Indian Periodicals, Literature. These contain information about all the subjects.

Discographies

These are the list of gramophone records in Indian music. This is unique published source of audio materials that contains information about the main artist, raag, compositions and accompanied artists. Only few books are available in this field.

1. ***Kinnear, Michael, S.:*** A discography of Hindustani and Karnatic Music. Westport (USA) Green Wood press. 1985, 594p.
2. ***Sangeet Natak Academi :*** Tape recordings Catalogue. New Delhi, Sangeet Natak Academy 1976.
3. ***Danielou, Alain:*** A catalogue of recorded classical and traditional Indian Music. UNESCO, 1952, 235p.

Raga Indices

These are the alphabetical lists of ragas. From these the researchers may know the book and specific pages that contain information about the particular raag. Only two raga indices have been published so far.

1. ***Moutal, Patrick:*** Hindustani Raga-s index New Delhi. Munshi Ram Manohar Lal, 1991, 238p.
2. ***Moutal, Patrick:*** A comparative study of selected Hindustani Ragas. 3 used on contemporary practice. New Delhi, Munshi Ram Manohar Lal, 1991, 578p.

Encyclopaedias

An encyclopaedia is a book, giving information on all branches of knowledge of a specific subject. It is an ideal book, which deals with concepts. An encyclopaedia is a storehouse of knowledge giving all information of significance. However, it is best used for finding answers to background questions related to general information and self-education. One often turns to encyclopaedias for one's everyday information requirements. e.g.

(*a*) ***Encyclopaedia Americana,*** New York, Grover, 1976, 30 vols.
(*b*) ***International Encyclopaedia of the Social Sciences.*** New York, Collier and Macmillan, 1968, 17 vols.

There is no encyclopaedia exclusively on Indian music. Some information on Indian music is given in Encyclopaedia Britannica and Encyclopaedia of Religion and 270 Ethics. Grove's Dictionary of Music and Musicians also covers some aspects of Indian Music.

ALL INDIA RADIO

Radio, Television, Films and Photography are the most fascinating branches and have gained extra-ordinary importance in recent decades. Developments in electronic and satellite communication are giving a new impetus to TV and Radio. The term mass communication stands for dissemination of information ideas and entertainment by the use of communication media. The media include those, which are modern means of communications such as radio and television, film, press and publications. Infact, they co-exist with the important traditional media such as folk dance, drama etc.

"Research on relative effectiveness of different media of communication include —

(*i*) What role the media play
(*ii*) Has they motivate the people of bring about change in their value orientation and perception
(*iii*) What media are relatively more effective.[27]

Radio broadcasts started in India in 1927. In 1936, the name of service was changed to All India Radio (AIR). Since 1957 it is known as Akashwani and now AIR is the biggest media organisation. It is servicing as an effective media not only to inform and educate people, but also to provide healthy entertainment. Music was largely under the patronage of princely courts during pre-independence days. With the abolition of princely states after 1947, the task of preserving the musical heritage and propagation of music in all its variety, especially classical music, was taken over by AIR. Through the regular broadcast of music programmes, from all AIR stations in the net work AIR has contributed largely to bringing about an awareness and appreciation of Indian music, classical, light folk and tribal.

About 38 per cent of the total broadcast of AIR at present constitute music programmes. This includes classical and light classical music, light devotional, folk, film as well as classical and light western music. Apart from the regular music programmes. AIR started way back in the 1950's some of the major network programs namely the national program of music and the Radio Sangeet Sammelan. A few years later the national programme of regional and light as well as zonal hook up concerts by young artists were linked to these programs. Through these programmes, AIR brings to its listeners the best of music available in the country on its network.

In order to create better appreciation of the musical heritage of the country especially among the younger generation, AIR broadcasts music lessons and music appreciation programs regularly from various AIR stations. New talent is scouted through the regular music auditions as well as annual competitions. One of the significant achievements of AIR national programmes and Sangeet Sammelan concerts is the integration of Hindustani and Karnataka styles, which are the major styles of music in the country.

Another important milestone in AIR's music programs was the inception of national orchestra known as AIR Vadya Vrinda in Delhi 1952. This orchestra unit consisting of both Hindustani and Karnataka musicians has made remarkable experiments in orchestration of the Indian music. AIR pays equal attention to the preservation and development of folk and light music. Besides the national program, AIR relations broadcast regularly folk and tribal music of various regions.

Some of the major music events held in different parts of the country are also covered by AIR. Two major festivals, excerpts from which are broadcast on the National as well as zonal hookup level are the Thyagaraja and Tansen Festivals. The music archives of AIR are among the most important collections of music records in the country.

Recording of Old Masters in AIR Archives

Sr. No.	*Name of the Artist*	*Duration*
1.	Abdul Karim Khan	20 mts.
2.	Abdul Wahid Khan	120 mts.
3.	Allauddin Khan	240 mts.
4.	Ali Akbar Khan	720 mts.
5.	Amir Khan	1020 mts.
6.	Asad Ali Khan	60 mts.
7.	Bade Gulam Ali Khan	840 mts.
8.	Barodekar Hirabai	640 mts.
9.	Begum Akhtar	2460 mts.
10.	Bismillah Khan & Party	1500 mts.
11.	Bundu Khan	160 mts.
12.	Dagar Brothers	600 mts.
13.	Faiyaz Khan	1700 mts.
14.	Kumar Gandharva	200 mts.
15.	Ghose Pannalal	720 mts.
16.	Girja Devi	140 mts.

(*Contd.*)

Sr. No.	*Name of the Artist*	*Duration*
17.	Hangal Gangoo Bai	340 mts.
18.	Joshi Bhimsen	560 mts.
19.	Mansoor Malikarjun	1740 mts.
20.	Omkar Nath Thakur	920 mts.
21.	Paluskar D.V.	1420 mts.
22.	Ravi Shankar	380 mts.
23.	Subbalaxmi, M.S.	1500 mts.
24.	Vilayat Hussain Khan	2360 mts.
25.	Siddeshwari Devi	1000 mts.
26.	Vyas Narayan Rao	160 mts.
27.	Kanthy Maharaj	60 mts.
28.	Pandist Krishna Shankar Rao	300 mts.
29.	Patwardhan Vinayak Rao	760 mts.
30.	Yusuf Ali Khan	300 mts.

Source : U.L.Baruah. This is All India Radio, p. 349.

Names of Music Artists of Different Radio Programmes and Radio Sangeet Sammelan

1.	Parveen Sultana	Vocal
2.	S. Bala Chander	Veena
3.	Rajan Mishra Sajan Mishra	Vocal
4.	Uma Shankar Misra	Sitar
5.	Ragunath Seth	Flute
6.	Mehmood Mirza	Sitar
7.	Kumar Gandharv	Vocal
8.	Sheik Hussain Saheb	Clrionet
9.	Amjad Ali Khan	Sarod
10.	A. Subba Rao	Vocal
11.	Bismillah Khan & Party	Shenai
12.	Bhimsen Joshi	Vocal
13.	Shiv Kumar Sharma	Santoor
14.	Buddaditya Mukherjee	Sitar
15.	Prabha Atre	Vocal
16.	Imrat Hussain Khan	Sitar
17.	Jaya Biswas	Sitar
18.	Hari Prasad Chaurasia	Flute
19.	Kishori Amonkar	Vocal
20.	Tejpal Singh and Surinder Singh	Vocal

(*Contd.*)

Sr. No.	*Name of the Artist*	*Duration*
21.	Asad Ali Khan	Been
22.	AIR Madras Vadya Vrind Unit	—
23.	V.C. Jog	Violin
24.	T.N. Krishnan	Violin
25.	Debabrata Chaudhuri	Sitar
26.	Chittu Babu	Veena
27.	Buddhadev Dasgupta	Sarod
28.	Jitendra Abishcki	Vocal
29.	Naina Devi	Vocal
30.	Kishan Maharaj	Tabla
31.	Abdul Halim Zafar Khan	Sitar
32.	Pandit Ram Narain	Sarangi
33.	Sabri Khan	Sarangi
34.	N. Rajan	Violin
35.	Sulochana Brahaspati	Vocal

Table I
Music Programmes

Year	*B'east Hrs. Total*	*Devoted to Music Hrs.*	*Percentage*
1937-38			74.00
1960	1,08,256	50,981	47.06
1961	1,17,265	51,184	46.70
1975	2,97,481	1,21,285	40.80
1980	3,91,246	1,58,831	40.60
1982	4,31,653	1,55,869	36.11
VIVIDH BHARATI			
1960		7,123	
1961		7,931	
1975		1,41,198	
1982		1,40,675	

Sources:
1. Broadcasting in India, G.C. Awasthy, p. 33.
2. Mass Media in India, 1978, I&B Ministry, p. 23.
3. Indian Broadcastilng Media, Year Book 1982, K.S. Duggal, p. 3.
4. Mass Media in India, 1981-83, I&B Ministry, p. 137.

Table II
Statement Showing Students of Music Influenced by Radio Programmes of Classical Music

Total Number of Students Interviewed (Music College and School)		48
Listen to classical music prog. Broadcast from radio		
	Regularly	17
	Frequently	11
	Occasionally	16
	Never	4
Listen to Sangeet Sarita Prog.		
	Regularly	35
	Frequently	3
	Occasionally	8
	Never	2
Influenced by Sangeet Sarita * or other Music Prog.		43

* Students were also influenced by other means like Parents, concerts and relative etc.

Table III
Compositon of Music Programme

Music	*Hrs*	*Mts*	*Percentage*
Classical	52,143	42	33.46
Folk	16,100	41	10.34
Light	33,625	46	21.57
Devotional	21,927	58	14.06
Film	27,150	58	17.42
Western	4,920	52	3.15
	1,55,869	57	100.00

Reference from 'Broadcasting' New Patron of Hindustani Music (B.N.Goswami). Sharda Publishing House, New Delhi, 1996.

Table IV
Comparative Listening Percentage of Sangeest Sarita Programme

	Delhi		*Bombay*		*Calcuttaa*		*Madras*	
	Weekdays	*Sunday*	*Weekdays*	*Sunday*	*Weekdays*	*Sunday*	*Weekdays*	*Sunday*
Urban								
Base N	586	586	600	600	600	600	590	598
Light Music	4	4	4	3	1	0	1	4
(Mini)(Nonfilm)								
Sangeet Sarita	18	20	20	20	5	3	6	5
Film Music (Max)	36	38	39	43	17	16	7	6
Rural								
Base N	297	296	299	300	299	298	300	288
Light Music	2	4	6	13	1	0	1	1
(Mini) (Nonfilm)								
Sangeet Sarita	8	13	25	21	1	1	3	2
Film Music (Max)	26	30	39	39	22	19	6	7

Table V

Percentage Listening of VB Classical Music Programmes

	Delhi		*Bombay*		*Calcutta*		*Madras*	
	Weekdays	*Sunday*	*Weekdays*	*Sunday*	*Weekdays*	*Sunday*	*Weekdays*	*Sunday*
Urban								
Base N	586	599	600	600	600	600	590	598
Sangeet Sarita	18	20	20	20	5	3	6	5
Swar Sudha	3	0	7	6	2	0	2	1
Anuragini	0	—	3	—	1	—	1	—
Rural								
Base N	297	296	299	300	299	298	300	288
Sangeet Sarita	8	13	25	21	1	1	1	2
Swar Sudha	2	5	13	9	0	1	1	2
Anuragini	3	—	2	—	0	—	0	—

GRAMOPHONES, TAPES, C.D.

Sound recording and reproduction is one of the most significant contribution of modern technology. Probably for the first time in human history, It has become possible to copy, store and reproduce sound using a suitable medium. This has opened a variety of new possibilities particularly in the field of music. We can now record songs of our favourite artists and enjoy listening to them any number of times at our leisure. Also now it has become possible to preserve the music of great artists for posterity. This also enables us to trace the growth of music, Lot of research is going on to develop new techniques and new material for recording and storage of sound. The field is relatively new and constantly changing with the addition of more and more new information.

With Edison's invention of the phonograph in 1877, it became possible to store sound. Technology and provided different formats for recording viz Flat discs, Plastic records, spool tapes, audio and video cassettes and the most modern compact discs-C.D.s. With this, various reproduction machines were invented such as talking machines, gramapohones, record players and changers, wire and spool tape recorders, audio/video, tape/ cassette recorders, compact disc players. Both sound recording and reproduction witnessed the changes in technology ranging from mechanical to electrical and now the optical methods using laser technology. The practical history of music's audiovisual aspect can be traced by allied arts like sculptures, paintings, manuscripts etc. Due to the absence of the above scientific developments, it was not possible to present the audio performance of the artist in a ready form. But now these inventions helps us in knowing the names and listening to the performances of different artists. It also helped in knowing the forms of various 'raags' and 'raginis', which were rare.

Gramophone Records

We can't tell how many old 78 of pure and light classical music were made by the different gramopbone companies during this long period, but the number will not be less than thousands. In the early part of this century, lots of classical and light classical songs sung by 'tawaifs' were recorded largely at Calcutta.[28] This is the only document left in the form of recordings showing how classical music was sung in India at the turn of the century. The great masters like Pandit Vishnu Diagambar Paluskar,Balkrishnabua Ichalkaranjikar, Bhaskarbua Bakhale, Alladiya Khan Saheb and several other renowned musicians of that period, did not give recordings for reasons unknown and so we are left with imagination only. Fortunately, several musicians of the later period made gramophone records The list of these artists is very long but to name a few:

GRAMOPHONE RECORDS

	Artist		*Content*		*Raag*
1.	Akhatri Jann (Begum Akhtar)	78/359	Sude A (Bhajan)	Khuda Khuda na sahi	
			Side B (Gazal)	Har ek Bat pai kahethe	
2.	Achhen Bai	78/P246	Side A (Dadra)		Piloo
			Side B (Holi)		Kafi
3.	Bade Gulam Ali Khan	78/H.886	Side A (M.Khyal)	Rut Basant may	Adana Bahar
			Side B (Thumari)	Baju Band khul khul jayae	Bhairavee
4.	Dilip Chandra Bedi	78/H.404	Side A (Khyal)	Jowan jat sajani	Vedi Lalit
			Side B (Khyal)	Rang rang phul khilat	Behar
5.	Hira Bai Barodkar	78/GE 5030	Side A (Kajari)	Mera Bawari rama	Piloo
			Side B (Bhajan)	Girdhar Gopala	
6.	Kumar Gandharva	78/H 11344	Side A (M.Jhaptaal)	Sakhi Mori rim jhim	Durga
			Side B (Teental)	Shyam Sundar madanmohan	Bhairvee
7.	Naryan Rao Vyas	78/N.5741	Side A (M.Khyal)	Lagan Mori lagei	Naiki Kanada
			Side B (Thumri)	Ada jan lati hai	Khamaj
8.	Pt. Omkar Nath Thakur	78/6GE 3185	Side A (Thumri)	Nandiya Kaise neer barun	Tilang
			Side B		
9.	Shamshad Begum	78/GC-12 13403-13405	Side A (Dadra)	Kaise Katage raitiya	Bhairvee
			Side B (Jhoola)	Aaj bagiya may phul	Sarang

10.	Siddheshwari Devi	78/GE 23153	Side A (Holi)	Udat abhir gulal	
			Side B (Dadra)	Sawariya pyara ray	
11.	S.N. Ratanjankar	78/H.381	Side A (M.Khyal)	Pyare Lalla	Piloo
			Side B (M. Khyal)	Barsan ke badal	Sur Malhar
12.	Zohra Bai	78/GC-4	Side A (Tarana)	Na Dhir Dhir Dani	Todi
		13182-13185	Side B (Gazal)	Tere Kuchache say	Kalingra
13.	Gangoobai Hangal	78/FT.3108	Side A (M.Khyal)	Rang kar rasiya avaye	Puriya
			Side B (Tarana)		
14.	Gauhar Jan	78/P.17	Side A (Thumri)	Nahaq laye gahenuva	Kafi
			Side B (Thumri)	Ziya pe laghe	Gara
15.	Vinayak Rao Patwardhan	78/FT.5271	Side A (M.Khyal)	Sumri honam	Jaunpuri
		(V-2-26/2)	Side B (M.Khyal)	Dhekho saki aaj	Malhar
16.	K.L. Saighal	78/K.271	Side A (Holi)	Hori ho brij raj	
		(K.L 24/4)	Side B (M.Teentaal)	Jhulan jhulaori	
17.	D.V. Paluskar	78/GE.30291	Side A (Filmsong)	Kaliyan sang karat	Bahar
			Side B (Filmsong)		
18.	Jankibai of Allahabad	78/FT 2297	Side A (Thumri)	Ab na bajavo kanaha	
			Side B (Thumri)	Bisreyho na balam	
19.	Vilayat Hussain	78/A 245038	Side A (M.Khyal)	Saiyan paro nahi	Gaur Sarang
			Side B (M.Khyal)	Ajhuna aye sham	Bhimpalsi
20.	Nathu Lal	78/P.3394	Side A (M.Khyal)	Bhajan bin beet gaye	Bilawal
			Side B (Bhajan)	Jhageye brij raj	Vibhas

INSTRUMENTALIST

No.	Artist	Record No.	Contents
1.	Ali Akbar Khan (Sarod)	78/N.92569	Side A Raagmala Misr Mand Side B Raagmala Misr Mand
2.	Bismilah Khan (Sehnai)	78/N.14564	Side A Raag Malkauns Side B Raag Todi
3.	Kishori Lal (Harmonium)	78/P.1447	Side A Raag Bhairvee Side B Raag Asavari
4.	Manohar Barve (Orchestra)	78/N.5989	Side A Raag Jogiya Side B Raag Bhairvee
5.	Ravi Shankar (Sitar)	78/N.87538	Side A Raag Sarang Side B Raag Sindh Bhairvee
6.	Pannallal Ghose (Flute)	78/N.15928	Side A Raag Khamaj (Thumri) Side B Raag Khamraj (Dabra)
7.	Ram Narain (Sarangi)	78/N.92610	Side A Raag Puriya Kalyan Side B Raag Gunkali
8.	Vilayat Khan (Sitar)	78/GE 3346	Side A RaagMadhuwanti Side B RaagMadhuwanti

9.	Birendra Kishor Roy Chowdhari (Veen)	78/2NG 180	Side A Raag Basant Side B Raag Basant
10.	Bashirkhan (Harmonium)	78/P.1484	Side A Raag Bihag Side B Raag Multani
11.	Chhotey Khan (Sarangi)	78/JNG 143	Side A Raag Darbar Side B Raag Bhairvee
12.	Gajanan Rao Joshi (Violin)	78/N.15915	Side A Raag Tilakkamod Side B Raag Sarang
13.	Imdad Khan (Sitar)	78/P.1460	Side A Raag Bhairvee Side B Raag Asawari
14.	Khan Sahab Abdul Karim Khan (Veen)	78/GE 17505	Side A Raag Darbari Side B Raag Pilu
15.	Hussan Lal (Violin)	78/FT 10010	Side A Raag Alahiya Bilawal Side B Raag Todi

L.P.s Gramophone Records (Vocalist)

No.	Artist	Record No.	Side	Song	Raga
1.	Abdul karim Khan	LP/33ECX 3253	Side A (M. Khyal)	Ab mane maan	Basant
			(Thumri)	Piya kay milanki	Jogiya
			(Thumri)	Prem Sewa sharan	Bhimpalasi
			(Thumri)	Aaj Suhaag	Sankra
			Side B (M. Khyal)	Chandra ka hi jaun	Dev Gandharv
			(M. Khyal)	Mander bhaje	Sudh Kalyan
			(M. Khyal)	Ab kan kant	Anand Bhairvee
			(Thumri)	Piya bhin nahi avate	Jhinjhoti
2.	Amir Khan	LP/EASD. 1357	Side A (V. Khyal)	Jai Mata vilaumbh	Hansdhwani
			Side B (V. Khyal)	Jinkay mann ram	Malkauns
			(M. Khyal)	Aaj more ghar aiyla	Malkauns
3.	Ashwani Bhinde	LP/ECSD 2973	Side A (V. Khyal)	Piya nahi aaye	Patdeep
			(M. khyal)	Jako mana	Multani
			Side B (V. Khyal)	Gumaan jaga	Darbari
4.	Bhimsen Joshi	LP/EASD. 1513 (B.C.D.F. 22/2)	Side A (V. Khyal)	Piyare gar lago	Poriya
			(M. Khyal)	Gadi ye genat jat	Poriya
			Side B (V. Khyal)	Tu rum kan re	Durga
			(M. Khyal)	Chatur sudar	Durga
5.	C.R. Vyas	LP/ECSD. 2974	Side A (V. Khyal)	Daar Daar Paat Paat	Shivmat Bhairav
			(M. Khyal)	Taal Swaron ki	Shivmat Bhairav
			Side B (V. Khyal)	Peyarwa ke	Poorvee
			(M. Khyal)	Tarana	Poorvee

6.	Dagar Aminuddin	LP/EASD 1420	Side A (Dhrupad)	Aye hay ghatta	Miya Malhar
			Side B (Dhrupad)	Shiva addi mada	Bhairav
			(Dhamar)	Kunjan may khilate	Bhairvee
7.	Faiyaz Khan	LP/EALP 1292	Side A (M. Khyal)	Tadphat Hoon jaise	Lalit
			(M. Khyal)	Unsang lagi akiyaan	Ramkali
			(M. Khyal)	Gharwa may sang	Todi
			(Dhamar)	Aari maero	Desh
			(Thumri)	Baju band khul khul	Bhairvee
			Side B (M. Khyal)	Jhan jhan payal	Nat Bihag
			(M.Khyal)	Neyen dekho	Sughrai
			(V. Khyal)		Darbari
			(M. Khyal)	Man mohan brij	Paraj
			(M. Khyal)	Phulwan ki gandh	Jaunpuri
			(Dadra)	Chalo kahe ko	Bharivee
8.	Girja Devi	LP/ECSD 2590	Side A (V. Khyal)	Meka chaen na avae	Deshi
			(M. Khyal)	Ghund ghund lavo	Deshi
			Side B (V. Sitar-khani)	Jham Jham ke	Yaman
			(Dadra)	Tum sachi kaho	Yaman
9.	Gulam Mustafa Khan	LP/ESCD 2471	Side A (V. Ektaal)	Nish din tum haro	Bhupali Todi
			(M. Teentaal)	Unsay ja hamri	Bhupali Todi
			Side B (V. Ektaal)	Saij nis din	Bageshwari
			(M. Teentaal)	Piyarwa garwa	Bageshwari

(*Contd.*)

10.	Hafiz Ahmed Khan	LP/POLYDOR	Side A (V. Ektaal)	Peer paraye	Basant Mukhari
		2392.931	(M. Teentaal)	Manat nahi mora	Basant Mukhari
			(Thumri)	Morae nayena	Bhairvee
			Side B(V. Tilwara)	Tori saugandh	Rasranjani
			(M. Teentaal)	Kaise kate aye	Rasranjani
11.	Pt. Jasraj	LP/ECSD 2705	Side A (V. Ektaal)	Shri Kamleshwari	Bilaskhani
			(M. Teentaal)	Ja jarey kaguva	Bilaskhani
			Side B (V. Ektaal)	Preet mori laag	Gorakh Kalyan
		(M. Teentaal)	Nek kirupa kar	Gorakh Kalyan	
12.	Jitendra Abhisekhi	LP/ECLP 2367	Side A (V. Ektaal)	Sat guru raho man mey	Bilaskhani
			(M. Teentaal)	Tejrey abhiman	Bilaskhani
			Side B (V. Ektaal)	Hay ishwar	Marwa
		(M. Teentaal)	Aau guniyan	Marwa	
13.	Kumar Gandharv	LP/ECLP 2360	Side A (V. Khyal)	Sudh na rahi	Lagan Gandhar
			(M. Khyal)	Baje re mora	Lagan Gandhar
			Side B (V. Khyal)	Sab ras ek bhayo	Patmanjari
			(M. Khyal)	Yad aaway teri	Patmanjari
14.	Krishan Rao Pandit	LP/ECSD 2453	Side A (V. Tilwara)	Lal manavan may	Todi
			(Chatvrang Ektaal)	Sanch sukh gavo	Todi
			Side B (V. Ektal)	Mere albhela	Hamir
			(Tappa Punjabi)	O miyan janewale	Kafi
15.	Kankan Banerjee	LP/ECSD 2990	Side A (M. Khyal)	Ram jum badriya	Gaur Sarang
			(M. Khyal)	Balma na ja	Hamsdhawani
			(Tarana)		Hamsdhawani
			(M. Khyal)	Lat uljhi	Bihag

		(M. Khyal)	Dekho more rang	Bihag	
			Side B (M. Khyal)	Mohammad Shah	Miyan Malhar
			(Tarana)		Chanderkauns
			(Tarana)	Mata kali Ka	Adana
16.	Prabha Atre	LP/ECSD 2490	Side A (V. Ektaal)	Kal nahi avave	Maru Bihag
			Side B (V. Ektaal)	Tan man dan topae	Kalavati
			(Thumri)	Kaun gali gayo	Miskhamaj
17.	Parveen Sultana	LP/ECSD 2731	Side A (V. Ektaal)	Tarase nain	Kusumi Kalyan
			(M. Teentaal)	Aale mohe	Kusumi Kalyan
			Side B (V. Jhumra)	Bin dekhe mohe	Mangal Bhairav
			(M. Teentaal)	Dhay dhing dhing	Mangal Bhairav
			(Thumri)	O more ram ji	Bhairvee
18.	Roshanara Begam	LP/ECSD 14620	Side A (V. Ektaal)	Vidha bhai ranin	Lalit
			(V. Ektaal)	Basant key din	Bhatiyar
			Side B (V. Ektaal)	Rasiya na ja	Maru Bihag
			(V. Ektaal)	Mundri mohe	Adana
19.	Rajan Sajan Misra	LP/ECSD 3135	Side A (V.Khyal)		Gurji Todi
			(M. Khyal)	Tarana	Gurji Todi
			Side B (M. Khyal)		Jog
			(Bhajan)		Jog
20.	Singh Bandhu	LP/ECCD 2840	Side A (V. Jhumara)	Sumiran ko	Nat Bhairav
			(M. Teentaal)	Hun tero nam	Nat Bhairav
			Side B (V. Jhumra)	Aari dan dan	Kalawati
			(M. Teentaal)	Aaj mil gavo	Kalawati

INSTRUMENTALIST

No.	Artist	Record	Contents
1.	Allauddin Khan (Sarod)	LP/ECLP 2757	Side A Raag Kaushi Bhairav Side B Raag Hem
2.	Ali Akbar (Sarod)	LP/EALP 1301	Side A Raag Multani Side B Raag Hindol Hem
3.	Abdul Halim (Sitar)	LP/ECSD 2808	Side A Raag Arabi Side B Raag Multani
4.	Hari Prasad Chaurasia (Flute)	LP/ECSD 2388	Side A Raag Marwa (Dhun) Side B Raag Des
5.	Lal Mani Misra (Vichitra Veena)	LP/H. 72086	Side A Raag Anand Bhairav Side B Raag Multani
6.	Robin Ghose (Violin)	LP/ECSD 2510	Side A Raag Pahadi Jhinjhoti (Dhun) Side B Raag Aheer Bhairav (Dhun)
7.	Sharan Rani (Sarod)	LP/ECSD 2421	Side A Raag Puriya Dhanashree Side B Raag Bajeshwari
8.	Shiv Kumar Sharma (Santoor) Hari Prasad Chaurasiya (Flute)	LP/ECSD 2747	Side A Raag Jhinjhoti Side B Raag Misrapiloo
9.	Raghunath Seth (Flute)	LP/ECCD 2704	Side A Raag Kalavati (Dhun) Side B Raag Hemant Raag Misapiloo(Thumri)
10.	Rais Khan (Sitar)	LP/ECSD 2412	Side A Raag Darbari Side B Raag Tilak Kamod

Esp Gramophone Record (Vocalist)

1.	Ghulam Mustafa	EP/7EPE 1522	Side A (Thumri)	Sham bhaye bin	Misra Piloo
			Side B (Dadra)	Chen nahi paiho	
2.	Rasoolan Bai	EP/SEDE 3301	Side A (Dadra)	Kankar mohe lag	
			Side B (Dadra)	Pangatwa na	
3.	Shobha Gurtu	EP/7EPE 4072	Side A (Thumri)	More saiyan nahi aye	Piloo
			Side B (Thumri)	Bherin ratiyan	Tilak Kamod
4.	Sunanda Patnayak	EP/7EPE 3038	Side A (Bhajan)	Tu Dayal	
			(Bhajan)	Prabhu mere	
			Side B (Bhajan)	Maya anjan	
			(Bhajan)	Man gavo ran ho ram	
5.	Nazakat Ali	EP/7EPE 1235	Side A (M.Teentaal)	Aere piya	Gorakh Kalyan
	Salamat Ali		Side B (M.Teentaal)	Sunder Nayen	Todi

INSTRUMENTALIST

1.	Anant Badekar (Been)	EP/7EPE 1568	Side A Raag Malkauns Side B Raag Malkauns
2.	All Rakha (Tabla)	EP/7EPE 1252	Side A Taal Roopak Side B Taal Teentaal
3.	Chandra Sekhar (Surbahar)	EP/7EPE 1590	Side A Raag Des Side B Raag Chandra Kause
4.	Shashi Mohan Bhutt(Sitar) Vishwa Mohan Bhutt(Guitar)	EPS/7EPE 4021	Side A Raag Hemant Side B Raag Madhuwanti
5.	Devbrat Chaudhuri (Sitar)	EP/7EPE 1853	Side A Raag Des Side B Raag Bhairvee

This list is of course incomplete and several known artists can be included. Similar listing can be made of the musicians from South India and of the instrumentalists. These great masters have cut several 78s and presented their art in a mere three minutes duration. Unfortunately, very few of us know about them today. The records made by them are difficult to find, so we require preserving in a very small sub set of the total recording viz., pure and light classical music. With gramophone records and cassettes one can establish archives, so that these treasures will be preserved for the generations to come and they would be available. This is all the more important since the information inscribed in these grooves represents audio history of our musical culture and they will also serve as a source of reference to the researchers intending to study musical history and the heritage of India.

Old Recording (Gramophone) Companies

(*a*) Gramophone company of India Ltd

(*b*) Twin Record Company

(*c*) Gramophone disc Record Company

(*d*) Hindustan Record H.M. V. & Syndicate broadcast India

(*e*) V. Musical products Ltd. Madras.

(*f*) Breaka Grand Records

(*g*) Valabhadas Laxmidas Company, Bombay

(*h*) Gramophone Monark Record

New Gramophone Companies

1. Polydor Music of India International Company
2. His Masters Voice (HMV)
3. E.M.I.
4. Colombia Record Company
5. C.F.P. Record Company
6. M.F.P. Record Company
7. Odeon Record
8. Regal Record Company
9. World Pacific Company
10. T. Series Company

Cassette Tape Recorders

In audio or auditory equipment, a widely used aid is the cassette tape recorder or a two in one i.e. a radio plus a cassette tape recorder, where we have a facility for instantly recording a required radio broadcast. Nowadays the cassette recorder has become very common and is widely used. This helps one to listen and to note down compositions down to the minutest details. This is one of the finest aids to a student, and a researcher for the purpose of documentation.

With the advance of technology, the world has gone through many major changes. With the very essence of life style changed, the music world could not be an exception. Music was restricted to prestigious institutions, darbars and auditoriums, but availability in the form of cassettes and discs, it has made an immense impact on the world of music. Future generation hence forward will hear not only about the great masters but the great masters themselves. "All music institutions, artists, music lovers, possess their own collections of recorded music. In fact, now a student of music simply cannot afford to ignore recorded music. He is able to learn and know so much from it all the different styles of rendering the same raga its variations different compositions, different talas and so on. Though we are discussing vocal and instrumental music even a student of a classical dance form benefits greatly from recorded music because dance and music go together (the word Sangeet includes vocal, instrumental music and dance. Geetam Vadyam cha ntrutyam che trayam sangeetemuchyate)."[29]

Recorded music has widened our areas of study and specialization. One can choose a particular subject and so research on it. It is now possible to have music of your choice whenever and wherever you want. We can conclude that audio visual aids are not designed to replace or revolutionize but to supplement and modernize other methods. They are vital to the learning of music. These devices help to make learning more meaningful, more interesting and more effective. Thus, the advancement of modern technology is sure to help Indian artists and musicians in preserving their age old traditions and the cultural heritage of music for the use of tomorrow artists and scholars.

Cassette Tape Recorders

Sr. No.	Artist	Contents	Manufacturer	Cassette No.
1.	Pt. Ravi Shankar (Sitar)	SideI Alhiya Bilawal Side II Rasiya	Gramohone Co. of India Ltd.	6TCS 02B 2459
2.	Vilayat Khan (Sitar)	Side I Yaman Side II Jaijaiwanti	Gramohone Co. of India Ltd.	6TCS 04B 7106
3.	Abdul Halim Zafar Khan	Side I Anjun Lahren Side II Saraswati Ranjani	Gramohone Co. of India Ltd.	STCS 04B 7284
4.	Nikhil Banerjee (Sitar)	Side I Sohni Side II Megh	Gramohone Co. of India Ltd.	STCS 02B 2406
5.	Vilayat Khan (Sitar)	Side I Gujari Todi Bismilah Khan (Shehnai)	Gramohone Co. of India Ltd. Side II Bhairavi Thumri	STCS 02B 1153
6.	Various Artists (inst.)	Side I Classical Music of India Bismilah Khan, Ram Narayan, Ravi Shankar, Ali Akbar Side II Shiv Kumar, Hari Prasad Brij Bhushan, Vilayat Khan Pannalal Ghosh, Bismilah Khan	Gramohone Co. of India Ltd.	STC 04B 7458
7.	Alla Rakha & Zakir Hussain	Side I Matta Taal Side II Jai Taal, Pashto	Music Today Living Media India Ltd., G.K. Block, C.P. New Delhi.	A 91013

(Contd.)

Sr. No.	Artist	Contents	Manufacturer	Cassette No.
8.	Music Composed by Vamraj Bhatia (Orchestra)	Orchest (Element of Earth)	Music Today Living Media India Ltd., G.K. Block, C.P. New Delhi.	M 95007
9.	Music Comosed by Zakir Hussain (Vocal)	Orchestra (Element of Space)	Music Today Living Media India Ltd., G.K. Block, C.P. New Delhi.	M 95011
10.	Pt. G.K. Ginde (Vocal)	Lecturer Demonstration on Malhar ke Prakar	Megna Sound (India) Pvt. Ltd. Bombay.	C4 HV 2049
11.	Pt. Shiv Kumar Sharma	Music of Mountains	Music Today	M 93028
12.	Shahid Parvez (Sitar)	Side I Deshkar Side II Yaman	Music Today	M 92022
13.	Folk Artists (Vocal)	Himachal Folk	Music Today	P 93003
14.	Girja Devi (Thumri Vocal)	Thumari & Dadra (Shringar Series)	Music Today	B 93005
15.	Bismillah Khan (Shehnai) Kishori Amonkar (Vocal)	Side I Hamir Bahar (Basent Bahar) Side II (Basent Bahar)	Music Today	A 91021
16.	Bhimsen Joshi (Vocal) Ravi Shankar (Sitar)	Side I Bohar Hindol Bahar (Basent Bahar) Side II Sindura Mishra Kafi	Music Today	A 91022

17.	Kumar Gandahrav (Vocal)	Hamir Raag (Baithak Series)	Music Today	A 93013
18.	Shobha Mudgal (Vocal)	Side I Hori Sawami Side II Chaiti, Kajri, Baramsa Song of the Season Series)	Music Today	B 94004
19.	Gangubai Hangal (Vocal)	Side I Bihag Side II Bageshree	Music Today	B 91005
20.	Bhimsen Joshi (Vocal) Lata Mangeshkar (Vocal)	Side I Ram Bhajan Side II Krishan Bhajan (Ram Shyam Gun Gaan)	H.M.V.	SPHOS 853034
21.	Hari Prasad Chaurasia (Flute)	Various Compositions Music of the River	Music Today	M 93027
22.	Rajan Shajan Mishra	Chaiti	The Gramophone Co. of India Ltd.	STCB 04B 1522
23.	Amjad Ali Khan (Sarod)	Side I Miyan Ki Malhar Side II Megh Malhar	The Gramophone Co. of India Ltd.	STCS 04B 7737
24.	Amir Khan (Vocal)	Side I Jog Side II Darbari	The Gramophone Co. of India Ltd.	STCS 04B 7374
25.	Various Artists (Vocal)	Vol. 1 Thumariyan (Sajan Na Aaye)	The Gramophone Co. of India Ltd.	STCS 04B 7732

(*Contd.*)

Sr. No.	Artist	Contents	Manufacturer	Cassette No.
26.	Raag Rasa Vaibhav (Vocal, Instrumental)	Side I Introduction, Shanti Ras Side II Shanti Ras, Karuna Ras Shringar Ras	The Gramophone Co. of India Ltd.	STCS 04B 850328
27.	Various Artists (Phukar) (Vocal)	Miyan Ki Malhar, Megh, Megh Malhar, Sur Malhar	The Gramophone Co. of India Ltd.	STCS 04B 7598
28.	Ravi Shankar (Sitar) Ali Akbar Khan	Side I Dhun Raag Kafi Side II Bilaskhani Todi	The Gramophone Co. of India Ltd.	STC 02B 6128
29.	Prof. Debu Chaudhuri (Sitar)	Side I Raag Bisweswari Side II Des, Desh Dhun	Rhythm House Clasic the Return of Aestheticism	230 888
30.	Pannalal Ghosh (Flute) Side II Shri	Side I Yaman India Pvt. Ltd.	The Gramophone Co. of	STC 04B 7182
31.	Vilayat Khan (Sitar)	Side I Darbari Kanada Side II sindhu Bhairavi	The Gramophone Co. of India Pvt. Ltd.	STC 04B 7338
32.	Various Artists (Vocal)	Raag Rang Berang	The Gramophone Co. of India Pvt. Ltd.	STC 04B 5040
33.	Parveen Sultana (Vocal)	Side I Madhuwanti Bhajan Side II Gorakh Kalyan, Thumri Misra Bhairavi	The Gramophone Co. of India Pvt. Ltd.	STC 04B 4009

34.	V.C. Jog Hari Prasad Charuasia (Flute)	Side I Jog Side II Hamsadhwani, Holi Misrakafi	The Gramophone Co. of India Pvt. Ltd.	STS 04B 3986
35.	Shobha Ghurtu (Vocal)	Thumari	The Gramophone Co. of India Pvt. Ltd.	STC 04B 7326
36.	Various Artists (inst.)	Side I Ahir Bhairav Nat Bhairav Pilloo Side II Bhoop, Des, Pahadi	The Gramophone Co. of India Pvt. Ltd.	STCS 04B 1109
37.	Arjan Shejwal (Pakhawaj)	Side I Chawtaal Side II Dhamar, Mattatal	The Gramophone Co. of India Pvt. Ltd.	6TCS 04B 7147
38.	Ramnarain (Sarangi)	Side I Saraswati Side II Meru Bihag, Piloo, Thumri	The Gramophone Co. of India Pvt. Ltd.	6TC 04B 7171
39.	Produced with the Book Thomar Mercotty (Rudra Veena)	Rudra Veena : The Theory and Technique	of Tantric Music with the Book — The way Music.	Book ACC No. 9469B
40.	Mehmood Dhoulpuri	Side I Todi, Hansdwani Side II Hori, Maand, Rasia, Pahadi, Bidai	Amritvani Delhi	CC 5043

COMPUTER DISCS

The emergence of digital computers soon after World War II brought in one of the most sophisticated equipment to the service of mankind. Since digital computer is an information — transforming device, its use is bound to be all persuading. No discipline of study remains untouched by computers. The use of digital computer in fine arts and music started as early as in 50's. The creation of music by artificial means has been subject of considerable interest in the past few years especially since the introduction of sophisticated equipments capable of handling and processing information. These have resulted in the production of some delightful music. However in India, not much work has been done in this direction. Thinking about the possible uses and therefore impact of electronic and computerized sounds on Hindustani classical music. One can visualise: (*a*) As Max Mathews forward to foundations of Computer music, this sophisticated instruments will require lot of learning before it can be used to give expressions to ones artistic creations. Hindustani/ Karnatak instrument players will take some time before they start using it as a regular instrument for delineation of raags and secondly (*b*) for vocalists and players of traditional music instruments. 'Riyaaz' and creations of new 'Alankars', which can be assimilated by the performer so that his next line performance can be more attractive with, added embellishments. In order to get a better impression of the research applications of digital computers, in Indian Classical music, it will be helpful first to review the work carried out by Mrs. Khandekar concerning what she calls the simulation model. "In her thesis, attempts have been made to simulate raags of Hindustani music she has tried through experimentation to build a model which will produce a rendering of a raag given certain parametric information as input. Detailed study of some rendering of well-known musicians was made and the starting strategy of the simulation model was reached. The raags chosen for simulation were Yaman, Marwa and Malkauns which are typical of the three jatis *viz.* Sampoorna, Shadav and Audav The model is capable of rendering any raag which satisfies the criterion that the 'Aaroha' and 'Avaroha' notes are the same. The rendering is sufficiently interesting and has several good features. The thesis gives the system diagram of the model. Printed output of the final experiments has been provided in the appendices of the thesis. One of the important concepts in designing the model was the automation of the mukhda as also creating an auto structure, which was supposed to give 'Raag-hood to the rendering.'[30]

The thesis makes a good survey of literature, which in it could be instructive to those who would want to take up research work in this area.

References

1. Indian Sculpture and Paintings, pp. 143-45.
2. Indian Dance, p. 20 (Rina Singha & Ragnd Mossey).
3. Arts and Crafts of India and Pakistan (Shanti Swarup).
4. Classical Indian Dance (Kapila Vatsyayan), pp. 3-73.
5. Mary VII, Sept. 1954, No. 4, pp. 14-15.
6. Arts and Crafts of India and Pakistan (Shanti Swarup), p. 24.
7. Historical Study of Indian Music, p. 326.
8. Raga and Ragini (O.C. Ganguly), p. 101.
9. Archaeology of Indian Musical Instruments, p. 19.
10. Musical Instruments in Indian Sculpture, pp. 23-24.
11. Indian Music, B.C. Deva, pp. 129-30.
12. Methodology in Indological Research, M. Srimannarayana Murti, p. 91.
13. The Manuscript is preserved in the Durbar Library at Kathmandu (CF. H.P. Sastri) Catalogue of palm-leaf and selected paper Mss. 1. Introduction of Cecil Bandall, p. 52. 140 and plate.
14. Music Research Perspectives and Prospects Reference Indian Music edited by R.C. Mehta, pp. 2-3.
15. On Music and Musicians of Hindustan, Ashok D. Ranade, pp. 25-26.
16. Srivastava, Sahab Lal, Folk Culture and Oral Tradition, Abhinav Publications, New Delhi, 1974, p. 9.
17. Vasina, Oral Tradition: A Study of Historical Methodology, Penguin University Books, 1973, p. (xiii).
18. Preminger, Alexander, S., Princeton Encyclopaedia of Poetry and Poetics, Princeton, 1974, p. 591.
19. Winternitz, M., A History of Indian Literature, University of Calcutta, 1962, p. 29.
20. Ancient Indian Education, Brahmanical and Buddhist, Motilal Banarsidass, New Delhi,1969, p. 211.
21. Understanding Indian Music, G.M. Joshi, p. 39.
22. Understanding Indian Classical Music, G.N. Joshi, p. 41.
23. Hindustani Music, Ashok Ranade, p. 103 (Gharanas and their Contribution) 104.
24. Hindustani Music, Ashok Da Ranade (Gharanas and their Contribution).
25. On Music and Musicians of Hindoostan pp. 36-37.
26. Bhatkandes Contributon to Music, Shobana Nayar, p. 341.
27. Media Communication and Development, S.C. Sharma (quoting Wilbur Sherama).
28. Preserving the Recorded Sound : 78RPM. Shri Suresh, S. Chandwankar, World of Gandharvas, (60 Musical years), p. 159.
29. Recorded Music Disciples Treasure (Smt. Asha Deodhar): World of Gandharvas, p. 175.
30. Music Research: Perspective and Prospects, Reference Indian Music, Computer Application to Music, Some Thrust Area (N.C. Khandekar) edited by R.C. Mehta, p. 79.

Appendix

INTERVIEWS

Smt. Gangubai Hangal interviewed by Dr. S.S. Gore

1. How do you think music has been affected by scientific advancement and inventions? Do you perceive any remarkable change in music, brought about by the advent of science?

Yes. I do perceive a marked change. Let me explain. It was the gramophone, which was responsible for my turning to Indian Classical Music. When I was a child, every tea stall and pan shop round the corner used to play gramophone records. They were exclusively of classical music. This atmosphere, knowingly or unknowingly, might have shaped by childhood tastes.

The gramophone company used to organizer's 'gatherings' of artists at Bombay, for the purpose of collecting recordings. My first recording was made in 1932 and I first sang for the radio in 1936. There were only two radio stations in those days, but people were very keen listeners. The periodical 'Radio listener' was avidly studied programmes of one's choice were marked and enthusiastic discussions followed the broadcasts. This is how one-stepped into the limelight.

But the radio imposed the time confines upon music. A raga recital had to be accommodated in a three and half minute record. A radio broadcast would hardly be of some 20 minutes duration and it was so different to sing inside a closed studio with none but the microphone and the accompanying artists to applaud one's efforts. Devoid of the appreciative audience half an hour would seem like hours. This had an adverse effect one one's raga exposition. The artificial time restriction soon developed into a built in short coming in the artist's rendering of a raga.

2. Would you explain how the nature of the music concert changed in the course of time?

My earliest memories are of private concerts 'baithaki' arranged as a part of a some domestic celebrations such as a wedding, a naming ceremony and so on. The news was conveyed by word of mouth and a few listeners would come together.

In Dharwad I heard Abdul Karim Khan, Sundarabai and Hirabai singing in the jalsa, a more formal type of concert than the baithak which would be organised by a small group of well to do music lovers. I heard most of these concerts standing outside the auditorium as the hall used to be packed with invitees the prestigious guests of honour. I used to take a peek and see how the musician appeared in real life. This interest on part of the listeners also seems to have waned today, may be as a result of the 'tapes'. Friends jokingly comment "Gangubai, we have you in our drawing rooms under lock and key and we'll hear you at our own convenience".

I don't think the TV has done much for the spread of music. Faiyyaz Khan used to sing the 'thumri, and then the 'tappa'. 'Natyasangeet' came at a much later stage. Natyasangeet came at a much later stage. But not so with a present day music concert it consists of 'thumri', 'dadra', tarana' and 'bhajans' besides the classical music proper. In fact a present day audience cannot conceive of a music concert without the inclusion of these forms.

The music conferences (sangeet sammelan) of olden days were also quite different. Performances at the music conferences were a hall-mark of all that was novel and significant in the field of music. The modern conferences have become impersonal and artists appear to be quite indifferent to audience response as well as to their own performance. The same impersonality and lack of support with audience is also evident in the present day concerts. The singer who sits on a stage has little or no connection with the large crowds packed inside a dark auditorium.

The financial factor was not so crucial in my times. The standard rates in Hubli were Rs. 25 for a concert. Then people started coming from Bombay with offers of Rs. 125. How could an artist demand for more'? I felt, 'when organizers have already offered so much! This reaction is strikingly different from that of a contemporary artist who, once he has reached the heights of fame, can strike and bargain at whatever rates he fancies for.

The conventional 'baithak' used to be a lengthy affair involving the minimum of 4 to 5 singing hours. A single artist at a conference use to get one whole evening reserved for him. Sometimes one had to make a number of appearances at a single music conference. At present four artists render their musical skills within five hours. How is an artist likely to find true self-expression in these so-called musical events?

3. **Do you think that wider exposure to music has lead to a breakdown of the traditional 'gharanas discipline'? if yes, how far do you welcome this change?**

I see nothing wrong in the wider exposure to music. We used to listen to students from other gharanas. My guru never discouraged it. By listening to others one can improve and develop one's own music. But more mechanical imitation at the cost of one's own discipline is objectionable. Take the modern practice of singing notations or 'sargam', it is a device invented for playing to the gallery. There is nothing wrong in notation basically, for the whole structure of music depends upon it. But it is a mistake to equate 'sargam' with music. People employ the device, for it facilitates toying with the 'tala' and audiences applaud such exercises. But this has sacrificed an important aspect of music I mean the tan.

The 'sargam' is a recent phenomenon introduced in the last 40 years or so. It is true that Khansahib Abdul Karim Khan used it; but it was used in the last phase of his career and that too for the purpose of recordings. He was impressed by Karnatic music, during one of his visits to Madras and accepted some of its features. But he never used the 'sargam' in excess. Those who sing it for fashion often commit a technical blunder for fashion often commit a technical blunder. For instance, while passing from, sa to ga they do touch the rishabha note. But they neither pronounce it, nor do they express it through gamak.

Running for the search for novelty is not really imperative I remember Ustad Abdul Karim Khan telling Raghunathrao Limaye that he would render nothing but raga 'Puriya' for one whole month and he claimed the listener would never find it monotonous. I do not deny that a musician has to make some compromises for the sake of his listeners. I myself at the beginning of my career sang every form of semi classical music, except the 'gazal'. Now a days I sing only classical. But then, I sometimes do sing the raga of my listeners choice.

4. **What are your views regarding the changing pattern of relationship between the Guru and his disciple? What do you think about the contribution of music institutions?**

The gurukul system, according to me, is the only true method of music education. I have absolute faith in it. In my time there were no music schools and no university examinations in music. I had to depend exclusively upon the guru. He taught me only three ragas. 'Todi', 'Multani' and 'Puriya' to be sung in the morning, afternoon and evening respectively. These three were the only ragas I practiced during the riyaz. Others I picked up on my own. Guruji encouraged no questions. We were simply told to follow all his instructions. The kind of devotion one had for the guru has now become a thing of the past. The modern students do have respect for the guru, no doubt; but it cannot be compared to our brand of devotion. Availability of recorded music has possibly contributed to this situation. We found ourselves exceptionally fortunate in finding a good teacher. Nowadays the guru considers himself lucky if the comes across a deserving disciple. We never dared to suggest that the guru put in a word to recommend his disciples. The present day gurus on the other hand, are often seen pleading with organisers for a programme for one of their disciples. Music students these days, quickly come into the limelight and soon pass into oblivion. They do not receive proper training and guidance, it may be. Or perhaps they are too busy with the modern struggle for survival or preoccupied with their school education and so on.

Music at me institutional level has rarely produced great artists. There are so many of them taking lessons at the same time that a teacher cannot give any individual attention. They rarely come to realise the value of 'riyaz'. They pick up a greater amount of theory and turn into scholars, appear for exams and get degrees. In the process, they forget all about music as an art. I remember singing raga Suha at pt. Ratanjankar's Music college in Lucknow. The students started whispering amongst themselves when I began to sing. Later I was told by Mohanrao Kalyanpurkar that the students had been discussing whether my raga was Suha, Sugrai or whether it was Juhasugrai. Those children were knowledgeable but I wondered how much sheer joy they gained from music I expressed my anxiety to Ratanjankar and asked him how these students could possibly become great artists. He answered that his aim was to produce discerning listeners ***kansens***—and this target he was sure to realize. I believe that everybody can always find time, provided one has the sufficient, motivation. The modern students have other preoccupations besides music, as I said earlier that there is also the financial aspect involved in one's choice of a vocation in life.

5. How far do you think technological advancement can contribute to the education of music?

Music is not something one learns from books. The other media, I honestly feel, are nothing but obstacles in the path of music education. You see, there is no alternative for the guru. Every aspiring musician has to, first and foremost, discover his own limitations. The guru guides a student taking into account factors such as his temperament, his self confidence and the type of voice which the student has. Faithful limitations of the guru help the disciple to become a musician. Becoming an artist requires something more — it is one's own contribution to the knowledge one has acquired from the gurus. But in this process too, I believe, the guru can be of very great help. Learning from more than one guru, according to me, does not increase the disciple's insight into music. Finding the right guru is the luckiest things that can happen to a student. The radio I think is the best educational medium, so far as music is concerned. Live programmes are fertile sources of creative inspiration pre-recorded cassettes are useful only if the student aims at limitation of specific styles or nuances.

When we the aged artists come together, our conversation often leads to the younger generation which suffers from the lack of from training/ practice (talim) as well as from in depth study. We feel anxiety for their future and for the future of our music. Then I'm reminded of a proverb in Kannada. 'The cradle swings from one extreme to the other. But it always passes the centre and that is where it comes to rest, once the oscillations are over". This is also the case with progress. Your technological advances will move the world of music from one extreme to another until a balance is struck. Some time or the other, you are sure to find 'the golden means', a perfect balance, in future.

Smt. Gangubai Hangal — Senior most Vocalist of Kirana tradition student of Sawai Gandharava.

Dr. S. S. Gore, M.D. — (General Medicine) consulting Physician presently President Hubli Art circle, Hubli.

Dr. Smt. N.Rajam
interviewed by Shri Kumar Paramanand

1. **Our first question relates to scientific innovations. How do you look at it? Are these useful.**

Look, the scientific innovations are just marvelous, there can't be two opinions about it. For example we have direct communications with persons in any quarter of world. We can reach any part of world in hours. It is only possible because of science. All these things are useful.

2. What about music?

Oh. Your tape recorder is the best example. A very useful thing the recorder, particularly for music students. Agreed, that it cannot replace the guru; but after all we can put it to its proper use. One cannot remember all the details while taking lessons. Here it can be put to best use. In olden days barring a few things, students or listeners just could not remember many a detail. Now it is possible. We can, by repeatedly listening, recollect and understand all relevant details. One can even listen to one's own performances for improvements. It allows us to understand others' styles in detail.

3. What about its utility in education?

Imagine you are taking lesson from a guru. If you record the lesson itself and repeatedly listen to it at home, would not that help you? Now out life to day is fast, time is short and hence this process is the best one to enlighten students. Listening to music has to play a great role in a student's education. The more music you hear the better chance you have to improve. Records are meant for such use. You can have lots of music and various formats. Artists and styles you love can be listened to and that too whenever you find the time for it. Scientific gadgets are useful in education, certainly. The University Grants Commission has been using the TV medium for lessons in a big way.

4. How can this be used in institutions?

To me, institutions have greater responsibility to take advantage of such facilities. They can develop libraries comprising of various artists, different gharanas, music of earlier periods, that of contemporary musicians and so on. By adopting the process mentioned earlier students, can be better enlightened. An institution can introduce listening sessions, offer listening facilities and make students listen to a lot during their training periods. By this method we can solve many problems we face today. We do not know how musicians of earlier periods performed, what were the styles, what are the changes that took place since then etc. By collecting and preserving music available now, we can make it possible for future generations to study, assess and compare the music of this day. Looking in broader terms, posterity can have glimpses of our cultural richness.

Dr. Smt. N. Rajam — A violinist enjoying top ranking status is popular in field. Trained under the training of great Pandit Omkar Nath Thakur. She is a Professor at Banaras Hindu University's Music Department.

Sh. Kumar Paramanand — A young and energetic musician. He has received intensive training from Kumar Gandharava.

Dr. Prem Lata Sharma
interviewed by Smt. Kalyani Inamdar

1. What are your views regarding the availability of advanced scientific gadgets? Do you think they are useful in music education? If yes, please explain how they can be best utilized.

The main contribution of science has been in the preservation of sound. It did not seem possible a century ago. Gramophone records were the first steps taken around 1880 and then the 1950s we have had tape recorders. Music can be preserved and replayed now. Then there is the large-scale spread of music through radio broadcasts and the visual aspect of it conserved and relayed at will, through the medium of the television. Of course much depends on how wisely and discerningly we utilize the gadgets made available by science. I don't feel any blame can be attached to scientific progress, in itself.

Personally I think we have not yet explored their potentials fully. Your second question relates to music education. There, recording equipment has two man uses. First of all a student can record his live sessions with the guru and by repeatedly listening to it try to understand his own shortcomings. This way he can improve upon his performance. Secondly, he can evolve his own collection and by listening to it, develop his own consciousness of music. I don't think anyone in our country has seriously employed recording facility to perform these functions. The only exception, as far as I know, is the Sangeet Research Academy, Calcutta.

2. Do you think scientific technology can help an artist's own development in any way? How would it affect an artist, say a vocalist, with a small voice?

A microphone would surely be an asset in enlarging a small singing voice. The reach of voice used to be an important consideration in the pre-microphone era. The person with a small voice used to pay great attention to the cultivation of voice and to its employed in music. He simply had no alternative. Now microphone have totally changed our conception of voice culture. A present day signer does not have to worry about teaching an audience of one thousand or one hundred. No matter if he can hardly make himself audible to the audience of a dozen listeners. The microphone takes care that his voice reaches anywhere and everywhere. I won't say this is either good or bad. This is merely a statement of facts. But I repeatedly say that the microphone should not be used indiscriminately. We often indulge in excessive use of loud speakers, even when there is a small auditorium and the microphone is not really required.

I have also said that music recording should serve as an aid to human memory. It can never substitute the human brain itself. Making things by heart was much emphasised in the pre-recording days. Now things can be stored on tapes; but again not excessively. The human memory needs to be exercised as well. Taxing the memory does not harm our intellectual faculty. On the other hand, such exercise helps to sharpen it. There is yet another way in which science has brought about change in the education of music. Before the revolution in communication technology took place, teachers used to guard their disciples from 'outside' influences. Exposures to other musical influences were strictly prohibited. Such a taboo can no longer exist today, for a student inevitably listens to a lot of recorded music, belonging to different musical styles and gharanas. This is once again an area where I restrain myself from making any value judgements. How far one should maintain the rigid discipline of a gharana is a question involving a choice of values. It could be argued that too rigid an adherence to tradition might hamper the progress of music. I do agree that a 'school' of music in the sense of being a steady evolution of music through a series of teacher and disciples — Guru shishya parampara contributes positively. A restrictive framework, on the other hand, would have a negative effect on the development of music. One way or the other, no one can deny that intermixing of musical styled, a free interchange of aesthetic principles is the trend of the day. Nothing that we can do can alter this trend. We should take into account this phenomenon as a fact of our contemporary reality.

3. What are your ideas about its most effective use to the students and the future generation?

I have already said that we should begin by drawing a firm line between the uses and abuses of scientific technology. Recording should be used sparingly in music education and as an aid to memory. It provided ideal material for analytical discussions. If used indiscreetly, recording would only result in mass production, which fails to serve any purpose. Take the example of printing. A book in ancient days existed in manuscript form and was a very rare and precious possession. Professional scribes inadvertently altered a few words here and there when they copied it out manually. These minute changes caused great debates and discussions. So keenly did people think about every word which was written down in books. Then printing was invented and the text could be mass produced. This has diminished the value of books so far as the average reader is concerned and since the explosion of communication media further mechanisation has set in. This mechanisation of life is causing great concern in many foreign societies and clubs have sprung up with the sole aim of saving children from mass media, such as the Television. The mass media have levelled down all individuality in the past. These regional flavours are being lost, day by day. The same is reflected in the field of music.

4. How can music be preserved to enhance the culture of the country?

The best enhancement of culture would result from the creation of live preservers of culture. Music cannot live merely through the preservation of recordings. The music of maestro will survive only if he can produce in his lifetime, a few disciples each of whom is capable of producing a few more. Culture is not something that thrives on machines, if you think you has saved culture by simply recording music, you are surely mistaken. Your recorded music will only be useful to a researcher and this has some value surely, but it cannot amount to the enhancement of culture. Many institutions along with the Sangeet Natak Academy have emphasised this documentation aspect of sound preservation, particularly since the Indian independence. But they have not been able to preserve culture. On the other hand, culture is on the decline. Recorded music, microphones and the disco have reached out villages today and people have forgotten their native musical traditions. The rapid spread to TV as resulted in further erosion of their living cultural practices. We are much too insensitive to view the phenomenon in the proper perspective and our bureaucratic superiors are no better. On the institutional level we sometimes are on the right track when fellowships are awarded to students to learn from a guru, who is the last survivor of a musical tradition. To put it in a nutshell, preservation of culture requires great conscientiousness, sensitivity and methodical planning. We would go a long way by cultivation of these qualities. But the way things stand at present, we are doing great harm to the cause. It seems as if we were set on destruction.

Dr. Prem Lata Sharma — Educationalist, ex-Vice Chancellor, Khairagarh University.

Smt. Kalyani Inamdar — Novelist, poetess and music critic.

Dialogue
Shri Hari Sahastrabuddhe and Smt.Veena Sahastrabuddhe

1. **Can you give us a detailed idea of the material you have collected?**

I have collected Veena's concerts. There are approximately 120, C-90 tapes at the date of this recording which is August, 1992.

2. **In what manner did you accomplish the task of your collection? How long did it take you to go about it? And what were the means you adopted to fulfill it?**

Well, I have been using an independent recording machinery, separate from the public address system, mostly, in the recordings that have made myself. At other concerts I have taken the help of either the public address manager or individual recordists who was doing it other than myself.

3. **What is the method of presentation of the collection that you possess?**

It is on C-90 cassettes mostly. Some are on C-60s.

4. **Did you face any difficulties in this project? If so, what are they? And how you eliminate them?**

No difficulties whatsoever.

5. **What according to you, is the use or utility of this collection?**

Veena's students already use it in order to prepare for their concerts, whenever they want to sing a particular raga, they can take that raga from the collection and hear it.

6. **What are the special efforts that you put into make this collection possible?**

Oh. I collected the equipment, imported some, I carry four bags of equipment to the concerts which I record myself. And there is nothing I expect a medal for.

7. **Did you use any specific machines or tapes? What special precautionary measures did you adopt?**

I have been using TDK and Sony C-90 tapes in the past I have now switched over Meltrack C-60s. I use my Sony FX 210 whenever I record or when a friend records whatever machine he is doing it on. I generally record with Dolby, as this particular recording is done for example. That can make the recordings more versatile. It can be heard on more machine that way.

8. What advice would you give to those who are beginning or already have began their own collection?

Most important, maintain a catalogue from the first day of your collection. Later you will find it much harder to catalogue what you have got. So do it from the beginning.

Artists and Disciples

9. How do you view the new scientific advancement and its availability? Do you in your opinion consider it useful? If so why? Is the availability of scientific technology useful in the education and training of students of art? Does it help in widening the span of an artist? If yes, in what manner?

Let us consider two inventions in sequence. First is the microphone. With the microphone the demand on the tongue power of a singer is reduced tremendously and therefore, one can become more expressive in one's singing. Consider a similar effect produced by the video camera. Without the help of such a device, audience sitting at a distance from the stage can only see the gross movements of hands and legs and therefore one's acting has to depend on gross movements of the body. Facial expressions have little significance! But once you have a video camera pointed at your face, even the slightest twitch of a facial muscle is seen by all your spectators, and therefore, acting can become more subtle, more expressive, more far fetching. The microphone does the same to the human voice and to the sound of many of the acoustic instruments that Indian music uses. The second very important invention is the magnetic tape for recording sound with the help of a tape recorder and player, you can listen to your own singing, you can listen to the singing of others, you can listen to many more artists than you could possibly in person; you can hear every line of a passage in music again and again, if you wish to. These opportunities are just not there without a tape.

Veena, S. : I think there are two basic uses of the tape recorder. First, for absorbing the style of an artist by hearing him or her a lot. Second, for learning bandishes. Before you can do that, you must learn the fundamentals of music and understand the styles of the artist whose tapes you are learning from. I have used LP records and tapes extensively since 1968.

10. What are your ideas regarding its most effective use to the students and the future generation?

Hari, S. : I believe that every educational course in music must include a significant part of listening. Therefore, in institutions which teach music there must be listening booths where there are tape recorders, players and head phones, where the student can listen to what he or she wants to, without disturbing others.

Veena, S. : I ask my students to record the lessons, I give them, together with all my commentary over and over again at home. This reduces the number of sessions required and makes the students more aware of the subtilities.

Connoisseurs

1. What are your specific interests? Vocal, instrumental or any specific personalities?

Reasons

Hari, S. : Well, I get to hear a lot of Veena's singing for obvious reasons. But I tend to hear virtually any vocal that is available within the limitations. I used to hear a lot of instrumental music. My interest in it has waned out during the years.

Veena, S. : Basically, I like to hear any classical music, vocal or instrumental if it is good. I am not partial to any gharana. I hear them all.

2. Has your interest helped percolation in your future generation?

Hari, S. : Well, both our children share our music but do not share our preference for Hindustani classical music.

Veena, S. : I think, because of me, my children have seen how a musician conducts herself in life.

3. Do you see change in taste over the times? And can you specify reasons?

Hari, S. : The pace of life has changed. As a result people are beginning to prefer shorter concerts. People are beginning to insist on concerts at pre-specified times, no delayed according to the whims of whosoever. People are beginning to demand more and more recorded music they can purchase. The reasons are obvious.

Veena, S. : I think, today's audience have wider exposure to music. In the older days people may have spent many hours listening to music, but they only heard the artists who gave concerts in their city. Today one can hear artists from all over the world singing in divert styles. Therefore I believe that the musical world of a listener so much richer today.

Smt.Veena Sahastrabuddhe : Performing vocalist, Former H.O.D. of Music, S.N.D.T., Pune.

Shri Hari Sahastrabuddhe : Computer Engineer, H.O.D. of Computer, Pune University.

Shri Ulhas Baspat
interviewed by Smt. Shruti Sadolikar-Katkar

Pandit Ulhas Baspat is an accomplished santoor player who also had sound training in vocal music as well as the tabla.

1. How and when did you come in contact with classical Hindustani music?

Although my father, Y. G. Baspat was a police officer, he had been trained in vocal music. He used to sign 'different ragas' and compositions in leisure hours. That influenced and interested me.

2. You also had very sound training in tabla. When and how long did you learn? Do you play any other instruments?

As I told you vocal music did interest me but it was the tabla that fascinated me from my earliest days. It took me some years to actually start learning it. But I did at the age of 5-6 years. I was trained by Pt. Ramakant Mahapsekar to play solo tabla. At the same time I played on the butbul tarang as a toy. That gave me the feel for the key board which made it easy for me to learn repeating harmonium. I had also started to play the violin seriously. But at one point I came across a discussion about certain instruments and their famous players, wherein I discovered that not a single artist besides Pt. Shivakumar Sharma performed on the santoor, at that time. This triggered of my curiously I had listened to Pt. Sharma, way back in 1964-65 where he had played raga Kalawati. I had also liked his playing but after reading about this piece of information I became really keen to know more about santoor.

3. How did you learn to play the instrument? Was it the method of tuning it or was it practicing the use of sticks?

As Pandit Sharma was the only player of santoor, there wasn't any music class where I could get to learn it. The day I got my first santoor horne, I spent all my working hours getting to know all about the instrument. I studied in depth, how it was made how it could be tuned and how to use the sticks and thus learnt to play it quite on my own.

4. How did you learn to tune the santoor in all the twelve notes?

I had seen people use the swaramandal in vocal concerts. It was known that the swaramandal has to be tuned in the notes employed in the raga to be sung. Similarly the strings of the santoor. I assumed would be tuned according to the notes of the raga to be played. I wondered why the bridges on both sides of the instrument were not used fully and started tuning my santoor right from the first day, in all the twelve notes. It is called 'Chromatic tuning' fixed tuning. I developed my own style of playing after a lot of reflection.

5. How did you learn the technique of instrumental music?

Smt. Zarine Sharma the Sarod player tought me the 'tantakari', 'ang', 'alap', 'jod' 'zala' and other aspects of instrumental recital.

6. Do you think your training in tabla helped you?

Yes, it very much did help me and I honestly believe that every performing artist ought to have a fair amount of knowledge of 'laya' and 'tala'.

7. Both. Pt. Ginde and Pt. Sadolikar belong to different gharanas, namely Agra and Jaipur. How do you reconcile both?

The Jaipur style of singing is dominated by undercurrents of laya. It is 'talpradhan'. It is this aspect that helped me to assimilate it with style of playing . I am very comfortable with this style of alap and tan. Pt. Ginde explains the raga with especial attention to the balance between musical phrases and combinations of notes and their aesthetic appeal. This has widened my knowledge of ragas.

8. Have you tried to overcome any other invitations of the instrument by some other means?

Yes, producing 'meend' was practically impossible on this instrument. I gave a lot of though to this serious limitation and invented a method peculiar in its own way, by designing my sticks differently. I have the legal patent for it with this technique. I can play 'meend' on any note that is available on the 'santoor'. It is very scientific and reliable method. Rest all depends on the capability of the player. I employed this technique immediately.

9. Did you face any criticism for trying the 'meend' on this instrument?

My audience has never failed to appreciate my 'meend'. Many contemporaries find it difficult to digest the fact.

10. Does the meend help you play ragas like Marwa, Todi better?

Yes specially the degree of flatness (Komal, ati komal) can easily be played without losing the character of the note.

11. What do you think of the Western notation methods?

As far as notating the minute details of a composition is concerned, I can say that it is the most correct method. But one must understand that western music is played by many instrumentálists at a time and if the notation is not accurate to the last detail, it would create chaos. Our music is 'one person music'. It is highly individualistic, giving more importance to individual improvisations. Hence in our music a very accurate notation method does not play a role as important role as it does in western music. If I am given a certain piece in staff notation I can easily play it.

12. Do you use chords in your performances?

Just as you use the balance between the vadi and the samvadi notes of the raga there are certain other combinations of notes which add to the beauty of the raga. My knowledge of the chores helps me to use such combinations in my performances.

13. Have you composed music?

I did compose music for two ballets in Bharat natya mandir 'Swapna-shilpi' and 'Snehasarita', where I used all Indian instruments.

14. Your career is almost self-made. Do you have any disciples who can play the way you do?

As of today I have not come across any one who will put in enough hard work and meet my satisfaction. To add to this there are many misunderstandings about this instrument such as, santoor is very easy to play; even a mouse running across it will give your music and so on. I am of the opinion that every instrument has its limitations and so to play it, one has to put in a lot of effort and he devoted to it. People lack the patience and music cannot become instant music.

15. You manufacture your own instruments, I heard.

Yes. Because the santoor available in the market do not meet my requirements, I have made three Kashmiri santoors and one Irani santoor (after studying a photograph of that instrument). I also have a Chinese santoor.

Sh. Ulhas Baspot — Upcoming santoor player

Smt. Shruti Sadolikar Katkar — Bombay Vocalist of Jaipur tradition, groomed by her father and Smt, Gullu Bai, Visiting Professor of Music in Netherland.

Pt. Bhimsen Joshi
interviewed by Dr. Shrirang Sangoram

1. Panditji, what, in your opinion are the plus and minus points in the old Guru-shishya (teacher-disciple) system in music?

To my opinion there are no minus points or drawbacks at all in the guru shishya system, if of course it is handled ideally. In fact this system has proved to be the most fruitful in grooming the disciple as a successful performing artist. In the first place it inculcates faith and modesty in the trainee.

2. But it is often observed that in this old system theoretical knowledge in the formal structure of music is not given much importance. Most of the emphasis is laid upon the imitation of the Guru.

No, it really depends upon the disposition of the guru. My guru Pandit Sawai Gandharva did not like blind following only. He was of the opinion that the shishya should add his own ideas and imagination to whatever he gets from the guru and should develop his own style. Now about the theoretical knowledge or the grammatical aspect I would say that the essential elements of this are sufficient in the 'Guru shishya' system. Because if the shishya devotes much of his time to the theory only, it will affect his excellence in his performance. Hence much more importance is given to the practical side. It has happened that sweet voiced music students having indulged in the scientific details of the music to the utmost, have failed to achieve the ideal height in the musical performance. On the contrary some of those whose voice is not that sweet and melodious could earnquite a name as a performing artist, just on the basis of unmatched riyaz (i.e. practise) and sell polishing. I may say that some of our inborn sweet voiced singers unfortunately become a prey to their conceit and pride. In short, we can say that as far as the performance aspect is concerned, there is nothing to beat the guru shishya system.

3. What are the limitations of the institutional training in music?

This question of yours is the counterpart of the former one. It is clear that in this system grooming of a student as an excellent performer is hardly possible. Limited time and fixed time table is its special feature. Let me tell you about one of the great personalities in our music Dr. S.N. Ratanjankar, Principal, Morris (now Bhatkhande) College of music, Lucknow. Many performing artists got training under him. He would engage his classes in the college, but for special students he used to give training after the office hours, for which there was no pressure of time limit.

4. It is claimed that the current usage of cassettes, records, etc. has helped to minimise the lengthy procedure in the Guru shishya system. Your reactions?

I do not believe in such indirect short cuts. The recorded music cannot take place of the direct training. One must exert. Perseverance is a must in music. We fail to realise the gravity of effortless achievements and run after the momentary impressions of the recorded music.

5. How in your opinion, the modern aids of music listening (like gramophone records, cassettes, video recorders) have affected the process of music learning?

The music learners, nowadays are after quick success. They all along are after momentary novelty. The guardians of the sprouting music learners are anxious to see that their sons/daughters should since on T.V. Now, here, I can agree that these new media do help in enriching the musical experiences of the common listeners.

6. But in the current age, the records, cassettes etc. have become quite inevitable.

Yes. I agree. But as far as the music learners are concerned the significance of the recorded music is valid only after the learner is well groomed in a particular musical system or school (which we call as gayaki) and has achieved a particular level in the practice of the melodic tunes or swara.

At this level the learner can take help of the tape recording machine for his personal study or sadhana, in the old days the ustads or guru would always preach that you should devote yourself to continuous practice, but they would not tell as to which lessons are to be practiced. Even the clear words in a song or bandish were not clearly taught. And the disciple was not in a position to get his doubts cleared.

7. Do you think it was ideal?

Not at all. But the teachers or gurus would always come across such students who would leave the learning within six months period. Hence the guru used to examine the student's urge for learning and then only he would accept him in his personal folds. The old teaches always had a hard and taskful examination of the learners and then only they used to teach the deep structure in singing or instrument playing.

8. How far has the radio affected the overall styles in the presentation of khayal etc.?

The first thing which the radio programmes have introduced is the time sense in presenting a khyal. My experience tells me that a period of 40 minutes is quite optimum for the comprehensive artistic presentation of a khyal. I can say that the radio has indirectly trained the artists to given an enriched musical experience to the listeners even in a short period of the ten minutes. Look at the old 78 rpm records. What a crystalline experience they render just in thee to three and half minutes. Here I am reminded of 5 minutes duration records of my Grand Guru Ustad Khan Sahib Abdul Karim. What a complete feeling those records give!

9. What is your opinion about introducing listening periods in the music training centres and music colleges?

Doubtlessly it is a useful innovation in the pedagogy of music. Suppose if the students carefully listen to 100 cassettes of one raga, say Yaman, certainly they will get a wider perspective of that raga. But let me be clear that the cassettes will never be a substitute to the live training given by a Guru.

Pt. Bhimsen Joshi — Senior vocalist of Kirana tradition, Student of Sawai Gandharva.

Sh. Srirang Sangaram — Professor of Hindi, music critic and keen follower of musical world activities.

ARTICLES

Inscriptions on Music in Tamilnadu

By Gowri Kuppuswamy & M. Hariharan

Authentic chronicled history of India begins with the rule of Mauryan dynasty in the north and of the Cheras, Pandyas, and Cholas in the South. There is no gainsaying the fact that royal interest in literature and the fine arts including music was evident even at the time of the Mauryas (325-188 B.C.) and continued during the reign of the Sunga dynasty (188-76 B.C.) and the Kanva Dynasty (76-31 B.C.). However, sustained encouragement and patronage to music can be said to have commenced only with the rulers of the 'Gupta' dynasty. Chandra Gupta (320-330 A.D.) and Chandragupta II (374-413 A.D.) deserve particular mention in this context. The latter was better known as Vikramaditya and it was in his court that renowned poets like Kalidasa and Ashvagosha flourished. The Pallava rulers of Kanchi, Mahendravaranami and Narasimha Varaman (7th cent.) were also great patrons of music and dance. The former's name is associated with the famous Kudumiyamalai inscription (600-625 A.D.) concerned with the evolution of musical notation. In the list of illustrious Tamil monarchs whose deeds have illuminated the pages of India's musical history, there are few that have better earned a niche in the temple of fame and a place in the hearts of their country men through their contribution to art than Mahendravaraaman, I, the accomplished musician and musicologist. His inscription stands as a fitting monument to his attainments in the field of musicology wherein he has portrayed, in a characteristic manner, the notation of music as was neither current in his time or was invented by him.

To reveal the art history of music further, art forms like inscription, painting, sculptures, frescos etc. are being consulted during the last few decades. In this paper we shall attempt to bring to light some of the inscriptions found in Tamil Nadu and a few in the adjoining states, with themes relating to music and musicians. Many Chola kings whose reign extended over the 11th and 12th centuries encouraged and nourished musicians and other artistes in diverse ways including munificent gifts of land (in some case even whole villages) as evident from numerous inscriptions and edicts ascribed to this period. Musicians were greatly encouraged and music itself was given a very important place in the life of the people, especially in the field of devotional music. The rulers were themselves knowledgeable patrons and were able to enjoy and appreciate good music. The music of those days was, however, different from the music, as we know it today. Though they were not conversant with the Raga system, music has evolved continuously from the sangam age down to the present and this progressive evolution was definitely encouraged by the Cholas. It is obvious that during the chola period music must have been a harmonious synthesis of song, dance and drama. It is also clear that there was a large body of literature on music, both theoretical and practical with which the patrons were familiar in those times.

The music was one of the fine arts, which flourished under the generous, and discerning patronage of the Cholas is also proved by the data provided by several inscriptions of this period. Some refer to the singing of Tiruppadiyam in temple set to tune; some others mention musicians, instrumental accompanists and types of musical instruments. There is, however, no direct evidence about manner in which the science of music was practiced or the type of music in vogue then. But considerable research in this direction has been mooted. As will be obvious from the inscriptions, rulers of the Chola reign made several endowments for the regular recital of the Tiruppadiyam in temples and public places. Rajaraja I endowed land for fifty persons called "pidarara", forty eight of whom were to sing, one to accompany in Udukkai and one on Maddatam daily in the Big temple at Tanjore. Another inscription of Rajaraja from Tindivanam refers to an endowment of land for the musicians playing on the Vina as well as singing of the Tindisvara temple at Kidangil. According to another inscription on the north wall of the Tyagarajaswami temple at Tiruvarur ascribed to Rajaraja I, music was to be provide during the time of Sribali services by seven persons three of them on maddalam, one on patakam and one on sekandigai.

The epithets Torukkaruvi, Turaikkaruvi, Narambukkaruvi and Kanchakkaruvi. There were also sufficient inscriptions to confirm the presumption that music recitals were solo, vocal and instrumental, the forty eight 'pidarars' of big temple already referred to as beneficiaries of Rajaraja I could not have sung the tunes individually. It is probable that there were musicians attached to the palaces and they gave recitals for the delectation of the king. From the inscriptions at palur, Tirvavaduturai, Andanallur and Virddhachalam it is apparent that music culture was widely prevalent. It is interesting to note that the gifts of Rajaraja I came largely from the booty captured in victories on the battlefield and included well over 41500 kalanjus of gold, 50650 kalanjus of silver etc. About 180k kalanjus of paddy a year were set apart to maintain 212 male musicians, drummers etc. They included three persons to sing ariyam and four others to sing the ahamargas and desi type of music. A choir of fifty on a daily wage of 3 kurunis of paddy was appointed to recite the Tiruppadiyam to the accompaniment of musical instruments. 48 singers consisting of Brahmins, Devadasis etc. were brought to the Tanjore temple from various other temples in 1014 A.D. during the 29th regnant year of Rajaraja I. Some other inscriptions refer to the endowments given by this monarch.

Regarding Rajaraja III, there is an inscription of Tiruvottiyur during his 10th regnant year, which refers to the king listening to music recital on the 8th day of the Avani Tirunal Festival. His consort Puvanamulututaiyal was well accomplished and proficient in music. An inscription of this king during his 10th regnant year registers a Vinaikkani an endowment offered to one who played the Vina in the temple. It is interesting to learn from a source that the Tevaram songs of the first three Nayanmars were inscribed on copper plates through the efforts of Kalingarayan, the commander-in-chief of Kulottunga I. During his time the recital of hymns was considered a privilege and Kulottunga conferred this privilege on particular individuals. There were also musicians attached to the court called 'panars' who set hymns and songs to tunes and trained signers to render them. An inscription from Tiruvidaimarudur' describes panar called Thirmurti Cholan Piran alias Panappru singing in the local temple after receiving appropriate training. Like other employees musicians too were paid in kind and were also provided with living quarters.

Given below is a list of inscriptions relating to music found in Tamil Nadu and adjacent states.

Gift of land for reciting the Tiruppadiyam in the temple at brahmadesam, North Arcot District during the time of Rajaraja I alias Rajakesarivarman in his 16th year of reign (ARIE. 199 of 1915). Gift of land by the residents of nerkuppai alias Mudukunram on the northern bank of paravurkunram to the local temple of Mahadeva for reciting the Tiruppadiyaam hymns during the time of Rajaraja I in his 18th regnant year (ARIE.40 of 1918). The 11 verses of Tevaram sung by the saint Tirugnanasambandhar in praise of the sacred Vidaivei were engaged during the time of Rajakesarivarman alias Tribhuvanachakravarti Vikrama Choladeva at the Punyanathasvamin temple at Tiruvaveduturai, Nannilam Taluk (ARIE.8 of 1918).

An inscription of the time of Parantaka in his 25th year of reign in front of the central shrine at Siddhalingamandala mentions gift of land for providing music thrice a day during the time of worship in the temple of Vyagrapadaesvara (ARIE 387 of 1909). An inscription of the 5th regnant year of Rajaraja II on the south wall of the Mandapa in the Virattensvara temple at Valuvar, mentions gift of money for getting the Tiruvambavai recited before the deity during the Tiruvadirai festival, with an endowment of 30 Kaus (ARIE 421 of 1912). An inscription records that the king granted to certain individual the privilege of singing the Tiruppadiyam in the temple, besides a certain amount of land in his 2nd year of reign.

An inscriptions of the 10th year of the reign of Rajaraja I on the south wall of the central shrine in the Tintrinisvara temple at Tindivanam refers to the grant of 2910 kuli of land for a musician who was to play on the Vina and a vocalist who was accompany to him (ARIE 141 of 1900). An inscription during the 27th year of Rajendra refers to the gift of land by the residents of Arpakkam for the maintenance of seven musicians for services in the shrine of Thirumagaral Udaiya Nayanar on the belt round the local Adikesava Perumal temple (ARIE 145 of 1923). An inscription of the 25th year of the reign of parantakaa I, refers to the maintenance of pipers in the temple and records a purchase of 11 ma of land for this purpose (ARIE 126 of 1925). An inscription of the 13th year of the reign of Parakesarivarman, refers to a gift of land by Somban Arulan to 9 persons for beating drums in the temple of Tiruvelladai Mahadeva. (ARIE 434 of 1918). Another inscription of the 6th regnant near of Vikrama Chola on the south wall of the Mandapa in front of the central shrine in the Karkatesvara temple near Vepattur records a gift of land to a private individual for playing on the vina before the deity (ARIE 47 of 1910).

An Uttiramerur inscription records a grant of land for provision of music during Sribali at the temple of Uttiramerur. (SII Vol. in No. 194). Another inscription from the same place of 26th year of the reign of Rajaraja I records grant of land 2 persons for singing Tiruppadiyam in the temple at Tirunallam Udaiyar. Another inscription in the same temple refers to the daily allowance of paddy to forty eight persons appointed for reciting Tiruppadiyam in the temple and for two persons who were accompany them on drums one on Udukkal and one on Kottimaddalam (SII. Vol.II No.65). An inscription of Dharmasagar records the gift of two portions of land for musicians, instrumentalists, etc. Another inscription of Pillalemeri records the grant of nineteen houses in the fort of Pillalamari to the musicians and dancers.

By virtue of the simplicity of language and the tremendous enthusiasm by the kings who patronised musicians and music through various measures, the music of the Chola period had its unhindered continuance in the later times as well. Till the end of the Chola era, a single system of music was followed in the whole country with local variations it was only afterwards that the division into Carnatic and Hindustani music came into vogue. The Chola period was an age of renaissance in many ways. The rulers of the dynasty founded by Vijayalaya were all ardent followers of Saivism. They made music part and parcel of the daily life of the people and emphasised not only the spiritual and emotional but, even the educative aspects of this fine art.

Musical Instruments in Indian Plastic Art: Strings

By S.Krishnaswami

Though ancient literature, anthropological and ethnographical evidences provide fund of information on the role of musical instruments through the past centuries, much information could be obtained through the study of the great wealth of instruments depicted in ancient Indian sculptures and paintings for the proper appraisement of the magnitude of the contribution made by the Indian artists who have produced some of the greatest masterpieces of art on instrumental material from Bharhut, Bodhgaya, Sanchi, Mathura, Konarak, Kausambhi, Gandhara, Ajanata, Amaravati, Nagajunakonda, Ellora, Badami, Belur Halebid from the shore temples of Mahabalipuram to the mighty temples of Chidambaram, Kumbakonam, Bhubaneshwar, Madurai, Khajuraho, Srirangam, Rameshwaram, Suchindram, Trivandrum, from the wall paintings in the caves of Bagh and Ajanta to the temple paintings of Tanjavoor, which throw light on the various stages in the evolution, development and usage's of hundreds of varieties of instruments during different epochs of Indian history, thus preserving the cultural heritage of India. All these sculptures and paintings belong to the period between 2nd cent. B.C. to 17th cent. A.D. and their historical value is very great.

Incidentally it is worthy while to mention that in the north after the domination of the muslims, a new influences began to take effect in the art of India in music, architecture and painting. A number of mughul and rajasthani and many of the rag-ragini paintings contain musical instruments used during this period just as the sculptures paintings of ancient temples and monuments did earlier. Before introducing the subject, I would like to emphasize that

> "EVERY THING IS MORE ANCIENT THAN THE FIRST INSTANCE IN WHICH ONE NOTICES ITS EXISTENCE, AND EVERYTHING LASTS MUCH MORE THAN THE PERIOD AT WHICH IT SEEMS TO STOP".

The instruments, used by the modern classical musicians, the vina, sitar gottuvadhyam, surbahar etc. are very beautiful to look at for they are shining, slick and streamlined and ornamented with ivory and capable of producing the various nuances of the highly developed and complicated styles of Indian music. Yet they are descended from very primitive instruments used by our ancestors several centuries ago. The vina, venu and mridanga are the most important instruments representing the string wind and percussion variety and I now take up the vina which has a notable history in its evolution and development.

Early Beginnings

The first stringed instrument invented by men was surely the hunter's bow. As a hunter or an archer, when the primitive man shot his arrow, he must have noted that the bowstring produced a pleasant humming sound and he enjoyed the twangling of his bowstring. He later found that the sound was amplified and the resonance increased when he plucked the string near his mouth cavity or by resting the bow upon a hollow material. The development proceeds through different stages, during which the mouth serves as a sound amplifier, later replaced by a gourd or other hollow material, which evolved into the actual body of the instrument. The early man probably discovered that the sound varied with the length of the string of the bow. Different strings of varying lengths were tied round a hunting bow to produce different sounds. He also found out that a tightened string produced a sound higher in pitch than a slack one. This is the basic principle of the harp, the famous stringed instrument used universally by the ancient people all over the world. The principle of the ancient harp is that a series of strings tied parallel to one over the other and set in vibration by fingers or plectrum, each string produces one note.

The fact that a piece of string stretched over a hollow body such as a pot or a vessel produces a sound relatively great volume when caused to vibrate was known to . man very early. This principle was used to increase the volume of sound by fastening one end of a string to such a kind of resonator. Later he gave one end of the bow the shape of a hollow boat and stretched a skin tightly over it. Sever strings were merely tied round the bow shaft and they could be tuned by an elaborate process of unfastening and refastening. In modern times the tuning pegs have overcome this complicated process in many instruments.

Early Harps in Indian Plastic Art

According to experts, examples of Indian plastic art begin from the 3rd cent. B.C. After the invasion of Alexander the great (326 B.C.) the dynasty of Maurya was founded. The representations of historical art on permanent material are from this period. The first sculpture which have any musical figurations belong to these Sunga and Kanwa dynasties and these figurations constitute the most ancient documents of Indian musical instruments which seems to be already organised and enable us to have an idea on the role of music played, in those far off days. The artists of ancient India have made very interesting sculptural musical scenes in the Buddhist monuments of Bharhut, Bodhgaya, Amaravati and other places and we find several female musicians playing bow-shaped harp vinas, narrow waisted drums, twin drums, flutes etc. and the instruments are the same whether it is palace dance or celestial one.

Pitalkhora Caves

During recent excavations in the caves of Pitalkhora near Ajanta, we find examples of a few fragments of bow shaped harps most of them broken and mutilated and experts place the period between 2nd cent. B.C. and 3rd cent. A.D. The number of strings seems to be seven in all the samples.

Greco-Buddhist Period

As north western empire was dominated by Greek traditions, its Buddhism found expression through Greek forms and Greco-Buddhist art was born and started at the beginning of the modern era and had its full development from 1st Cent. A.D. at Gandhara (Peshawar). The music of Gandhar presents the same phenomenon in the plastic art in the bowshaped harp, twin drums, transverse flute etc., along with greek influence on the costumes of the characters, Indo-greeks of gandhara seem to have represented the same type of bow shaped harps, the difference being that all the musicians are males whereas the Sunga and Kanwa sculptures, the instruments are played by women.

Sanchi

Sanchi is famous for its stupas and is intimately connected with the life of emerpor Ashoka the great. The ground balustrade encompassing the great stupa has four gateways (Toranas) which are elaborately carved and are among the finest specimens of early Buddhist at enriched with bass-reliefs depicting Buddhist legends (Jatakas) and events of Ashoka's life. There are many musical scenes which include bow shaped harps in the Sanchi torana which are played by plucking with fingers and with plectrums in the carvings.

Bharhut

In Bharhut are the remains of a stupa built during the Sunga empire. The most important is a panel showing a dance — the dance of the Apsaras, the music of the gods delighting by sport and dance. There are four dancers accompanied by musicians with various instruments including bow shaped harp. There are examples of harps played with plectrum and by hooked fingers.

Bodhgaya

Bodhgaya belongs to the Sunga period. There are many representations of the bow shaped harps of the Bharhut type. The instrument is not played but is worn on the arm with the resonator leaning on the hip, the strings towards the exterior and the arm passing over the strings and holds the resonator on the hip. There are many example in Bodhgaya harps with seven strings are held either by man or woman.

Amaravati

Amaravati is about 26 km. From Guntur (Andhra Pradesh) containing historic monuments belonging to the pre-christian era it was built in the 2nd cent. B.C. The sculptures portray various scenes in the life of Buddha, Jataka stories etc. The whole period of Amaravati ranged between 2nd cent. B.C. to 4th cent. A.D. The ancient musical art seems to have attained culmination point of its first period in Amaravati. Musical life under the Andhras seems to continue the tradition of Gandhara. Here we find the instruments like the bow shaped harps of Bharhut, Sanchi, Mathura, Gandhara and all of them more developed. The handle of the harps are more elegant curved slightly towards the exterior. The plectrum or the kona of Amaravati is definitely longer than that of the Bharhut. The instruments are placed on the left side but the left arm holding the harp against the player while dampening the strings, the strings are plucked with plectrums held in the right hand.

Nagarjunakonda

Nagarjunakonda is another Buddhist centre like Amaravati containing number of examples of musical scenes. In one of the scenes the "Descent of Bodhi Satva', a man is seen holding a harp which is hung on the left side with a sling and the left hand dampens the strings. From the number of rings seen on the staff, it appears, there are 10 strings. The period belongs to 4th to 7th cent. A.D.

Kangra

In Kangra, in a pillar capital there is a representation of a figure holding a harp with about 10 strings. The left hand holds the harp on the top and the right hand fingers pluck the strings. This sculpture belongs to 8-9th cent. A.D. We find the long plectrum (Kona) used in Bharhut for instance. It appears, in playing the harps the long plectrum was a characteristic, and there are reasons to believe that the auxiliary bone (check bone) of a goat was used as plectrum. In the 1st centuries of our era, first in the north of India, then in the south, the bow shaped harp with plectrums is abundant. But it is the harp without plectrum that is continued. We notice that most of the harps played with plectrum has the handle roughly made with no decoration or thinning at the end but those which are played without plectrum have the handle more elegant, curving towards the exterior and not only slightly curved towards the interior.

Aurangabad Caves

The period of Aurangabad caves is placed between 2nd and 4th cent. A.D. In some of the caves we find musical instruments in sculptures. The most interesting instrument is a very large harp held by a woman standing. Though the carving is not very clear, it appears this large harp is hung crosswise on her shoulder and there is another small figure by the side holding the resonator part of the harp. The right hand of the player seems to pluck the strings while the left hand holds harp at the top. No strings are distinguishable.

Harp in Literature and Technique of Playing

In the story of Udayana, got from the Serpent King Vasuki in the Nagaloka a vina called Ghoshavathi whose name itself suggests that it must have had numerous strings? With it, udayana captivated not only the heart of Vasavadatta, but captivated wild elephants of the forest, as a princely past time.

Different Varieties of Harps

We find two varieties of harps in ancient Indian sculptures. In the first one, the boat-shaped resonator appears fixed under one end of the staff or the handle. In the second the handle is fixed in the boat-shaped resonator itself. The harps of ancient India belong to one or the other. In the first type, one end of the handle is attached to one of the resonators and lies over it; the other extremity of the handle can be clearly seen lying over the resonator. In the second type one end of the handle goes into the resonator, the strings are tied round the handle at different heights and are attached to the bottom at the back of the resonator. The resonator is covered with skin and pierced in many places for the strings to pass through. Sometimes the harp is placed in front and the strings are plucked with hooked fingers.

In the 2nd and 4th centuries A.D. at Nagarjunkonda in the south, we find the handle is definitely going into the resonator and forms a sort of stick or protrusion on the back on which the strings are fixed. In another type, the harp has ten strings and is played by a squatting woman, the instrument lying on the side. It is played with a plectrum (Kona) which means, instead of playing on the correct string, the plectrum sweeps on all the strings and the left hand of the player climates or dampens the strings, which are not to be sounded. In Bharhut (2nd cent. B.C.) The harp played with kona and that plucked with fingers co-exist. Another example comes from Nagarjunakonda where the harp is not leaning on the thigh of the performer. The resonator is near her on the side at the left but her left hand and arm are holding it against her while dampening the strings, the right hand plucks the strings with a plectrum.

Dr. Ananda Commaraswami gives the descriptions of the ancient bow-shaped harp as under:

The old Indian Vina is a harp without a post; it has a hollow belly covered with a board or stretched leather. This belly is broader towards the back where its end is rounded, and tapers towards the front, where it is continued into an upstanding curved arm which often terminates in a little scroll like the head of a violin. The seven strings, one above the other, are stretched from this arm to the belly, forming as it were arcs to the crescent of the whole frame; they pass through holes in the flat surface (wooden or parchment sounding board) of the belly and must be fastened to its underside. Thew eight of the instrument lies well back. It is held in the left arm or in the lap with its thin arm projecting forwards and upwards. Sometime it is supported by a sling.

Technique of Playing Harp According to Natyasastra

Touching the string simultaneously with the two thumbs.

Touching a string with the left thumb after pressing it with the right one.

Striking with the left thumb only.

Striking with the left forefinger.

A single sweeping stroke with all the fingers of the hand

Striking the strings at lower end with the little finger and thumb of the right hand.

One stroke with the little finger and the thumb.

The use of the left palm for dampening the strings.

The use of both the thumbs clearly indicates that these techniques were for the harp type; moreover in the harp type vina the thumb, the little fingers and all the fingers are used simultaneously or in immediate succession. In the modern vina or sitar, the thumb has no sue and the little finger is used only for rhythm cum drone purposes. While playing harps in almost all cases, the right hand plucks or strikes the strings and the left hand is stretched along the strings to dampen them wherever necessary.

Diffusion Common Tradition

In the various items of musical instruments in the ancient sculptures, we find many similarities such as the same group. the same technique of playing and the some position in which the instruments are held and played. The bow shaped harp used as accompaniment to dances reveals that this type of vina was in vogue in all the centres referred to above and show the diffusion of the culture from a common tradition. The bow shaped harp vina is the first musical instrument of the string variety to be manifested in Indian plastic art and it is difficult to fix the date of its appearance. It might have been in existence before but it came to be pictorially recorded on permanent material towards the 2nd cent. B.C. and disappears in India in the 9th cent. A.D. but continued to be represented in the sculptures of certain parts of South East Asian regions like Java (8th cent.) and Cambodia (13th cent.) But it survives in the modern Saun of Burma and the Siamese Phin.

ORCHESTRA AND CHORUS IN ANCIENT INDIA

By Swami Prajanananda

It is generally believed that orchestras as well as chorus are of recent origin, and was introduced in India during the british regime. But this belief seems to be incorrect, as the sanskrit treatises on drama and music bear eloquent testimony to the fact that vrnda-vadya (samaveta-yantra-vadana) or orchestra and vrnda-gana (samaveta-sangita) or chorus were current in India even before the dawn of the Christian era. We find full description of the Mahavrata ceremony in the Srautasutras. It becomes evident that the wives of the priests and the young unmarried girls used to sing songs in unison, accompanied by dance. Now the songs of the wives of the priests and the maidens in same pitches and tunes might have been known as chorus (Samuha-ṣangita) in ancient days. Again, we find references in the Vedic literature that lutes (vinas) and drums (puskaras) and other musical instruments used to keep rhythm of the dances and songs of the dancers and singers, and those combined musical instruments were known as musical concerts or simple orchestras.

In the Ramayana, Mahabharata and Harivamsa, we often come across references about group-singing of the Brahmis and wandering minstrels on the occasion of the coronation, wedding, funeral ceremonies and other sacred sacrificial functions and rites, and they may be regarded as the group songs of chorus. Though different musical instruments, were used on different auspicious occasions and in wars and funeral ceremonies, they cannot be considered as orchestra proper. Yet the practice of orchestra (samuha-yantra-vadaha) was in vogue before the Christian era, as we find mention of proper forms of different kinds of orchestra in Bharata's Natyasastra, composed in the 2nd century A.D. Thus, as we find mention of Kutapa (vrnda-vadya) in the 2nd century A.D. Bharata of the Natyasastra fame has, therefore, mentioned about kutapa or orchestra and samuha-sangita or chorus as well as other ingredients for drama, dance and music, in the Natyasastra, and from them it becomes evident that though we find frequent references to kutapa or orchestra and chorus in different literature.

Now it is found that Bharata of the Natyasastra fame has described orchestra (kutapa) in connection with dramatic performance (natyabhinaya). He has also mentioned about group singing or chorus as well as the grammar and science of drama, dance and music. The sculpture and bas-reliefs of the pre-Christian and early Christian eras supply palpable evidences of group recital of musical instruments (vrnda-vadana) and group singing or chorus (vrnda-gana), as prescribed in ancient India. In the Sitabenga cave in the Madhya Pradesa (2nd century A.D.) a dramatic stage has been exacavated in front of which there exists a music hall and a seat for the players of musical instruments, which go to prove that a simple type of vrnda-vadana or orchestra was in practices in the dramatic performances during the early Christian era. In one of the Ajanta caves (2nd-7th century A.D.), a dramatic stage and a stage-room are depicted. In front of the stage, some dancing girls (naris) have been painted in dancing posture, along with an orchestra to keep rhythms of dance as in actuality. That simple orchestra was composed mainly of flutes and drums. On the bas-reliefs of the railings of the Barhut stupa (2nd century B.C.) are to be found a band of players of musical instruments as if engaged in keeping rhythms of dance? Usually the orchestra or musical concert consisted of some harp shaped lutes (veenas) drums (puskaras) and cymbals. In the paintings of Bagh (4th-6th century A.D.) we also come across scenes of group dances and concerts in the Cave Nos. 4 and 5, consisting of drums, flutes, cymbals and music sticks, accompanying the dances of fair maidens. In different inscriptions, especially of the Magadha and Maurya-Seythian periods, we find references of group dance, group singing, concert and orchestra.

Now the question arises whether the scenes of vrnda-vadya and vrnda-gana (orchestra and chorus), as engraves in different railings and caves of the Buddhist stupas and Hindu temples are to be termed as orchestra and chorus proper. It is a moot point. But it should be earmbered in his connection that a definite form of concert and orchestra (kutapa or vrnda vadya) had already taken shape in the pre-Christian era, and Bharata has described it in the Natyasastra. The music experts and scholars have undoubtedly made a distinction between a concert and an orchestra. Concerts, they say, is a combination of voices or sounds or it can be said to be a musical entertainment, whereas an orchestra is a body of instrumental performers or a combination of different classes of musical instruments. In fact, a concert is a musical entertainment of concerted pieces, symphonies, etc., sometimes interspersed with songs, performed by an orchestra of many musical instruments.

Now, the term orchestra has been derived from the Greek term orcheomai meaning "dance'. In ancient Greek theatres, it stood for the space allotted to the chorus of dancers; in modern theatres, the part of the building assigned to the instrumentalists; and in the modern concert-rooms, the place occupied by the instrumental and vocal performers. The word orchestra was also used to denote the musicians collectively with the instrumentalists. Regarding orchestra and orchestration of the ancient Greeks and the western nations, Prof. Percy A. Scholes is of opinion that "the idea of combining instruments is probably as old as instruments themselves, but the principles of what may be called systematic combination (and the art of orchestration is just that) were very slowly realized".

"Between the Hayden-Mozart period and the Strauss period," says Prof. Scholes, "have come the work of the later Beethoven and of Wagner, and this great expansion of orchestral media, with its consequent enhanced variety, increased dynamic power, and greater aptitude for dramatic characterization, represents the influence of the romantic movement plus that of the efforts of instrument makers during the greatest age of invention the world has yet seen." Thus we see that in the ancient Greek theatre stages there were orchestras, but they were only the semi circular or square spaces in the front of the stages, where chorus danced and sang, and they were not meant for group playing of the musical instruments proper. Similarly in Hellenistic theatre stages in Graeco-Roman theatres, in Roman theatres, in Elizabethan theatres, in Italian Renaissance theatres, such semicircular, diagonal or square orchestras were in existence for songs and dances, and not for players of the musical instruments. This is also true of the theatres of modern France and Germany.

Though it is a fact that theatre or stage and drama (play or abhinaya) are by no means one and the same thing, though they stand in close relationship to each other, yet they have each its own boundary. Again it should be remembered in this connection that chorus or group songs, dance and music were connected all with theatre and drama, at least in ancient times. In India also, dance, music and concert or musical entertainment and accompaniment were closely connected both with the stage and dramatic play (abhinaya). In India, the germ or nucleus of geya-natakas can be traced to the early 12th century A.D., when Kavi Jayadeva composed the Gitinatya, Gitagovinda. The opera in India was not merely a fantasia, but was a combination of poetry, music, dance and symbolism. The orchestra (samuha-vadya) was also a part and parcel of the Indian opera (Gitinatya).

But it is a historical fact that orchestra (vrnda-vadya) evolved in India in the beginning of the Christian era, and as has already been said, Bharata's Natyasastra generally proves its prevalence. Bharata has styled orchestra (vrnda-vadya) as Kutapa. Besides kutapa or Indian orchestra, mention of assemblage of different musical instruments is to be found in different religious, royal and domestic functions, but they were not the orchestras or concerts. As for example, in the second chapter of the Natyasastra (Kasi edition), Bharata has mentioned different wind and percussion instruments on the occasion of the laying of foundation stone of the theatre-stage. "These halves (behind him) should be again divided equally into two parts, one of which will be made the stage (ranga-sirsa) and the part at back the retiring room (nepathya). And during the ceremony (of laying of the foundation) all the musical instruments such as conchshell, dundubhi (drum), mrdanga (earthen drum), panava (small drum or tabor) should be sounded."[1] Then Bharata has definitely mentioned about Indian orchestra or kutapa in the second chapter.

"For (in such a playhouse) made free from the interference of wind, voice of actors and singers as well as the sound of musical instruments will be distinctly heard."[2]

Now, it was customary to represent the kutapa or vrnda-vadya after the ceremony of laying of the foundation stone of the stage and in the beginning of the worship of the presiding deities. Bharata has used the word 'kutapa' in different senses. As for example, sometimes as different musical instruments and sometimes as orchestra or vrnda-vadya. Similarly the commentator Abhinava Gupta has used the word 'Kutapa' in three different ways. The word kutapa sometimes denotes four kinds of musical instruments like tata, vitata, ghana and susura; sometimes orchestra and also sometimes musicians and players of different musical instruments. Then Bharata goes on to describe the arrangement of musical instruments (kutapa-vinyasa) which was known as pratyahara. Regarding the detailed arrangement of the musical instruments (kutapa-vinyasa) and their names, Bharata has said, "The arrangement of the musical instruments (kutapa) is called the pratyahara. The appearance of singers is called the avatarcana. The commencement of vocal exercise for singing (pargita) is called the arambha or beginning. Adopting the musical instruments for playing them in due manner is called the asravana. Rehearsing (lit. dividing) the different styles (vrttis) of playing musical instruments is called the vaktrapani. The strings of instruments are adjusted duly during the parighattana. The samghotana is meant for rehearsing the use of different hand poses (for indicating the time beat). The playing together (in harmony with one another) of drums and stringed instruments is called the margasarita. The asarita is meant for practicing the beat of time fractions (kalapata). And the applications of songs (gitavidhi) is for singing the glory of gods".

Bharata has said that the arrangement of musical instruments (kutapa) used to be made exclusively in connection with the presentation of dramas. The kutapa consisted of four kinds of musical instruments, and Bharata has elaborately dealt with them in the atodyavidhi in the 28th chapter.

From this we come to know that ancient Indian orchestra consisted of vaipancika or vainika, vamsa-vadaka, mardalika or panavika or dardurika. It can be divided into four main classes, players of lute or veena, flutists, drummers and players of cymbal. The players were of three classes, uttama (best) madhyama (medium) and adhama (trite). The orchestra (kutapa) was arranged like alatacakra i.e. in a circle. These have been fully dealt with by Sarangdeva in the Sangita Ratnakara (vide III, prakirna chapter).

Sarangdeva has described the natya-kutapa i.e. combination of musical instruments (meant for drama). The natya-kutapa was divided into three classes according to their merits, and they were uttama (best), madhyama (medium) and adhama (trite). When these three types of kutapa were used to be combined, they came to be known as vrnda or combination (or cluster). The combined musical instruments or instrumentalists (vrnda) were in their turn divided into best, medium and common.

1. The best type of vrnda consisted of four main singers, twelve accompanying singers, four flutists and four drummers;
2. The medium type of vrnda consisted of two main singers, four accompanying singers, two flutists and two drummers;
3. The common place (kanistha or adhama) type of vrnda consisted of one main singer, three accompanying singers, two flutists and two drummers.

According to Bharata, these vrnda or combined musical instrument players and musicians were called kutapas or orchestras : Sarangdeva holds a different view to some extent. According to him vrnda, known as kutapa, was really the natya-kutapa (orchestra proper) and exclusively meant for use in dramatic performances.

It has already been said that the natya-kutapa was also divided into three classes, best, medium and common place: "etesam ca patranamuttamamadhyamadhamatvena kutapasyapi travidhyam". Simhabhupala has used the term vrnda and samuha or samghata to mean 'collection': "Samghatah samuho vrndamuchate". The vrnda or samuha-vadya was also of different classes, such as kutapa vrnda i.e. collection of different musical instruments, vamsika-vrnda i.e. collection of flutes only, gayani vrnda i.e. collection of singers, kolahalakhya vrnda i.e. collection of various musical instruments.

It is a fact that though the gayani-vrnda or the musicians in the gayani-vrnda were accompanied by different musical instruments and were connected with the dramatic plays, yet they used to sing songs for the drama in unison, which was nothing but chorus (samuha-samgita or vrnda-gana). Like kutapa orchestra, the musicians used to create the ethos in dramatic plays. The vamsika-vrnda were composed only of flutes, and consisted of one main flutist and four subsidiary ones.

All over the world well trained orchestras provide the musical accompaniments in opera plays. In opera, dance is only incidental, and the dramatic action and conversation (abbinaya) take prominent role. In South India, different operas (geya-natakas) were written by great composers in different times. The charitrams, written in songs and verses, were produced as opera. The charitrams were known as the geya-charitrams. It has it been said by Prof. Sambamurthy: "A well trained orchestra is absolutely necessary to provide the music accompaniment in operas. In a properly balanced orchestra, constituted with an attention to tone colour effects it is possible to achieve brilliant results".[3] It is thus found that an orchestra is necessary for an opera or geya-natya.

Prof. Sambamurthy has further said : "Kutapa is the term for orchestra in ancient Indian music. There are references to tata-kutapas or stringed bands and avanaddha-kutapa or bands of drums. The kutapas provided musical accompaniment to the dramas in ancient times. In late times, the term sangita-melam came to be used to denote orchestras, playing classical music. The orchestras, designed to play folk music, were called by such names as naiyandi melam urumi-melam etc."[4]

It has already been mentioned hat genuine evidences regarding the existence of orchestra and chorus, accompanying dance and drama, are found in the sculptures and bas-reliefs of different Buddhist Stupas, railings and gates, monasteries and Hindu temples of ancient India. Evidences are also discernible :

1. in the paintings of the Ajanta-caves, in one of which is depicted a theatre stage and green-room with a dancing girl, dancing with her attendants, and female musicians are keeping the rhythm of the dance:
2. representations of dancing figures on the Barhut railings;
3. the vrnda-vadya and dancing figures as well as figure of a dancer and female players of musical instruments at the Bagh cave paintings are worth mentioning.

The orchestra party and the dance motif of a dancing girl (nati), as depicted in the pawaya at Gwalior of the 4th century A.D. is also very significant in this context. The orchestra, as depicted here, consists of a sarode-like veena, one harp-type of veena, flutes, drums and cymbals From all these it is evident that a simple form of orchestra was in practice in ancient India, approximately in the 2nd century B.C. The modern type of orchestra evolved in India in the beginning of the British rule, as it has been fashioned after the orchestration in the West. But that does not mean that there was no orchestra in India before the British came. India had orchestra and chorus of her own, and that orchestra consisted of purely Indian musical instruments, based on melody and melodic elaboration.

MUSICAL INSTRUMENTS DEPICTED IN THE SCULPTURES OF NAGARJUNAKONDA, ANDHRA PRADESH

By K.Krishnamurthy, Nagpur.

The musical instruments[5] depicted in the sculptures of Nagarjunakonda present a pleasing variety, reflecting intensely on the creative genius of the master-musicians of the day. The types represented in the sculptures are dealt with in these pages, basing mainly on the information supplied and supplemented by the ancient Indian literature. At Nagarjunakonda the lithic representation of vina is quite interesting. In a sculpture which represents Indra's visit to Buddha in Indra sala guha is revealed a harp (See Plate No. 20) (Fig. 1). The harper pancasikha is shown playing the harp with fingertips or nails while standing. Again the sculpture depicting the renunciation scene reveals a woman with a guitar type of vina on her lap. (See Plate No. 20) (Fig. 2) She is shown playing upon it with her fingertips or nails. Likewise the sculpture portraying the transportation of Gautama's jewelled turban to heaven reveals among the band of musicians, a man playing the guitar while standing. (See Plate No. 20) (Fig. 3) He is playing it with his finger-tips. The guitar has five small pegs to regulate the tuning by tightening and loosening them. Elsewhere a peculiar lute or vina (See Plate No. 20) (Fig. 4) gets its depiction. A woman is shown playing on it, while standing. She is keeping it slanted to her left shoulder and playing it with finger. The vina has a vary narrow string-board and the strings are stretched almost half of the entire length of the lute. Thus this lute is unique in its representation among the vinas depicted in Nagarjunakonda sculptures. In a way it reveals some semblances to the sitar of North India.

Conch (Sankha)

This comes under sushira (wind instrument) category. The oldest of the wind instruments was probably the buffalo horn, a specimen of which may be seen in the Indian Museum, Calcutta. The conch is also an old instrument and in fact it is the harbinger of the trumpet. In ancient literature it is said that the conch was used for both pugnacious and holy purposes. The warriors carried the conches along with them in the battle-fields.[6] They were so important and propitious that each hero of the bygone ages named his conch.[7] Thus Pancajanya of Krishna and Devadatta of Arujuna acquired their names.[8] Incidentally Kautilya testifies to the use of sankhas in the war.[9] In temple ritual it either gives an opening fanfare or plays a sort of rhythmical accompaniment. In orchestral bands the conch has its own place. It is blown in two ways. It can be blown either by keeping the perforated tip of the conch into the lip direct or by connecting some ornamental pipe to it. However the process of blowing the conch was known as Dhamana (blowing) or purana (filling).[10]

The depiction of this instrument in stone is quite interesting. At Bharhut the conch with pipe often occurs invariably accompanied with dundubhi.[11] The shell represented in the monkey and elephant scene in which it is fastened at the end of the pipe is quite remarkable. At Amaravati both the varieties with and without pipes are available in lithography.[12] In one of the sculptures a group of eighteen women has been depicted playing upon the drums, a shell trumpet or sankha and two other instruments akin to the Assyrian harps. At Ajanta the representation of conches in the paintings is superb and sublime. In one of the paintings a palace scene depicts a woman holding a conch in her left hand while the right one is drawn close to her ear in the post of audition.[13] The other painting portraying presumably Mahajanka Jataka,[14] reveals a conch blower in association with a flute player and drummer. The sculptural depiction of the instrument conch at Nagarjunakonda is significant. A panel representing the transportation of jewelled turban of Gautama by Devatas with all pomp and splendour reveals a band of musicians. A conch blower can be seen among them, in action. (See Plate No. 20) (Fig. 5) But the conch is devoid of any metal pipe as evidenced in the sculptures of Amaravati.[15]

Drums

These fall under anaddha, the instrument of percussion. Varying in their sound and model they range from sonorous Pataha to dulcet sounding tabors. The drums used for funeral ceremony were called preta pataha, fearful in sound. Generally in the war held the drums like pataha. Dundubhi, anakas etc., were struck. It is stated that they were played with konas.[16] The auspicious drum pratahkala-nandi-pataha was struck in the early morning to notify the break of the day. There is another variety of drum known as Mardala which is usually suspended by the strap from the shoulder and played with koans. This is midway between the sweet noise produced by muraja and noisy pataha.

The melodious sound producing drums like muraja, mrdanga and puskara are generally used in the musical accompaniment. To this category also belong darduras, panavas and jarjharikas. The mrdangas have been further classified according to the positions to which they are held. They include ankya, alingya and urdhvaka.[17] The ankya mrdanga is played on the lap while playing the alingya is larger then ankya in size but is also placed on the lap while playing. However, the mrdanga is considered to be fairly ancient among drum varieties. It is said to have been devised by Brahma to act as an accompaniment to the dance of Siva in the hour of his triumph over Tripurasura, and Ganesa the son of Siva is said to have been the first one to play upon it. The mrdanga means made of clay presumably therefore its body should have been originally of mud.

The sculptural depiction of drums in plenteous and accords pleasing variety. At Bharhut two types of drums are carved in the sculptures. The smaller drums represented in the sculptures are shown in beating with fingers while the larger ones are suspended from the necks and struck with sticks. The former variety gets its depiction more than once. At Amaravati the sculptural delineation the drums are frequent and varied. The pataha, mardala and mrdanga get their portraiture frequently. All the types of mrdanga namely ankya, alingya and urdhvaka are to be seen in the sculpture at Amaravati.

At Ajanata its portraiture is profuse. A palace scene wherein dancing girls are painted reveals a woman playing exquisitely on a mrdanga.[18] Another painting depicting Mahajankaa Jataka reveals again a drummer in the group of flute player and conch blower.[19] In cave no. XVII on the left wall of the verandah above the ceiling door is painted the Wheel of Samsara which depicts a group of musicians. There a man with a dholak (double drum) slinging by a black leather strap from his shoulders is portrayed.[20] In the same fresco can be seen also a dholak and pair of tabalas. A painting on the base of a pillar of the ante-chamber portrays the musical instruments like triangular stringed instrument and double drums.[21]

The lithic delineation of drums at Nagarjunakonda is of special interest. The drums like urdhavaka mrdhanga, alingya mrdanga, mardala and pataha get their depiction significantly. A sculpture representing the scene of the transportation of the jewelled turban of Gautama by the devatas reveals a drummer in action. He is playing urdhvaka mrdanga with fingers and the drum is suspended by means of a leather strap from the left shoulder. (See Plate No. 21) (Fig. 6) The drummer is having his right hand upraised in the act of beating the drum while the left one is kept tangential to the drum. Another drummer (See Plate No. 21) (Fig. 7) from the same sculpture is discernible wherein he is represented as playing on urdhvaka mrdanga. But in this case the mrdanga is tied to the waist by means of a leather strap unlike the aforesaid mrdanga where it is suspended from the shoulder. Besides in this case the drummer is playing with konas. He is depicted in action showing both of his hands raised in the pose of beating the urdhvaka mrdanga. The sculpture representing the night before renunciation reveals against alingya mrdanga. (See Plate No. 21) (Fig. 8) Here a woman is shown with alingya mrdanga.

Another variety of drum mardala also gets portraiture in the sculptures of Nagarjunakonda. The sculpture depicting the transportation of Gautama's jewelled turban depicts a band of musicians, which includes a drummer playing on mardala. (See Plate No. 21) (Fig. 9) He is having the mardala dangling from his shoulder by means of a leather strap and playing it with a plectrum (kona). Again the same sculpture represents a drummer playing on pataha. (See Plate No. 22) (Fig. 10) He is in the act of beating the pataha with konas. Thus the delineation of drums in Nagarjunakonda sculptures is picturesque and realistic.

Cymbals

They fall under Ghana. They were plain and generally made of brass, copper or bronze. The sculptural representations of them are numerous. Both the Apsarasa scenes in Bharhut sculptures reveal cymbals.[22] Interestingly the relief from Jamalgarhi in Yusszai, depicting Renunciation scene reveals a group of girls playing on the musical instruments. There a harp, a flute, drums and cymbals are shown.[23]

In Ajanta paintings also many cymbals can be seen. In one of the paintings that reveal a palace scene is shown a musician holding the cymbals.[24] Another painting reveaiing Mahajanka jataka depicts the orchestra comprising five artists. Of them two are shown playing cymbals.[25] In plates VII a-b are represented two Kinnaras playing on flute and cymbals.[26] In cave XVII the painting portraying the wheel of Samsara depicts a party of musicians playing on cymbals.[27] The Nagarjunakonda sculptures are also not wanting in their representation of the cymbals. They are simple and they are presumably made of metal. The sculpture depicting the transportation of Gautama's turban to heaven reveals a fine example of cymbals. (See Plate No. 22) (Fig. 11)

Konas

They are used for beating the drums or for playing on vinas. At times in music parties the people will play with konas by striking them one against the other, individually or in-groups. The depiction of a man playing with kona individually at Nagarjunakonda, in the band of musicians, in one of the sculptures revealing transportation of Gautama's turband to heaven is quite befitting. (See Plate No. 22) (Fig. 12) Such wise the delineation of the musical contrivances in stone at Nagarjunakpnda is aesthetic and alluring, throwing a lucent light on the social history of the locality.

SAPTATANTRI VINA IN THE SCULPTURES OF THE BUDDHIST CAVES OF PITALKHOTA

By Swami Prajnananda, Calcutta

Musicians as well as musicologists and lovers of music generally miss or rather neglect to study the archaeological findings relating to music, excavated from the mounds of the ancient sites in different places in India. Treatises on music no doubt supply us much valuable material which throws light on the obscure and forgotten chapters of the history of Indian music. But it is a fact that the representation of musical instruments and different dancing postures with different hand posts (mudras) of different epochs carved on the stone walls and facades of different caves and temples of India furnish us materials for the proper appraisement of the culture of music as obtained in ancient India. Well has it been said by Garl engle is connection with music of the most ancient nations that sculptures and frescoes of muscial instruments and dance poses of different nations of different times supply us the knowledge of the culture and customs of the ancient peoples among whom music was common. The archaeological findings on music should therefore be regarded as one of the essential and valuable means for studying the historical evolution of music.

Apart from the study of the archaeological findings, we should also pay attention to the pages of the valuable ancient manuscripts and books on music. Blind faith and fanaticism in the name of love for tradition should not be allowed to blur our vision in the proper revaluation of the priceless treasure of the music of India. Representations of some of the musical instruments on stone have recently been excavated from the Buddhist caves of Pitalkhora, carved in the Satmala ranges, known also as Chandera. The earlier account of those caves says M.N. Despande[28] seems to have appeared in 1853, when John Wilson gave a very brief description of the Chaitya cave and the adjoining Vihara cave. Fergusson and Burgess have also given a more detailed account of the same in their monumental book, Care temples of India. Three Saptantantri-vinas have been found engraved on stone slabs excavated from the debris in the forecourt of cave no. 4 of Pitalkhora. Beside them, have also been found one fragmentary sculpture of a winged Kinnara and that of a flying Gandharva from the same site of the cave 4. Though the nomenclatures kinnara and gandharva are closely associated with music, as found in ancient lore, the epics and the classical literature of India, yet sculptural representations of gandharvas and kinnaras as found in the Pitalkhora caves are very peculiar in forms and features, for the winged kinnara have been featured with collared beads in the right hand and bowl of flowers in the left.

The Saptatantri-vinas, together with their plectrums have been vividly depicted in some sculptures in cave No. 4. The particular sculptures are three in number, two of which contain the representation of one female and one male musician. In one of the two, a woman has been portrayed in a reclining posture, playing a vina having seven strings with her right hand. From the fragmentary piece of the sculpture it appears that the vina depicted thereon resembles in shape the Egyptian harp. It is placed on the lap of the woman who holds the plectrum with her thumb and forefinger, and plucking the second string on the Saptatantri-vina. In the second one, a youth has been portrayed, holding a Vina against his right shoulder, and seven strings of the vina emanating "from an elliptical gourd with a curved handle at one end of which a retied the string." The Saptatantri vina was not a novel string instrument in ancient India. In the Rgveda we find mention of the vina, vana with hundred strings: "Vanam sata-sankhyabhis tantribhir yuktam vina visesam dhamante vadayante".

The Saptatantri vina is one of the types of vina or lute class of ancient India. The most ancient type of vina was in the form of a Bow, which was known as Dhanuryantram, a musical instrument fashioned after the hunting bow, having strings of gut. The bow or dhanuryantram is regarded as the forerunner of all classes of string instruments of the world. The vina with one string (Ekatantri) and the vina with two strings (Dvitantri or Dotara) were the primitive types of vina. In the Vedic literature, different kinds of vina have been mentioned. The name of the Saptatantri-vina has also been mentioned in later Classical sanskrit literature, Buddhist birth stories or Jatakas, Natyasastra of muni Bharata and other works on music. The vina with seven strings has also been described in the works of Kalidasa. The Saptatantri-vina perhaps resembled the Citravina as described by muni Bharata in his Natyasastra in the 2nd century A.D. Bharata has said,

> Saptatantri Bhaveo citra vipanci mavatantrika!
> Vipanci konavadya svat citra rangulivadana!! (29,114)

That is, the Citra vina, having seven strings was to be played by the finger, whereas the Vipanci vina, having nine strings, by the plectrum (Kona). Narada has also mentioned about the Vinas, Daravi and Gatra in his Naradi sikasa of the 1st century A.D. It is said that the Daravi vina, which contained seven strings, was used as an accompaniment in classical type of Desi or formalise regional music. We get also the reference to the Saptatantri Vina, during the time of the Pallava King, Mahendravarman, who lived in the 7th century A.D. It has been said that King Mahendravarman was himself an accomplished Vina player and that he received his training in vina from his learned teacher Rudracarya. The vina which he used to play was known as the 'Parivadini', having seven strings. Dr. Raghavan says in this connection in his illuminating article on "Music in the Deccan and South India" (vide "The Bihar Theatre', No. 7, January 1956). To the east of Kudumiyamalai inscription, there is a lable "parivadini-da" helping us to understand the notations given in this inscription, as pertaining to the music on the vina called Parivadini, a lute of seven strings". From this it becomes clear that the Saptatantri vina was in vogue among the Indian society. Our modern sitar with seven strings is but the modified form of the ancient Citra vina, though it is erroneously believed that the Indo-Persian poet Amir khasrau fashioned and introduced it into India for the first time. Most of the post Bharata musicologists have also mentioned about the Saptantantri vina in their works.

Regarding the forms of the ancient musical instruments of the vina class, it can be said that most of them were Bow-shaped, resembling the Egyptian harp, as has been said before. The representations of the three Saptatantri vina engraved or stone, which have been excavated from the Buddhist caves (Cave No. 4) of Pitalkhora, are Bow or harp shaped, and most of the ancient vinas, though differing in number of strings, were came same shape. Vinas featured in the sculptures of Gandharva (1st-2nd century A.D.) Barabadur (8th century A.D.), Amaravati (2nd-3rd century A.D.), Ajanta (2nd-7th centuries A.D.), Nagarjunakonda (2nd-3rd centuries A.D.), Satna (2nd-century A.D.), Mahabalipuram 7th century A.D.), and other places. Again, the vina which is embossed on the coin of Emperor Samudragupta II (4th century A.D.) is also of identical shape. Figures of Vinas prepend large in shape with a gourd at each and are also found in Mahabalipuram (7th century A.D.) and Ajanta (2nd-3rd centuries). But the sculptural representations of the Saptatantri vinas of the Buddha caves of Pitalkhora are of the bow or harp type.

FRETTED VINA IN INDIAN SCULPTURE

By Sh. G.H. Tarelekar

The Natyasastra says in chapter XXXIV that the two vinas citra and Vipanci are the major ones and those like Kacchapi, Ghosaka and others are minor ones. In Chapter XXIX, Citra is described as having seven strings and vipanci, nine strings. The former was to be placed by fingers, while the latter with a kona. Nanyadeva says that Citra with its seven strings is meant for the seven notes of the scale, while the latter provides Antara Ga and Kakali Ni with its two additional strings.

Guttilajataka (vol.11, p. 248) also gives the idea that the vina had seven strings for the seven notes of the scale. In the competition, Bodhisattva broke the seven strings one by one and still the notes could be continued. In Vinathunajataka (vol.11, pp. 224-226) the hunch back is compared to the vinadanda with broken strings.

This[29] old vina is the harp type one having a hollow belly covered with a board or stretched leather. The belly is broader towards the back where its end is rounded and tapers towards the front, and it is continued into an upstanding curved arm. The strings are stretched one above the other, from this arm to the belly. These strings vary in their length. Dr. Coomarswarmy says that it can be safely assumed that the same harp vina is referred to in the still earlier Vedic literature.

We find this harp vina (sketch 1) (See Plate No. 23) with minor variations in the available sculptures of the Sanchi, Bhaja, Bharhut (2nd to 1st cent. B.C.), Amaravati (1st to 2nd cent.A.D.), Nagarjunkonda (2nd to 4th cent. A.C.) etc. and even at Modhera (1st quarter of 11th cent. A.C.) and on Samudragupta's coin and in terracotta figures as well. (It was usually placed on the lap and played with fingers or Kona, the plectrum). At Bodhgaya, in one sculpture, it is held vertically in the left hand. Perhaps it was supported by sling over the shoulder sometimes. At Modhera also we get this type with five strings. One string might have been used in this type of vina to produce more than one note by stopping it and thus shortening its length to effect higher pitch. In the Sanchi museum (1st cent. B.C.) the vina (sketch 2) (See Plate No. 23) with seven strings is not of this harp type.

The other type of vina (sketch 3) (See Plate No. 23) represented in sculptures is like guitar. It is found in as early as Amaravati and Nagarjunkonda sculptures. Pawaya (Gupta period) has both these, harp and guitar type vinas. The Ajanata paintings (4th cent. A.C. to 6th cent. A.C.) have this guitar type with four, five or six strings. It was usually plucked by the right hand and played by the left hand. Pattadakal temple (8th cent. A.C.) has a sculpture (sketch 4) (See Plate No. 23) in which a vina with four strings is carved, slightly different from the guitar type. The violin type is said to be found in the Chidambaram temple.[30]

As regards the vina with one string, we have specimens in Ajanta, Badami (7th cent. A.C.) and Ellora (8th cent. A.C. to 11th cent. A.C.) etc. In one variety (sketch 5) (See Plate No. 23) it is placed on one hand and played by a kona or without it, with the other hand. It has a half gourd or a full gourd at the upper end. In Delwara temple (11th cent. A.C.) we get the vina (sketch 6) (See Plate No. 24) with one string and one gourd at the upper end or two gourds (sketch 7) (See Plate No. 24), one at each end, and played by the fingers. In the sculptures of Sarasvati of Pala period (8th cent. A.C. onwards), we get this vinā. But in all these types, the frets are absent. Somesvara (1st quarter of the 12th cent. A.D.) describes Kinnari vina with fourteen frets which were meant for the notes of the two octaves. Before that Nanyadeva (11th cent. A.C.) has also described the use of frets in connection with Kinnari. Sangita Ratnakara of Sarangadeva (13th cent. A.C.) also describes the Kinnari with fourteen frets and later on Kumbha as well. All these authors describe frets in connection with Kinnari vina.

I was able to get two specimens of fretted vina in Belur temple (1st quarter of the 12th cent. A.C.) In one case, the vina was broken and hence it was not possible to have a complete idea. But to the left hand side of the main entrance there is a small female figure (most probably that of a Sarasvati) sitting and playing on vina (sketch 8) (See Plate No. 24). It is played by fingers and has thirteen frets. Then in the temple of Vastupala and Tejapala (13th cent. A.C.) on Mt. Girnar I found another sculpture of fretted vinā (sketch 9) (See Plate No. 24), having thirteen frets and played with fingers. The late Shri Ramakrishna Kavi has described Matanga Kinnari with fourteen frets in his 'Bharatakosa', perhaps on the authority of Kumbha (beginning of the 15th cent.) Kumbha[31] describes three types of Kinnari, small, medium and big, as given in the Brhaddesi of Matanga. Matanga is dated by Shri Kavi as belonging to the 9th century A.C. But Nanyadeva mentions Matanga as Caitrika (one who plays on Citra vina). He has described Sarasvati vina according to Matanga. This vina was very important as it gave all the svaras, srutis and murchanas. The three types of Kinnari which have been described by Kumbha according to 'Bṛhaddesi' are treated by Sarngadeva as the desī (regional) Kinnaris, after first describing the small and the big Kinnaris. I doubt whether the word 'desi' in Sangita Ratnakara gave the idea of 'Brhaddesi'. The

reference to the Brhaddesi by Kumbha makes Matanga the originator of the Kinnari vina with frets. This view is mentioned by Prof. Brhaspati also.[32] In the largest type of Kinnari with three gourds the frets may be also eighteen according to Kumbha, for four more notes of the tara register, Sangīta Ratnākara allows the use of two or three more frets in addition to the fourteen. He has given[33] one view according to which the number of frets should be thirteen as well, Vema[34] says that the Kinnari was called Rudravina.

Mattakokila had twentyone strings for the notes of the three registers. Ghosa had one string and a gourd. It was the Prakrit, the original source of the other vinās of its type. Nakula had two strings and Tritantrika, three. Sangita Ratnakara says that the Mattakokila is the principal vinā. According to Shri Kavi, Bharata was the player of this vina. Prof. Brhaspati understands[35] the Vainika in the Nātyasāstra as Mattakokila player. The sanchi illustration where the vina is not bow shaped, seems to be the forerunner of the later Mattakokila or the Svaramandala of the medieval times. The guitar type vina with four, five or six strings could also give more notes by being pressed as in the case of violin. The vina with one string and gourd (which was sometimes half gourd also in the earlier period) was used to give all the necessary notes. Hence, Matanga says that Saraswati herself dwells in it. It had two gourds also. Upto the 10th century A.C. or even afterwards, we find this type. The frets were added to facilitate the production of the different notes. We get the earlier illustration of vina with frets at Belur. Nanyadeva of the 11th century mentions frets in connection with Kinnari. Hence I suggest that the fretted vina with frets for all the svaras came into vogue in India somewhere between the 10th cent. A.C. and the 11th cent. A.C.

MANUSCRIPT

This manuscript on music written by Tansen and based on Sangeet Ratnakar deserves mention.

The manuscript on music is based on Sangeet Ratnakar to start with, Tansen defines the three branches of music, vocal instrumental and dance. He, gives names of ragas and says that music has originated from brahma and believes that music give the best and the highest pleasure of life. He adds that pursuit of music gives comforting experiences easily and leads even to liberation. He emphasises the gains from music flow with the blessings of guru. He adds that it causes feelings of ecstasy and steers the sufferer to safety through storms in life. He makes mention of the vibration in views by seven swaras and the laya and the harmony they are capable

सं० र०
५

॥अथ मेघ भार्या॥मल्हारी देशकारी भूपाली पुन जान॥ बडहंस और टंक ले मेघराग के
॥गामान॥ अथ इन्द्र मत राग रागिणी॥ अथ पत्र राग नाम॥ पहिले भैरव राग
॥हे दुजे कौशिक जान॥ तीसरे हिंडोल बखानिये चौथे दीपक मान॥ पंचम श्रीराग कहे छटे मे
घ प्रमान॥ पांच पांच भार्या कही अष्ट पुत्र प्रति जान॥ भैरवी रामकली पुन टोडी गुनकरी ना
॥भैरव राग की रागिणी मत संगीत हि मारि॥ देव भावती बागेश्वरी ककुभ पन जमन मान॥
॥कल्याणी मत संगीत ते और शोभनी जान॥ प्रथम वसंती पंचमी देसी कान्हड़ा नारि॥
॥ललित हिंडोल सभी संग ते हिंडोल की नारि॥ धनाश्री सुलतानी नटी जयतश्री पुन आ
॥ना॥ भीमपलासी रागिणी दीपक संग बखान॥ मालवी त्रिवणी गौरी काफी टंकी

43

सं० र०
६

॥टंक के रहन कूम कुंभर दीपक रे मेवंत॥ मेघ मल्हारी गौड पुन गौड गिरी जल धार॥
॥नट मल्हारी सूर टुनिरा मल्हासी मल्हार॥ सुलतानी और धना श्री भीमपलासी
॥जान॥ बंबा धानी आडि रकी तृतीय प्रहर कर गान॥ जंगला मंगल पीलू पुन
॥सिंधु तैलंग परदीप॥ दीपक दीपकी काफी पुन चौथे प्रहर मलीप॥ जो नैं श्री
॥रूपी माल श्री मालश्री गौराह॥ गौड सारंग मारवा पुरवी औ पूरवाल॥ त्रिवणी

गो ॥श्री री बहुरी चेती टंकी मान॥ चौथे प्रहर दिन अंत में आट कर गान॥ प्रथम
गा ॥गार डानी संभ कल्याण सु धनी किन॥ तिम छीम एमन पुन श्याम हे मारती जान॥
॥जैता भूपाली पुरीया का केदार कर गान॥ प्रहर दूजा न जाने गुनी छायानट हू बरवान

45

॥ देकपल रनिशिके समेनायकी वक्तप्रमाना ॥ अष्टाद १ तिकान्हराकौशिककान्हर
॥ जान ॥ आडाना सहना सोभना तोलनसोतनी मान ॥ केदारा मलोला पुन नाटके
॥ सार बखान ॥ बिहागबिलाग रावित्ता रिपुनबिलागपुनबिनोद ॥ भरन अवन सेकी
॥ जो अरु शंकरा अमोद ॥ सारट देश सो रुष्टिकाति दुरासामेरि ॥ पाजरबंभानतो लावा
॥ वना कालंगरा आसेरि ॥ मालको १ और को १ की कुलनमका सजणोटा ॥ कोका
॥ कलिंगा की कोवरा अरुणोदय भैबाटि ॥ सोक सत खि और आ बलोशगगीरी
॥ गौरी जान ॥ देश दश के भेद में भिन्न भिन्न तेल नाम ॥ मारग मत आदिक कहे देश दिश हे
॥ धाम ॥ अनुद्रुत ॰ द्रुत ॰ लघु ॰ पुनि कुपु ॰ कुपुव दाम ॥ गुरु ऽ बखान ॥ तान सो सा

46

॥ ठ प्रसिद्ध है आदि ताल हि प्रमाण ॥ एक ताला धमार पुनि रूपक औ तिताार ॥ सुरफा
॥ क भाषतार औ चौताला अठताल ॥ के दस बारह बलि रे कांप च मुखीप दज़ार ॥
॥ तमा आड़ा चौताला पुन ब्रह्म ताल रुद्र तार ॥ अथ मारग ताल नाम ॥ चता
॥ लमार ग कहे शिव सुनव ते प्रगट भय ॥ तान सेन संगीत मत कहत जम बाहि जिनाय ॥
॥ पंच पुरुष हल के रुत हे पुन चाच पुट ही जान ॥ तान सेन सं गीत मत कहो गत थ
॥ मसान ॥ षट्पिता पुत्रक हे उद्घट्ट संप की धार ॥ तान सेन संगीत मत मारग ता
॥ ल विचार ॥ ताल नाम नि ॥ आदि ताल कहि ताल पुन त तीय च तुर्थ होय ॥ पंचम च
॥ निशंक सिंहविक्रम तान सेन कहे सोय ॥ इति ढोलक सिंह की कहे कर्प

47

to large. He describes the tones and tunes of different types of music. He enumerates tones their traits and different Moorchhana's used in ragas. Further he gives a list of main ragas and raginis and their description such as Bhairav, Malkauns, Hindo, Shree and Deepak. He lays down the preferences in which the ragas and raginis are used. Further he prescribes different times for singing different ragas. Next he gives details of different talas and how to use them finally he gives a detailed list of musical instrument then in use, such as been, Rabab, Swar Mandal, Tanbur, Dolak, Karlal etc. The study of the manuscript is interesting and helpful to students of music.

References

1. Bharta's Natya Sastra, Part-II, pp. 35-38.
2. Natya Sastra, Part-II, pp. 82-83
3. CF. Prof. Sambamurthy, History of Indian Music (1960), pp. 83-84.
4. *Ibid.*, pp. 86-87.
5. Yazdani: Ajanta IV, p. 57 xxxvii a.
6. Ramayana, vi. 63. Mahabharata, vi. 1, 15-18, iv 66, 11, iv-01-19.
7. S.B.E. 8-38.
8. Mahabharata, vi 1, 18.
9. Page 401.
10. Kadambari, p. 33.
11. Cunningham: Stupa Bharhut, p. 126.
12. C. Sivaramamurthy: Bulletin of Madras Government Museum, Amaravati Sculpture, Figs. 1 & 5.
13. Yazdeni, Ajanata 1, p. 15.
14. *Ibid.* 1, Pl. xvi/xviii, p. 22.
15. C. Sivaramamurthy: Amaravati Sculpture, pl. xiii, Fig. 5.
16. Ramayana, II 81, 2, VI, 60, 48-49.
17. C. Sivaramamurthy, Amaravati Sculpture, p. 148.
18. Yazdeni, Ajanata I, p. 17, pl. XII, XIII.
19. *Ibid.*, p. 22, pl. XVI, XVIII
20. *Ibid.*, IV, p. 24.
21. *Ibid.*, p. 106, pl. LXX, b.
22. Cunningham: Stupa of Bharhut, p. 126.
23. J. Burgess: Buddhist Art in nda, p. 129.
24. Yazdeni, Ajanta I, p. 12.
25. *Ibid.*, 1, p. 17, pl. XII, XIII.
26. *Ibid.*, II, p. 4, pl. VII, a-b.
27. *Ibid.*, IV, p. 24, 26.
28. Vide 'Rock-Cut' caves of Pitalkohora in Deccan, Published in Ancient India (Bulletin of the Arch. Surv. of India), No. 15, 1959, pp. 66-93.

29. The parts of Veena by A.K. Coomaraswamy, Journal of American Oriental Society, 1931, pp. 244-253.
30. Journal of the Music Academy, Madras, Vol. XIX, pp. 58-70.
31. तिस्र: किन्नरीवीषा: स्चुर्बृहद्देशी समाश्रिता: । बृहती मध्यया लध्वीत्यथासां लक्षणं बुवे।।

कुम्भ, भरतकोश, मंतग किचरी

32. Bharta ka Sangita Siddhanta, p. 297.
33. केचित्रयों दशेवात्र सारी र्निदघते बुधा: ।। VI. 306
34. एतास्तु किचरी: प्राहु रुद्रवीणाख्यया जना: । वेम:

Bharata kosa - Rudra Vinā

35. Bharata ka Sangita Siddhanta, p. 19 (F.N.)

Conclusion

Book written in Indian music shows that the studies are historical and descriptive with some analysis of practical music. This is only one type of research and scope of music research can be expanded. Prem Lata Sharma gives a striking image is to exemplify this narrowing of scope in music research: "Laksana is one foot of research. How long can we stand on one foot alone?" (Sharma, Problems, p. 30).

The topic taken up for research was Sources of Research in Indian Classical Music. The purpose was to specify guidelines for research in music since the research methodology books prescribed were found to be inadequate. The Hypothesis was that music being a creative performing art would not conform to the pattern of research used either by social science or humanities. Music has to be researched in a different fashion so that its results would benefit the researcher and the music world. Varieties of methods are necessary in research. Individual interview, observation, questionnaire are some of the techniques that have been developed in this descriptive. These techniques are useful for music research.

It is true that without historical knowledge of music, not only in India, but also of the world, becomes incomplete and can not be truly appreciated. So history is essential thing, which throw proper light on the all aspects of music and musical data from very earlier days up to this time. Music evolved in the pre-historic India, through in a very crude form. During Vedic period, the people developed the art of music and dance as essential. If we observe different phases of evolution of music, we will find that music has created a history of its own having different records, manuscripts, stone pictures, sculptures and paintings. And it can be said that the history of Indian music has preserved the glorious tradition from the most ancient time uptil now. Different stone figurines of singing, dancing and musical instruments are depicted in the railing, walls, and facades of the temples and from these we can say that India produced many stone figurines as the story teller. So from this we can proudly say that it has no missing link from the prehistoric time uptill now.

I have not attempted at writing or showing just a history of Indian music. More competent persons had done it earlier. Nor I researched for new material, as historians would like to do. I have just drawn material or the sources for research work in the Indian music. What I have actually tried to discuss with in a brief span is to link up the entire material in a systematic manner. The main object of this study is to find out sources by which we can easily study some pattern of the Indian music. The present Book is an outcome of the devoted study of the sources for research in Indian Classical Music. In this Book, wherever, I have quoted from the authentic references, I have acknowledged it all of them in the footnotes. The source, which provides materials for constructing a detailed study of music, is varied and extensive. I mainly employed sources from books, periodicals, and references, in music in the literature and private material.

Bibliography

1. Agnihotri, Vidhyadhar, *Techniques of Social Research*, M.N. Publishers, New Delhi, 1980.
2. Alamelu Govindrajan, *Music Miscellany*, Madras Kalashetra Publication, 1976.
3. Ahuja, B.N., *Audio-Visual Journalism*, Surjeet Publication, Delhi, 1992.
4. Agarwal, Vasudeva, *Studies in Indian Art,* Varanasi Vishwavidyalaya Prakashan, 1965.
5. Bhandarkar, Wilkinson, *Methodology and Techniques of Social Research*, 1986.
6. Coomaraswamy, Anand, *Rajput Painting* (vol.1 text) (being an account of the Hindu Paintings. Rajasthan and the Punjab Himalayas from the 16th to 19th cen. Described in their relation to contemporary though with text) Motilal Banarasidass, Delhi, 1977.
7. Celements, E., *Introduction to the study of Indian Music,* Gaurav Publications, 1981.
8. Chaudhary, Debu, *Sitar and its Techniques,* Allen Books & Co., Delhi, 1981
9. Dhar, Sunita, *Senia Gharana — Its Contribution to Indian Classical Music*, Reliance Publishing House, 1987.
10. Deshpande, Vamanrao, H., *Indian Musical Tradition* (An aestetic study of the gharanas in Hindustani Music), Popular Prakashan, Bombay, 1987.
11. Dhondyal, S.P., *Research Methodology in Social Sciences*, Friends Publication, [n.d.]
12. Deva, B. Chaitanya, *Musical Instruments in Sculpture*, Indian Institute of Advanced Study, Shimla, 1989.
13. Deva, B. Chaitanya, *Musical Instruments*, National Book Trust, India, 1977.
14. Deva, B.C., *Musical Instrument of India* (Their History and Development) Firma KLM Private Limited, Calcutta, 1978.
15. Deva, B. Chaitanya, *Indian Music*, Indian Council Goa Cultural Relations, 1974.
16. Durga, S.A.K., *Research Methodology for Music*, Centre for Ethnomusicology, Madras, 1991.

17. Ebling, Klaus, *Ragmala Painting,* Kumar Galery, New Delhi, 1973.
18. Goswami, A., *Indian Art and Heritage* (O.C.Ganguly) Oxford Book and Stationary Co., Calcutta, 1957.
19. Gaston, Anne Marie, *Siva in Dance, Myth and Iconography*, Oxford University, Delhi, 1982.
20. Guha, J.R., *Introducing Indian Art,* R & K Publishing House, New Delhi, 1963.
21. Gangoly, O.C., *Ragas and Raginis: A Pictorial and Iconographic Study of Indian Musical Modes based on Original Sources*, Vol. 1, text Munshiram Manohar Lal Publishers Pvt. Ltd., 1935.
22. Gupta, Santosh, *Research Methodology and Statistical Techniques,* Deep & Deep Publications, New Delhi, 1993.
23. Hariharan, M. & Gowri Kuppuswami, *Music in Indian Art*, Sundeep Prakashan, Delhi, 1985.
24. Havell, E.B., *The Art Heritage of India* (Comprising : Indian Sculpture and Painting and deals of Indian Art) (Revised edition with notes by Pramod Chandra) D.B. Taraporevals Sons & Co. Pvt. Ltd., Bombay, 1964.
25. Joshi, G.N., *Understanding Indian Classical Music*, Taraporevala, Bombay, 1977.
26. Kar, Chintamani, *Classical Indian Sculpture* (300 B.C. to A.D. 500) Alec Tiranti Ltd., London, 1956.
27. Kumar, Krishan, *Reference Service*, Vikas Publishing House Pvt. Ltd., New Delhi, 1978.
28. Kramsisch, Stella, *The Art of India*, Phaidon Publishers Inc., 1954.
29. Krishnaswami, D.R., *Methodology of Research in Social Science*, Himalaya Publishing House, 1993.
30. Koul, Lokesh, *Methodology of Education Research,* Vikas Publishing House Pvt. Ltd., 1984.
31. Lauania, M.M., *Logic and Methods of Sociological Research*, Research, Delhi, 1987.
32. Khanzode, V.V., *Research Methodology—Techniques and Trends*, APH Publishing Corporation, 1995.
33. Mathur, N.L., *Sculpture in India*, Minister of Education and Social Welfare and Culture, New Delhi, 1972.
34. Majumdar, R.C., *A Comprehensive History of India*, Vol. III, Part II, (A.D. 300-985), People Publishing House, New Delhi, 1982.
35. Mutatkar, Sumati, Editor, *Aspects of Indian Music*, (A Collection of Essays) J. Sangeet Natak Academy, New Delhi, 1987.
36. Murti, Srimannarayana, M., *Methodology in Indological Research.*

37. Misra, R.P., *Research Methodology,* A Hand Book, Concept Publishing Company, New Delhi, 1989.

38. Mehta, R.C., *Music Research Perspective and Prospects — A Reference Indian Music*, Indian Musicological Society, Bombay, 1994.

39. Nayar, Shobhana, *Bhatkhande's Contribution to Music* (A Historical Perspective), Popular Prakashan, Bombay, 1973.

40. Prem Latha, V., *Music through the Ages,* Sundeep Prakashan, Delhi, 1985.

41. Popley, H.A., *The Music of India,* Y.M.C.A., Publishing House, Calcutta, 1950.

42. Prajnanananda, Swami, *Historical Study of Indian Music*, Anandadhara Prakashan, Calcutta, 1965.

43. Prasad, Har, *Research Method and Techniques in Geography,* Rawat Publication, Jaipur, 1992.

44. Prajnanananda, S., *History of Indian Music*, The Indian Music Publishing House, Madras, 1960.

45. Prajnanananda, S., *Historical Development of Indian Music*, Firma KLM, Calcutta, 1973.

46. Ranade, Ashok D., *On Music and Musicians of Hindoostan,* Promila & Co. Publishers, New Delhi, 1984.

47. Ranade, Ashok, D., *Hindustani Music*, National Book Trust, India.

48. Shukla, D.P. & R.M. Trivedi, *Research Methodology,* College Book Depot, Tripolia, Jaipur, [n.d.]

49. Srivastava, G.N. Prakash, *Advanced Research Methodology*, Radha Publication, New Delhi, 1994.

50. Sharma, Nand Kishore/Sarita Sharma, *Research Methodology*, R.B.S.A. Publishers, Jaipur, 1996.

51. Swamp, Shanti, *Arts and Crafts of India and Pakistan,* Taraporevala's Treasure, House of Books, Bombay, 1957.

52. Sathanarayana, R. Kudumiyamalai, *Inscription on Music,* Public Srivaralakshmi Academy Publication Series, Mysore.

53. Sharma, Manorama, *Music Education — New Horizen,* Nirmal Publication, Delhi, 1995.

54. Sharma, Usha, *Heritage of Indian Music*, Vols. I & II, Printwell, Jaipur, India, 1996

55. Sahukar Mani, *Indian Classical Music*, Reliance Publishing House, New Delhi, 1986.

56. Saraswati, S.K., *A Survey of Indian Sculpture*, Firma K.L. Mukhopadhyay, Calcutta, 1957.

57. Sambamoorthy, P., *History of Indian Music, Ed. 2,* Indian Music Publication House, 1982.

58. Singh, Sadhu, *Research Methodology in Social Science*, Muradaya Publishing House, 1980.
59. Sculpture, *By Editors of Newsweek Books*, New York, Newsweek Books, 1965.
60. Sircar, B.C., *Indian Epigraphy*, Motilal Banarasidass, Delhi, 1965.
61. Thakur, *Bavender Research Methodology in Social Science,* Deep & Deep Publications, New Delhi, 1973.
62. Tarelekar, G.H. and Nalini Tarelekar, *Musical Instruments in Indian Sculpture,* Pune Vidyarathi Prakashan, 1972.
63. Verma, Gopal, R.K. Verma, *Methodology and Techniques of Research*, Anmol Publications, New Delhi, 1988.
64. Vatsyayan, Kapila, *Classical Indian Dance in Literature and the Art*, Sangeet Natak Academi, New Delhi, 1968.
65. Vir, Ram Avtar, *History of Indian Music* (Notation System) Pankaj Publication, New Delhi, 1978.

Journals (Articles)

1. Hariharan, M., Gowri Kuppuswamy, "Inscription on Music in Tamil Nadu", *Journal of Indian Musicological Society*, Vol. 22, 1991.
2. Krishnaswami, S., "Musical Instruments in Indian Plastic Art : Strings", *Journals of the Indian Musicological Society*, vol. 6, no 1, March, 1975.
3. Krishnamurthy, K., "Musical Instruments Depicted in the Sculputres of Nagarjunakonda, Andhra Pradesh," *The Journal of the Madras Music Academy*, vol. xxxv.
4. Prajnanananda, Swami, "Saptatantri Vina in the Sculptures of the Buddhist Caves of Pitalkhora", *Journal of Music Academy*, vol. 32, 1961.
5. Prajnanananda, Swami, (Ram Krishna Vedanta Math, Calcutta), "Orchestra and Chorus in Ancient India", *The Journal of the Madras Music Academy,* Vol. xxxv.
6. Tarelekar, G.H., Fretted Vina in Indian Sculpture, "*The Journal of the Madras Music Academy*", vol. lxxxv, Parts i-iv, 1965.

Index

Plate No. 1
VASANT RAGINI

Plate No. 2
GAURI RAGINI

Plate No. 3
SRI RAGA

Plate No. 4
MEGH MALLARA

Plate No. 5
BHAIRAV RAGA

Plate No. 6
BHAIRAVI RAGINI

Plate No. 7
HINDOLA RAGA

Plate No. 8
TODI RAGINI

Plate No. 9
DANCERS AND MUSICIANS FROM KHAJURAHO

Plate No. 10
STRINGED INSTRUMENTS

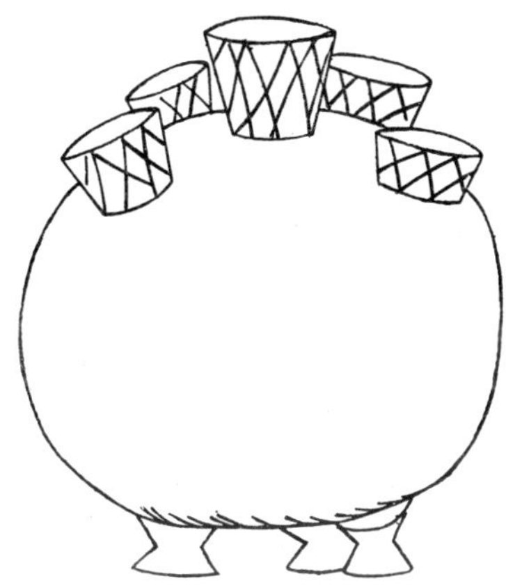

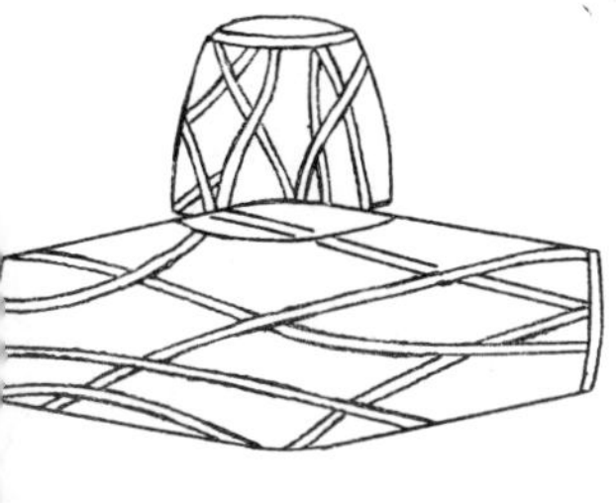

Plate No. 11
PUSHKARA VADYAM, PANCHMUKHAVADYAM

Plate No. 12
DAMRU, BARREL DRUM, WOMEN PLAYING DRUM

Plate No. 13
CUP SHAPED CYMBALS, JHALLARI, AVUJA

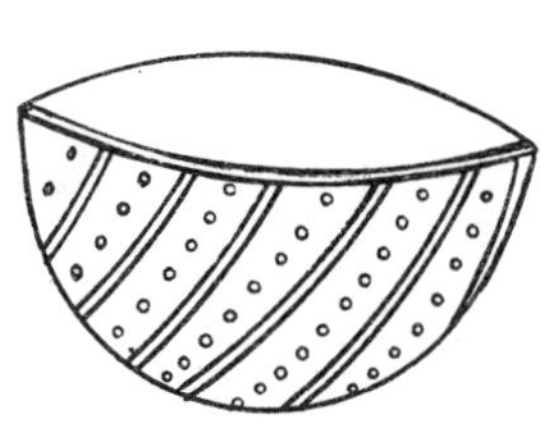

Plate No. 14
MARDALA, DUNDUBHI

Plate No. 15
PERCUSSION INSTRUMENTS

Plate No. 16
MUSICIANS FROM JAIN PAINTING (PALM LEAF); MUSIC PARTY, BAGH FRESIO

Plate No. 17
MUSICIANS FROM KANGRA PAINTING

Plate No. 18

MUSIC PARTY FROM AMARAVATI SCULPTURE

Plate No. 19
GOLD COIN OF SAMUDRA GUPTA

Plate No. 20
HARP AND CONCH FROM THE SCULPTURES OF NAGARJUNAKONDA

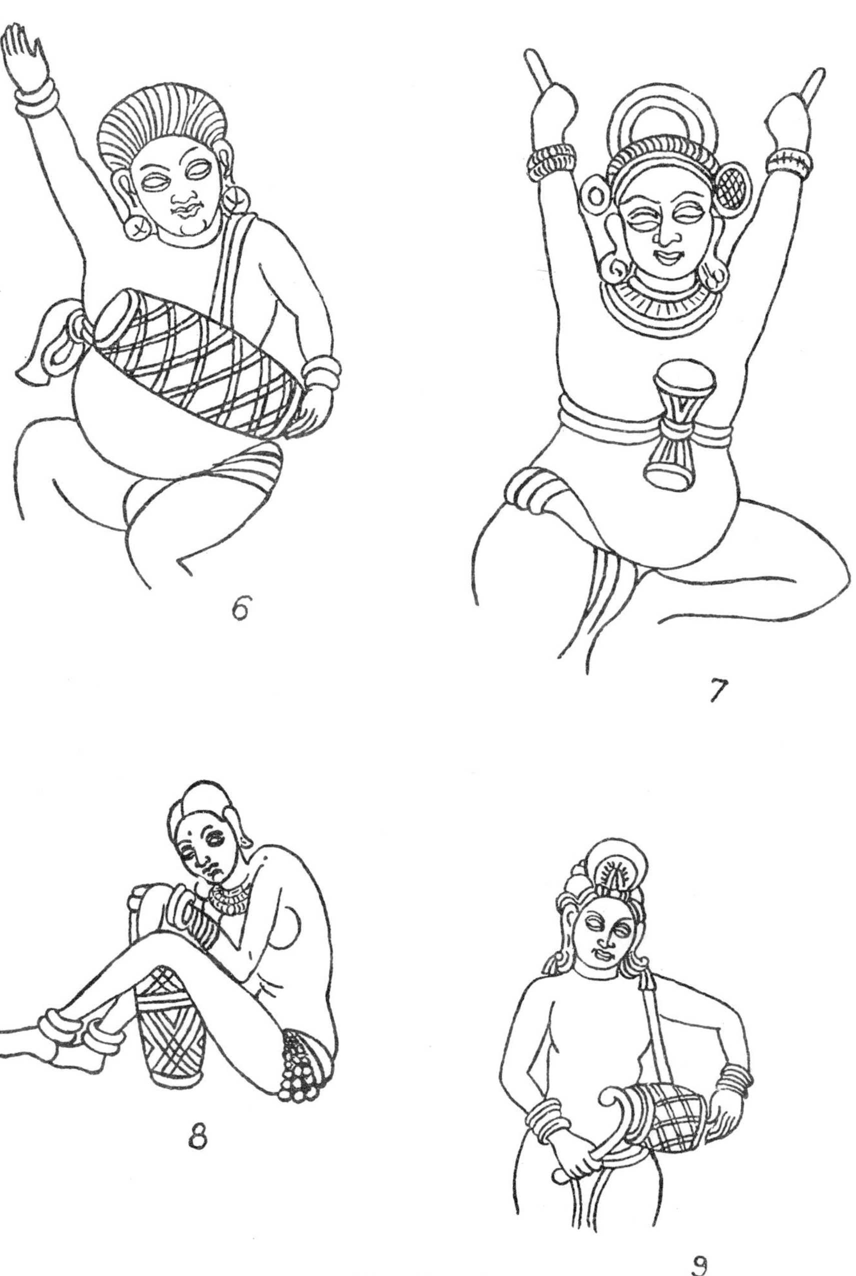

Plate No. 21
DRUM, MRDANGA AND MARDALA FROM THE SCULPTURES OF NAGARJUNAKONDA

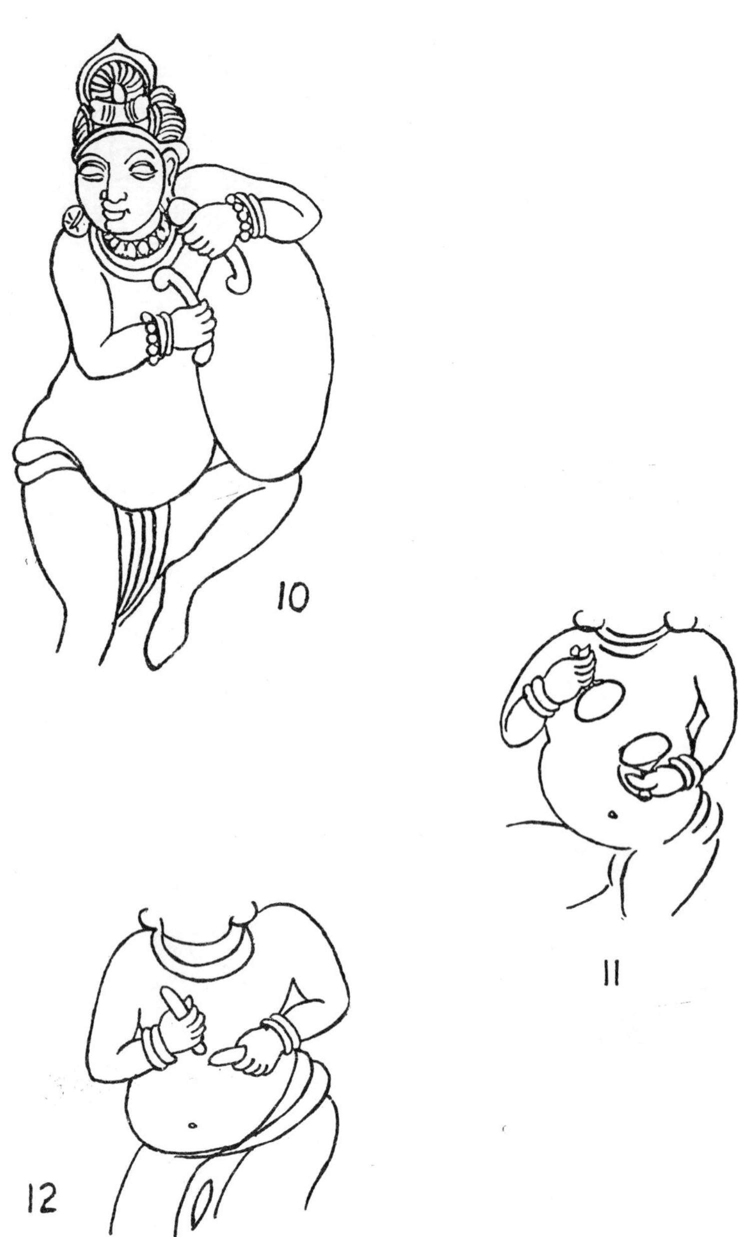

Plate No. 22
CYMBALS AND KONA FROM SCULPTURES OF NAGARJUNAKONDA

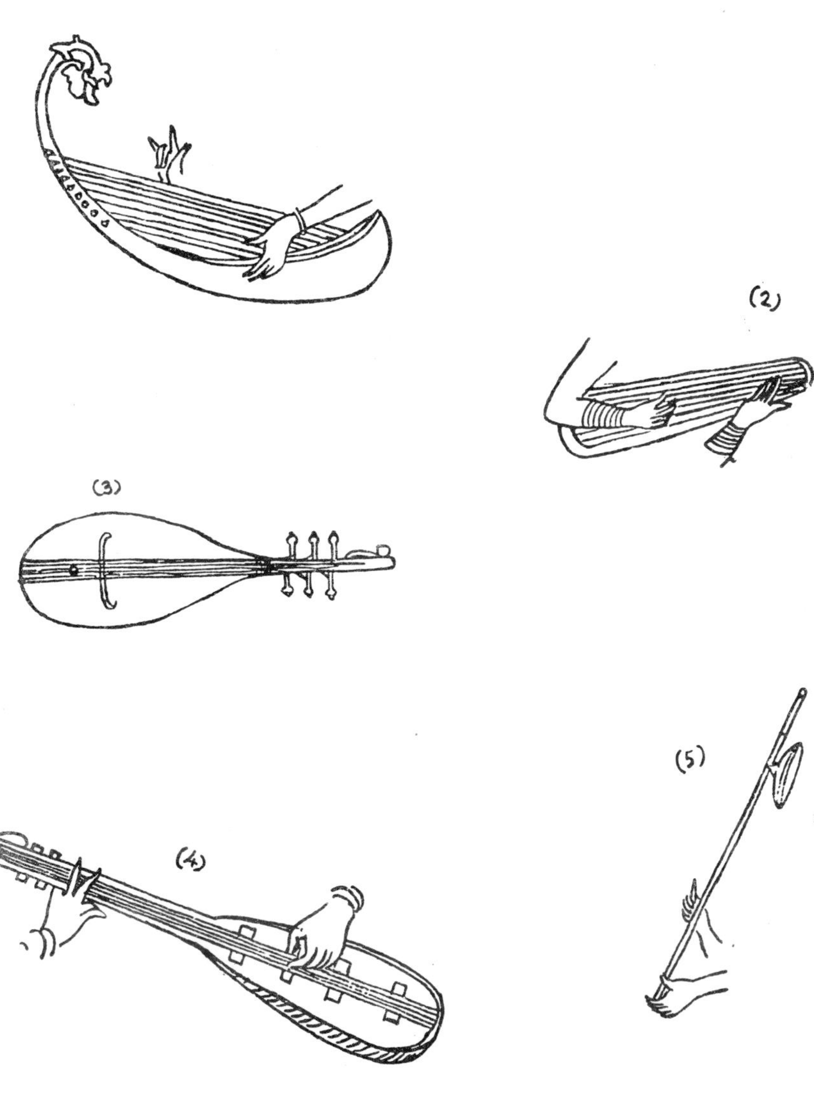

Plate No. 23
FRETTED VINA IN INDIAN SCULPTURE

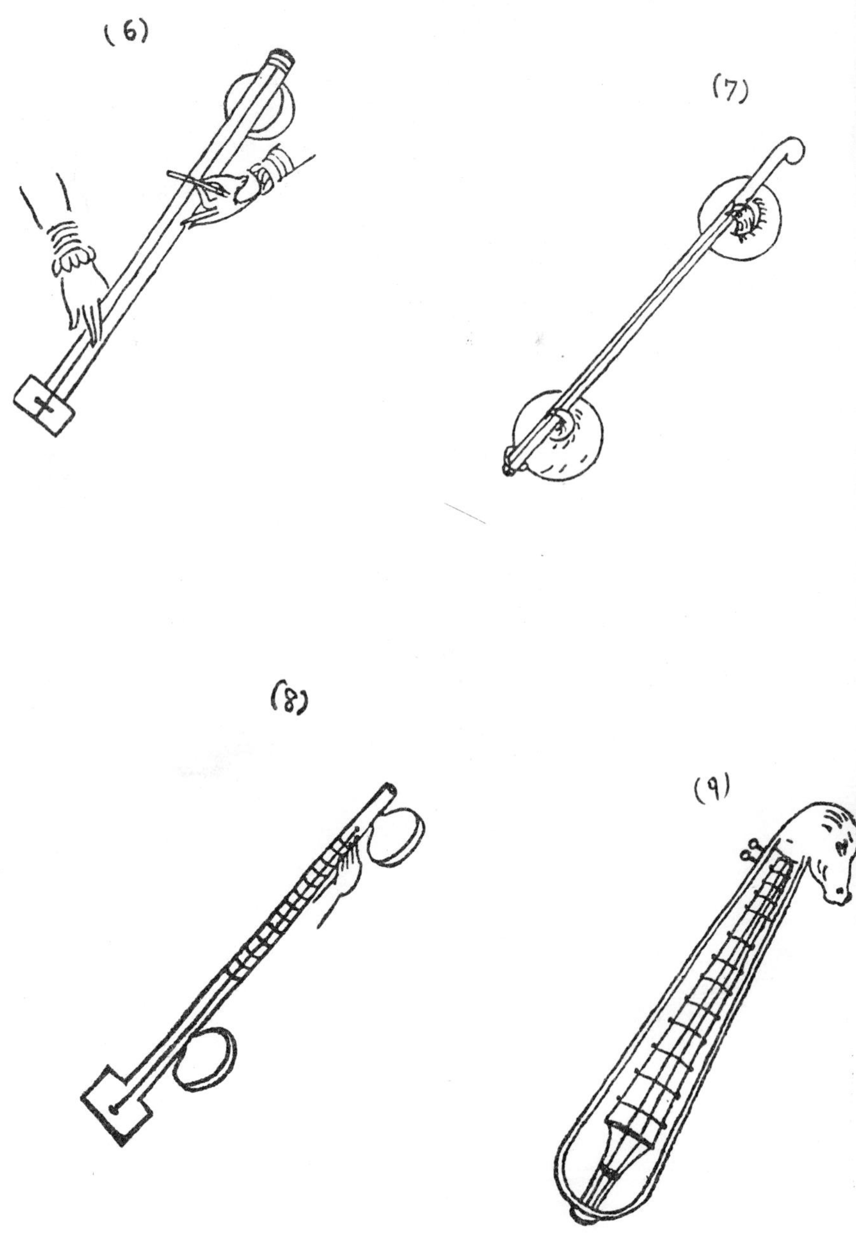

Plate No. 24
FRETTED VINA IN INDIAN SCULPTURE